RADIO LIVE! TELEVISION LIVE!

To the five most important women in my life:
to my wife, Cinda, for her love and support,
and to my daughters, Susan, Gail, Cathee and Nancy,
for allowing me to grow up with them.

RADIO LIVE!
TELEVISION LIVE!

*Those Golden Days
When Horses Were Coconuts*

═══════════════

ROBERT L. MOTT

McFarland & Company, Inc., Publishers
Jefferson, North Carolina, and London

ALSO BY ROBERT L. MOTT

*Radio Sound Effects: Who Did It, and How,
in the Era of Live Broadcasting*
(McFarland, 1993)

On the cover: Ray Erlenborn creating sound effects for the *Texaco Star
Theater* in 1939. The director on the right is Ed "Archie" Gardner of
Duffy's Tavern radio fame. *(Photo courtesy of Ray Erlenborn)*

Library of Congress Cataloguing-in-Publication Data

Mott, Robert L., 1924–
    Radio live! television live! : those golden days when horses were
coconuts / Robert L. Mott.
        p.   cm.
    Includes bibliographical references and index.
    ISBN 0-7864-0816-2 (illustrated case binding : 50# alkaline paper)
    1. Television broadcasting—United States—History.   2. Radio
broadcasting—United States—History.   3. Television authorship.
4. Television broadcasting—Sound effects.
PN1992.3.U5M63   2000
791.45'0973—dc21   00-20233

British Library cataloguing data are available

Manufactured in the United States of America

*McFarland & Company, Inc., Publishers
    Box 611, Jefferson, North Carolina 28640
    www.mcfarlandpub.com*

Table of Contents

Acknowledgments

The fact that I've chosen to write this book showing the lighter side of live radio and television does not mean I have trivialized the subject. It's just that I agree with Noel Coward when he said, "Who can truly say there is more truth in tears than in laughter?"

No book that attempts to present an accurate account of the past could be written without the cooperation and contribution of the people who were there. I therefore wish to express my thanks to the following people, both for their unselfish help in the writing of this book, and more importantly, for the enormous contributions they made to the Golden Age of live broadcasting: Jack Amrhein, Ted Baker, George Balzer, Barney Beck, Jackson Beck, Al Binnie, Bill Brown, Ray Brunelle, Tom Buchanon, Bill Cole, Keene Crockett, Ken Dufva, Ray Erlenborn, David Lee Fein, Don Foster, Monty Fraser, Opal Fraser, Mortimer Goldberg, Robert Graham, Grace Gustafson, Durward Kirby, Bill Levitsky, Jerry McCarty, Garry Moore, Ross Murray, George O'Donnell, Gene Perrett, Walter Pierson, Virgil Reimer, Jim Rogan, Red Skelton, Arthur Strand, Robert Turnbull, Ken Whelan, Orval White and Malachy Wienges. And to any of you whom I may have omitted, please accept my apologies.

Preface

This is a book about what many now refer to as the Golden Age of broadcasting. But to those of us who were there, it wasn't the golden age of anything. It was simply radio and television. We didn't even have to say it was live. Of course it was live; what else was there?

Having been both a sound-effects artist and a comedy writer during those exciting days, I hope you'll forgive any autobiographical improprieties you may encounter. Because this isn't a one-man-band book, I had an awful lot of help from friends and co-workers that I have cajoled, begged, threatened, bribed, or ass-kissed for their treasured remembrances. Together we have argued over dates, fought over names and places and laughed over past embarrassments and screw-ups. Then, when we finally agreed on what was the truth, it went in this book.

Exactly what is a "Golden Age" of anything? Is it simply a nostalgic love of days gone by? A nagging dissatisfaction with our own precious moments in time? Or is it a benchmark of distinction by which other periods of history are to be measured?

In order for a time in history to acquire that elusive golden quality, it must have more going for it than merely being old and *something* that happened in the past. It must involve people. People and an atmosphere of relative innocence and happiness.

Those days, it seems, are gone now. Today it's different, actually better in just about every way except that people are little involved in today's computerized workplace.

Not so back in the days of live broadcasting. And that's what this book is about ... the people and their hand-sweating, stomach-churning triumphs, trials and yes, monumental screw-ups.

Today those years are called the Golden Age. To those of us lucky to have been there, they were simply: live radio, live television. Those days when horses were coconuts.

CHAPTER 1

Before the Age Became Golden

If you believe a picture is worth a thousand words, what would you say a spoken word is worth? A million pictures? How about 30 million pictures? Because that's the estimated amount of people that laid down, sat up, stood, leaned, vacuumed, did their homework, went fishing, cleaned out the garage, did their homework, changed the baby, made love, and just about anything and everything else while listening to the most magical and accessible dream machine—radio.

Want to know what live radio was really like? Think of it as a cow. Yes, a cow. Now, what color is your cow? None of my damn business? Good. You're proving my point.

When television or films show a picture of a black and white cow lowing contentedly in a meadow, the viewer is immediately informed of a number of vital things. First that the animal is indeed a cow and that it's black and white.

This, then, is the power of films and television—to impart information quickly, and with little or no brain work from its audience.

Films and TV are both very public mediums, right down to the color of the cows they want you to see. What's more, (or worse) what they show is the same for everyone. No matter how you personally wish that damn cow was purple.

Purple cows, on the other hand, grew fat and lived to a ripe old age during the Golden Age of radio. And along with the purple cows, radio listeners could make some other changes. How about a gay Lone Ranger? an Hispanic Ma Perkins? or a black Jack Armstrong? Radio was that personal.

Was radio the theater of the mind? Yes. But it was the voices, music and sound effects that let you *see* what was happening on the stage. It was the sounds that took your imagination and gave it a good shaking. "Must your eyes do everything? Radio is only as good as you personally make it! So for goodness sake, put your ears and mind to work and listen!"

Before Horses Were Coconuts

Long before coconut shells could be used for the thundering hoofbeats of the Lone Ranger's great horse Silver, or Amos and Andy could delight a nation with their homey humor, someone had to invent radio. In 1895, someone did. Guglielmo Marconi, the man history refers to as the father of wireless telegraphy, was one of those someones. Heinrich Hertz was another. Hertz, a German inventor, discovered photo-electricity, a fundamental principle of what we now watch *Monday Night Football* on—television.

As incredible as it may sound, once radio had been invented, no one knew what to do with it. To some, radio was a miracle; to others it was frightening. The fact that voices and music could come out of the air and into a piece of living room furniture was just too incredible even to imagine.

Radio was unique. Nothing in the history of the world prepared people—at least most people—for this seemingly magic phenomenon. Fortunately, there were people of vision who saw the tremendous potential of radio. One such person was David Sarnoff, who as a young man was the wireless operator who had picked up the distress signal of the sinking *Titanic*.

When Sarnoff later became the head of RCA (Radio Corporation of America) he felt that radio's future was in supplying American homes with music. He further believed that the music and the airwaves were not to be contaminated by any form of crass commercialism.

But David Sarnoff's dream of a non-commercial radio soon received a rude awakening. On August 28, 1922, station WEAF in New York aired a commercial given by a Long Island real estate firm. What makes this so unusual is that the commercial wasn't simply the sponsor of the program, the commercial was the program! (And you thought today's TV infomercials were new!)

Some Early Live Radio Problems

The owner of WEAF was the American Telephone and Telegraph corporation, AT&T. They envisioned radio as little more than a long distance phone call. You have something to say over the radio? Drop your nickels into the coffers of WEAF and the air time was yours to discuss anything that was nearest and dearest to your heart. The problem was, what was dearest to some of those hearts was too raunchy for the home listeners.

To prevent material considered inappropriate from hitting the airwaves, the engineers in the control room were instructed to listen for anything suggestive, objectionable, or obscene. And if, or when, a paying customer got out of hand with his words, they were instructed to cut him off and switch to phonograph music.

This practice of keeping the airwaves squeaky clean was known as "hitting the button." What made this technique so efficient was that the people that overstepped good taste never knew that the microphone they were using had been cut off. It simply allowed the offender to keep talking into a dead microphone until their allotted paying time on the air was up.

Discussing, mentioning, or even suggesting anything remotely connected with anything below the belt was not the only topic that warranted a cut-off by the authorities of nervous early live radio. Discussions as seemingly innocent as "the proper way to brush your teeth" were considered too controversial on the grounds that it invaded the listener's privacy.

Shrewd performers soon caught on to what they considered radio's "unfair censorship of realistic public issues." One of the shrewdest was Olga Petrova. In addition to being a singer of some renown, she was also a strong supporter of women's rights and had a habit of letting her controversial views be known. Therefore, when Ms. Petrova offered WJZ, Newark, an evening of her acclaimed singing, WJZ was delighted—in a nervous sort of way.

When Ms. Petrova informed the station manager that in addition to her singing, she would be doing nothing more controversial than reading several classic nursery rhymes, the manager heaved a sigh of relief. But just to be safe, the manager told his engineer to listen like a hawk and keep his finger near the button.

That evening, listeners of WJZ heard Ms. Petrova give the following reading of one of Mother Goose's most enduring and innocent nursery rhymes, "The Old Woman Who Lived in a Shoe":

> There was an old woman who lived in a shoe, she had so many children *because* she didn't know what to do.

By the time the station manager realized what had just gotten out over the airwaves, it was too late. And the wily Petrova had once again escaped the engineer's fearful finger.

Today, thanks to high-tech engineering, preventing crank or obscene phone calls from being broadcast offers no problem—at least most of the time. Mortimer Goldberg, one of the first broadcast engineers to work with audio tape at CBS, New York, gives this explanation of how phone calls are monitored today:

> So many innovative processes emerged from the use of magnetic recording tape, but one in particular held, and still holds, a tremendous advantage, namely the seven second delay.
>
> Talk shows dealing with telephone calls from listeners leave the possibility of a caller uttering profane comments, which if broadcasted, would be embarrassing and offensive to many listeners. To avoid this, the so-called "live" show, is actually a tape of the show heard seven seconds *before* the show is actually heard over the air.
>
> Because of this seven second delay, talk show hosts are constantly reminding callers to turn off their radios. If they don't, the callers won't be listening to their real time conversation, but instead, what occurred on the program seven seconds earlier.

President Jimmy Carter being interviewed by Walter Cronkite. In addition, President Carter answered questions from the radio listeners. And just in case a Republican called, CBS was well prepared (photograph courtesy of Mortimer Goldberg).

While the modern talk show is on the air, the show's producer monitors the program and has access to a censor button. If a caller begins using unacceptable language, the producer has seven seconds to press the censor button. The program's content is then switched to an additional tape containing the program's identification which is exactly 60 seconds in length. Then at 53 seconds into that 60 second filler tape, the program is once again reintroduced and seven seconds later, the program resumes from the delay tape, ready again for the next off-color caller.

Despite Goldberg's explanation of these technological improvements over the old-time nervous finger, no system is absolutely foolproof. And to prove it, here is a conversation I heard on the radio while I was having lunch at a nearby CBS watering hole:

FEMALE: I just love your talk show.
HOST: Well thank you so much.
FEMALE: Are you married?
HOST: Yes I am.
FEMALE: Does your wife suck your cock?
HOST: Well—errrr—ahhhh... [*off mike to announcer in studio*] What did she say?
FEMALE: I said, does your wife...

This photograph shows the number of people involved in making certain the broadcast went without an incident. Off to the right are the tape delay cart machines. Over on the left, wearing the headset, is Mortimer Goldberg (photograph courtesy of Mortimer Goldberg).

At this point, everyone in the studio and listeners at home had a pretty good handle on what she had said, and she was cut off.

With all this advanced technology how could this have happened? It seems the producer, whose job it was to push the censor button, had to go pee.

Early Radio's Need of Talent

A popular act in vaudeville was billed as "The Famous Tap-Dancing Rooster." However, what the audiences actually saw in the theater was not so much a tap-dancing rooster as a chicken scratching the stage while a harmonica played "Turkey in the Straw."

This lack of the so-called dancing chicken's ability to live up to its promise prompted a noted radio columnist to write, "My advice to radio is … it's time to stop scratching and start dancing."

The Great Hunt for Professional Talent

Up until now, radio was able to acquire local talent by appealing to their ego. They provided limo rides to the station, bouquets of flowers, a lavish amount of flattery, but little or no money. Now their listeners began demanding better talent with bigger names. The problem was, the Ziegfeld stars the public wanted owned their own limousines and were already receiving huge salaries.

Ed Wynn, a major Broadway star, and later the star of his own radio show, was one of the few exceptions. On April 26, 1922, he took his Broadway stage hit, *The Perfect Fool*, over to Newark and aired it over WJZ's limited broadcast range. For the listeners fortunate enough to hear Wynn's broadcast, it must have been a night to remember. Certainly a welcome change from WJZ's parade of amateurs.

Radio's Money Worries

Now that radio was leaving the laboratory and entering homes, concerns on how radio was to support itself were reaching a crisis state in 1925.

Sarnoff and RCA suggested a separate organization that would put a levy on radio equipment sales. Other suggestions involved taxes on sales of equipment much like what was being done in England.

While the broadcast industry was trying to solve its financial problems, the advertisers remained on the sidelines. One reason for their indifference was that radio baffled them.

The advertising agencies were accustomed to selling their clients' products through newspapers and magazines. With radio, all the buying public could do was listen and try to imagine what a product looked like.

Another complaint from advertisers was "We know how many newspapers and magazines are being sold. But how do we know how many people are listening to the radio?"

That was radio's dilemma. Without advertising money, they couldn't afford the talent needed to attract the large audiences the advertisers wanted.

What radio needed, especially the small stations, was talent with a national reputation, like Ed Wynn, Al Jolson, and Eddie Cantor. Talent that would make people want to buy radios and listen! But unfortunately, what small station could afford such internationally known and expensive entertainment?

Radio Finds the Answer

One of the most significant dates in radio's history occurred in 1926. It was in that year that AT&T decided to get out of the broadcasting business and stick to what it knew best, charging a toll for its chain of telephone lines that radio needed to broadcast over long distances. And so in September it sold radio station WEAF to RCA.

What made this purchase so important was that it gave notice that the National Broadcasting Company (NBC was owned by RCA) was going into radio with all flags flying. It proved this by forming the first radio network.

This promise of supplying talent is what NBC offered these small stations. Talent with international reputations! Opera singers, symphonic orchestras, stars from the Broadway theater and, yes, maybe even a major college football game! NBC would even pay the stations for carrying this star-studded array of talent! How could the small stations go wrong?

They couldn't, and didn't! The listeners got the talent they always wanted, and NBC got their money by charging sponsors for the air time their commercials were heard over the stations in the NBC network.

At the time, NBC's network included 24 stations in 21 cities and extended from the eastern seaboard out as far as Kansas City. The inaugural program from this network was aired on November 15, 1926.

A few months later, on January 1, 1927, NBC put truth to one of its promises, airing the first network radio program to be heard coast-to-coast. And the program? A play-by-play football game from the Rose Bowl in Pasadena, California.

Because of the overwhelming popularity of radio and its rapid growth, the National Broadcasting Company began hearing grumblings from rival stations in the areas served by their network. These stations also wanted the advantages that a network affiliation could provide.

So NBC went to the drawing board to see what they could do. After the engineers were through, it was seen that the engineers had used a red and blue line to mark off the locations of the various stations involved. It was therefore decided that the two emerging networks were to be referred to as the Red and Blue networks.

The Other Networks

On February 18, 1927, CBS got into the act with a basic network of 16 stations. Several years later, on October 2, 1934, Mutual Broadcasting started out with a network of four stations.

In October of 1934, the Federal Communications Commission decided that NBC had used its pioneer status and preemptive maneuvering to unfair advantage, and for the first time in the fledgling industry that most American of marketplace charges, "monopoly," was flung. Not wishing to raise the ire of the FCC (or the U.S. government), NBC on October 1943 sold the Blue Network to the Wrigley Gum people. The Blue Network now became the American Broadcasting Company (ABC).

As of January 1949, the lineup of stations affiliated with the various networks looked like this: ABC, 272; CBS, 179; Mutual, 519; NBC, 170.

The Great Depression

Radio's emergence from the field of entertainment couldn't have happened at a better time for radio—or a worse time for the families of America. It was the time of the Great Depression and songs such as "Brother Can You Spare a Dime?" spoke of Americans, once happily work-weary, now bitten by hunger and without their characteristic vigor: "Once I built a railroad and now it's done. *Brother, can you spare a dime?*"

The problem was, whereas the song asked for a dime, coatless men, often college educated, stood on street corners in freezing weather selling apples and asking for only half that amount.

As a child growing up in the small town of Nyack, New York, I have faint recollections of what the Depression was like. I remember men—they called them "hoboes" in those days—knocking on the door and asking for food. And when our house suddenly lost electric power, it was my job to go down to the cellar and feed a quarter in the power meter.

This one-armed-bandit arrangement of paying for your electricity was provided by the electric company. It was better than having to cut off the electricity of the people that couldn't afford the one monthly charge of a few dollars.

It's little wonder, given moneyless times, that the nation welcomed radio with open and desperate arms. Not only did radio offer relief from the hardships and worries that plagued most Americans—it was free.

Overcoming a Few Hurdles

In the beginning, early radio posed more than just a few hurdles for the actors; for some, it was an insurmountable wall. No longer could you rely on costumes, or makeup, or props, or facial expressions to help you like you could in the theater. In radio, everything had to be pictured for the audience with just your voice going into something called a microphone.

To many actors, a microphone was more than just something to talk into; it was an ogre capable of ending a career. A monster that brought your voice to an unseen audience larger than any theater, ten theaters, hundreds of theaters—maybe even a thousand theaters!

To avert anxieties, engineers had the actors talking into microphones hidden under the skirts of lampshades. This rather bizarre practice was eliminated in 1924 when actors finally realized that talking into a lampshade not only made them feel idiotic, it was just as nerve-wracking as talking into a naked microphone.

One practice that wasn't abandoned as yet was the equally bizarre insistence upon the engineers of having a separate "girl" and "boy" microphone. The explanation given by the audio engineers had something to do with "the varying frequency responses in the timbre of the two sexes." As a result, the engineers made certain that the two microphones kept their distance from one another. One can only conjecture what hanky-panky went on at night when the engineer wasn't around.

Amos 'n' Andy Enter Radio's Picture

Despite the addition of professional talent, radio needed something it could call its own. Something family-oriented that the average American could identify with. But what?

Freeman Fisher Gosden ("Amos") was a product of the South. Born in 1899, he spent part of his childhood being reared by a mammy in a Negro household.

Charles Correll ("Andy") was born in Illinois in 1890. Correll met Gosden while they were both working for Joe Bren's company of minstrels.

After months of kicking ideas around, it was decided the two would put together a blackface act. Each had traveled and performed with minstrel shows for years and felt a blackface act was what he did best. They also knew of the demand there was for this form of entertainment.

The minstrel show is perhaps the only form of entertainment that America can call its own. Ironically it was started by slaves dragged to this country from Africa in chains.

In addition to all the privations the slaves suffered, they weren't allowed to communicate with one another in their native language. It was either learn English, or remain silent.

Because of these language restraints, the slaves turned to the one thing they all understood regardless of what tribes they came from: music and dancing. This became their method of communicating their hates, hopes, frustrations, despairs, and pains. In short, music and dancing weren't so much celebrations as they were outlet and relief from their sufferings.

The slaveowners, on the other hand, didn't see it that way. They saw the singing and dancing as an expression of contentment and happiness. And inasmuch as it didn't interfere with the slaves' field work, the owners even encouraged it. They particularly enjoyed watching their "darkies" put on a dumb (mime) show.

One of the tenets of comedy is not to provoke your audience. Especially an audience that holds your very life in their hands. So if you can't make fun of the owners, make fun of yourself: roll your eyes; shuffle your feet; fall on your rear end; do anything for a laugh! Yuk, yuk, yuk!

It wasn't long before the performers' outrageous satirization of themselves and fellow slaves became popular entertainment among slave owners. So much so, in fact, that neighboring plantations would pay the owners of these slave performers to have them come and entertain guests.

This was fine for the owners, but what was in it for the slave performers? Well, in addition to the small tips they were allowed to keep, it kept them out of the cotton, rice and tobacco fields. (Ain't that enough!) And what had started out as musical gatherings done by slaves for communication and relief from their sufferings soon became the basis for the minstrel shows.

White performers looking for something original to give their audiences soon adopted this form of entertainment. And to make it look "authentic" to their audiences, they blackened their faces with burnt cork, rolled their eyes, and even shuffled their feet.

Soon, to the people in the North—and to all Americans who had never seen blacks—this became the stereotyped picture of the Negro. Ironic that it was the slaves themselves who, in their efforts to escape suffering, were originally responsible for the portrayal.

Miller and Lyles

Flournoy Miller and Aubrey Lyles were two black comedians who did what very few blacks were doing in those days—they attended college. In fact, the two aspiring humorists graduated from Nashville's Fisk University. But because of segregation, they too found that one of the few places they could work was in the black minstrel shows that played only to black communities.

It was perhaps in these small productions that Gosden and Correll first saw the black duo perform and became ardent fans of Miller and Lyles. Of particular interest were the laughs the two black comedians always got with their way of "mutilatin'" the language by, for instance, making the two words "I'm disgusted" come out sounding like "I's reeegusted." Sound familiar?

Because of Miller and Lyles' tremendous popularity in minstrel shows, they were asked to audition at WGN, a Chicago radio station. The sponsor was to be Log Cabin Syrup.

As the two comedians walked into the station to sign their contracts, the management and syrup representatives were surprised to find that the black makeup the comedians wore in minstrel shows didn't cover white faces. As a result, the deal fell through.

The station continued to look for a Miller and Lyles type of entertainment. Two more veterans of the minstrel shows—this time the *white* minstrel shows—auditioned, Correll and Gosden.

Was the humor of Amos and Andy a degrading parody of African Americans? Is that what all this "I's reeegusted" way of talking was all about? Or were Gosden and Correll doing what Miller and Lyles would have done if they too had been white and accepted at WGN?

It's doubtful that the characters portrayed on *Amos 'n' Andy* were meant to be interpreted as the true Negro; neither were they intended to propagate stereotypes of the manipulative Negro, the lazy Negro, the uneducated Negro, the scheming Negro, or any other type of Negro. Amos and Andy were created to make Gosden and Correll a lot of money in an era when making a lot of money wasn't easy. And the best way they could do it was by performing the kind of comedy they were most familiar with.

Correll and Gosden were neither social reformers nor evangelists; they were entertainers. Did the duo's type of warm, character humor depend on Amos and Andy's being Negroes? No—but it certainly helped. Because these were the people the two grew up with and loved. In the hands of other, less sensitive entertainers, Amos and Andy would most likely have been mere joke-exchanging buffoons.

Though what Amos and Andy had to say was often mispronounced or contained malapropisms, wasn't this the way that most people spoke during those grim Depression times? Going to school cost money that could be better used to pay the rent and buy food. And besides, didn't Mark Twain and Abraham Lincoln often use this same technique to reach their audiences?

During the Depression when President Roosevelt was forced to close the banks to avert national chaos, he selected radio as the medium for explaining his reasons for resorting to such drastic actions.

Although Roosevelt was an excellent speaker with radio experience, he realized the unpopularity his closing of the nation's banks had caused. He also realized that most Americans weren't looking upon him as their president during these frightening times, but simply as just another politician telling them more lies.

Who then among his cabinet or economic advisors could he select to explain this intricate economic move he had made that would both be understandable to the average American and calm their fears? It only took the president a moment to select: Amos and Andy.

The next day when people discussed the *Amos 'n' Andy* program, the conversations centered not on the fact that the truth was spoken in the idiom of Amos and Andy, but on the fact that the truth was spoken at all. And if you couldn't believe Amos and Andy, who in the hell in America of those bleak days could you believe in!

Of final interest, when Johnny Carson's *Tonight Show* presented the wedding of Tiny Tim and Miss Vicki, it had an audience of 40 million viewers, one of its largest audiences ever. In contrast, radio's *Amos 'n' Andy* had an average listening audience each and *every* night of 30 million.

Radio Enters Its Golden Age

Whether the enormous popularity of *Amos 'n' Andy* opened the door for other shows or whether radio simply had come of age, the medium was now entering its most glorious period with such shows as *Molly Goldberg* (1929), *First Nighter* (1929), *Easy Aces* (1930), *March of Time* (1931), *Little Orphan Annie* (1931), and, on

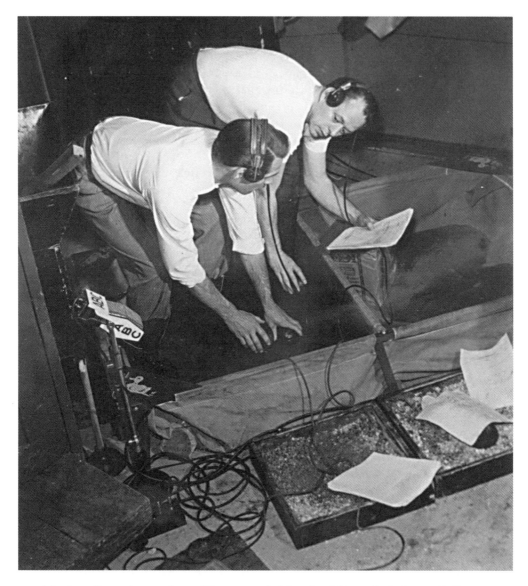

The Lone Ranger's great horse, Silver, not only "thundered," but splashed as well. Shown are Monty Fraser (NBC) doing hoofbeats in "an icy stream," while Virgil Reimer (NBC) tries to tell him where the hell they are in the script (photograph courtesy of Opal Fraser).

January 31, 1933, the airwaves suddenly erupted with the sound of a galloping horse, the "William Tell Overture" and a hearty "Hi yo, Silver!" *The Lone Ranger* had arrived!

Then, as the thundering hoofbeats of his great horse, Silver, drummed across the Western plains in search of evil and wrongdoing, little thought was given by the radio listener of how a great horse, or for that matter a little horse, could fit, let alone go kicking up its hoofs, in a WXYZ Detroit radio studio. Talk about an audience giving an entertainment medium dramatic license!

This, however, was the enormous power of radio. If the Lone Ranger cried out, "Hi yo, Silver, away!" that was good enough for any red-blooded listener. They knew those thundering hoofbeats would be there come hell or high water!

If Radio Was So Great, What Happened?

It's fair to ask why, if the medium was so wonderful, radio was unable to maintain its hold on the imagination of Americans. If the actors loved it, the writers loved it, and those of us who did sound effects loved it—what happened? The beginning of the end began with the networks' use of audio tape. As audiences became more sophisticated, they realized Ma Perkins and Helen Trent were no longer talking directly to them but were being electronically reproduced. With this knowledge, listeners felt that radio, which had once been so alive and exciting, had quietly become just another mistake-free, impersonal, electronic gadget.

But despite radio's no longer being live, and the resultant listener dissatisfaction, the real killer was television. And, ironically, it was the profits from radio that made it possible for television to survive its early lean years.

But was it simply an electronic box that was capable of showing only snowy pictures of cooking shows and old movies that really killed radio? Or did the death blow come from the advertisers? The advertisers that wanted their products not to be just talked about but seen—again and again and again!

It's one thing to give the buying radio listeners the freedom to choose what color they want their cow to be, but if you want to sell cigarettes, what better way than to show some rugged-looking cowboy lassoing a pack of Marlboros!

And what can you say about hemorrhoids on the radio? Isn't it better just to show a gorgeous, sexy woman? After all, does she look like the type to have the same embarrassing problem that you do? Of course not! How could she?—she's gorgeous. And be honest, have you ever seen a gorgeous woman scratch? Anywhere?

CHAPTER 2

Breaking into Radio

If ever there was an occupation that hired only the chosen few, it was radio. One reason was the Great Depression. The theaters that once glittered along Broadway's Great White Way were now dark. This meant that in addition to the hundreds of radio actors looking for the few jobs available in radio, stage performers were now vying for work in the popular new industry.

Because of the desperate times, any openings for work normally went to friends of actors already working in radio. Otherwise, if word got out there was an acting job open, even if the dialect was to be in Swahili hundreds of actors and would-be actors would show up in native garb swearing they were from the Bantu Province of Zanzibar!

To be a successful actor in radio you had to have talent, an excellent voice, be a quick-study, be able to portray a character with little or no rehearsal, be able to do two or more dialects, be punctual, be capable of taking direction, and be dependable. This meant, if you had a martini for lunch, you'd better chew a couple of coffee beans. It was a great deal better to have directors think you were hooked on caffeine than to have them think you a boozer. And finally, you had to give the impression you weren't the type that caused waves.

If the rehearsal meal breaks were often late or just didn't happen, you had a choice: report this grievous union infraction to AFRA (American Federation of Radio Artists) or spend a nickel and get a candy bar out of the hall machine. The wise actor always knew the nutritional value of a Baby Ruth or a Mr. Goodbar.

Finding work in radio required a great deal of hustle, luck and talent. No sensible working actor would jeopardize their own reputation by recommending someone they didn't feel was capable. In radio, the old show business winning smile and curvaceous body didn't get you a seat on the subway. It was what you could do with your voice that mattered.

The Radio Audition

Unless an actor was well known or was privy to a network of friends in radio, the best way to get an acting job in radio was to go through the emotional trauma of an open audition. Because you were in competition with so many other actors, these open auditions were referred to as "cattle calls."

When auditioning, the first thing you had to learn was that nervousness causes a shortness of breath and changes the timbre of your voice. It makes it sound thinner and sharper. To keep this from happening, you must stay relaxed. Even though your monthly rent or next meal is on the line, stay relaxed—damn it!

Now that you're relaxed, you have to make sure that your diction isn't careless or stilted. That your voice is well-rounded and you keep it interesting. That you don't go too fast or too slow. Remember that in radio, too long a pause can make listeners think there is something wrong with their radio. And finally, make certain you don't merely say the words: You have to make them come alive! Listeners can't see your tears; they had to *hear* them roll down your cheeks—one word at a time.

To show you how difficult and competitive these auditions could be, when John Hodiak, the future movie star, auditioned for the role of Li'l Abner back in 1939, he had to beat out 170 other Li'l Abners, all of whom had perfected the Dogpatch way of talking right down to pronouncing *pork chops* as the more countrified "po'k chops."

If you impressed the director, your name and how you did during the audition would be put on file. The following sample casting card was taken from Earl McGill's fine book, *Radio Directing*.

> Showed in general a warm, sympathetic quality. Voice is low; no great impact but controls it effectively. Readings are informed, times his reading well, has a well-controlled pace. Refined voice timbre makes his playing of common or tough character unbelievable. Do not when engaging him put too much dependence on his ability to double.

That last notation, "Do not ... put too much dependence on his ability to double," could very well have kept this actor from working in radio. Because as Cliff Norton, an actor in both live radio and TV's popular *Dave Garroway Show*, told me, "If you weren't star material in radio, the only way you could work was to be able to do a number of different voices and dialects."

Although this sounds like an exaggeration, it wasn't. Radio directors, unlike stage or film directors, didn't have the same casting problems encountered in visual media. In stage and films, looks were everything. You certainly couldn't cast a 70-year-old woman to play the part of a 5-year-old boy, could you? Radio did.

Because of the problems involved with hiring young children, and their pain-in-the-ass stage mothers, radio used women almost exclusively to play the part of young boys, teenaged girls, or in a pinch, 72-year-old women.

The possibility of employing one actor to play as many as three parts in the same show was one of the factors that limited the jobs available in radio. But what if a show's script required the sounds of an angry mob, or a cheering crowd, or the mob that watched Marie Antoinette lose her head to the guillotine? How large a cast would that need?

One. A sound-effects man with a crowd record. Not only would he furnish the *oooooh*s and *aaaaah*s from the bloodthirsty crowd watching poor Marie lose her head, he'd supply the sound of the guillotine (a heavy metal brake drum sliding down a long metal track and hitting three cabbage heads).

Perhaps, since this business of getting work in radio sounds so difficult and traumatic, one might wonder what happened to the actor's best friend in vaudeville, theater and films—the agent. You know—that unctuous hustler who, for 10 percent of their client's hide, wangled, finagled, cajoled, and did all the lying and bragging necessary to score a gig (and the commission)? Well, agents were virtually absent from early radio. Perhaps it was because many of those early 15-minute programs paid a whopping five dollars. Now let's see ... 10 percent of $5.00 equals 50¢. Does that answer your question?

The Old Clock on the Wall

Much has been written about radio as the "theater of the mind." And it was. But what really set it apart from the stage and movies was time. Time in radio was measured by how many ticks there were in a minute.

I remember when my daughters were young and I was working in live radio. I'd ask them to do something and they'd reply, "Okay, Dad, in a minute." And I'd reply angrily, "Do you know how long a minute or even a second is?" I also remember how many seconds they'd look at me like I was nuts.

I wasn't always so brusque, but when you work a job that's dependent on the big studio clock on the wall, you get that way. For instance: a radio show didn't last 15 minutes, it lasted *precisely* 14 minutes and 38 seconds. A half-hour show didn't last 30 minutes, it lasted *precisely* 29 minutes and 38 seconds. And at the precise moment, the network announcer would press the CHIMES button, which took *exactly* two seconds to activate. Then on the air you would hear the familiar NBC "*bing-bong-bing.*" That was the cue for the local announcer to come in and identify his station with its call letters.

The Announcers

One of the most prestigious and difficult jobs to get in radio was not that of the Lone Ranger or the Shadow or Jack Armstrong, it was the job of announcing for the Lone Ranger, the Shadow, or Jack Armstrong.

A radio announcer had to be able to read a script with one eye, while the other watched the clock—and the director. In addition, an announcer had to have a pleasant voice that was personable and convincing, but not *too* personable or *too* convincing—or too anything.

There could be no hint of a regional accent that could identify the speaker as someone coming from the South or North or East or West. And God help you if your roots were in any of the five boroughs of New York City! Especially, the Bronx or Brooklyn!

Or even way back home in Indiana!

Durward Kirby, in his book *My Life ... Those Wonderful Years*, had this to say about one of his first solo announcing jobs.

> My first radio remote [a program that airs from another location] was to announce an orchestra from the Indiana Roof Ballroom. After thirty minutes of announcing various orchestra tunes, midnight arrived and I signed off what I thought was a very fine show. I then received a phone call backstage from the chief announcer. He started out by saying how much he enjoyed the show. He then asked me a rather strange question.
> "Just one thing, Durward. What was that place you were at tonight?"
> I replied, "The Indiana Ruf, sir."
> "I've never heard of it."
> "Oh, sure you have ... that's where I just did the show."
> "Not according to your pronunciation, I haven't."
> "I don't understand, sir."
> "How do you pronounce this word: R-O-O-F?"
> "Ruf."
> "No, Durward, ruf is the sound a dog makes. As in, Ruf-Ruf-Ruf. Remember Durward, an announcer's voice is only as good as the words he uses *correctly*."

In addition to pronouncing *roof* "ruf," the next best way not to get hired was to have a voice that drew attention to it.

If for instance your voice was so deep and resonant that people often told you, "You ought to be an announcer on radio!" your chances of being a network announcer were extremely slim.

The job of the network announcer's voice was to sell products or announce things, not to be noticed and admired. And please don't even mention a voice that gives away the announcer's race, color, or creed! Certainly not if you wanted to be a network announcer! My God, what will the affiliates think!

Affiliate stations were the lifeblood of networks. They were also located in all parts of the country, from the Deep South, to the rocky shores of Maine, to the Midwest. Different parts of the country, different cultures, different ways of making a living, different prejudices.

Radio, in an effort to reach the greatest audience, made an all-out effort not to offend their listeners. If in doing so they shunned announcers and actors whose

Bob—
May your shadow
never grow less—
Durward Kirby

Durward Kirby was one of the most versatile, durable announcers in live broadcasting. In addition, his work in comedy sketches on the **Garry Moore Show** *set him apart as one of television's truly fine comedic actors (author's collection).*

color didn't happen to be white, it was a damn shame, but well, you know how it is. Besides, if radio could get an actor of German descent to play the part of an Irish cop, or an Irishman to play the part of a Nazi soldier, what's so wrong with a white man playing a black man?

Hell, wasn't this the voice-only medium of radio? Who's to know? The listener at home won't. I mean if that 72-year-old woman could get away with playing a 5-year-old boy, think of the fun it would be to a studio audience to see a white man play a colored woman!

On *Fibber McGee and Molly*, in fact, the part of the colored maid, Beulah, was indeed played by a white man. Marlin Hurt made a comfortable living impersonating both male and female African American voices in a manner that Gosden and Correll's *Amos 'n' Andy* never dreamed.

The people that ran the networks of course knew the anonymity that radio provided. No need for the minstrel show's noisome burnt cork, all that was needed was a voice—and, of course, the listener's imagination.

Because *Fibber McGee and Molly* was a comedy show, there is a somewhat logical explanation for this unusual casting. The studio audience assumed that the role of Beulah would naturally be played by the stereotyped Negro they were accustomed to seeing and hearing in the movies.

Therefore, when Beulah's name was called out on the program for the first time, and this man—this white male actor—turned around and answered, the audience never failed to laugh and scream their surprise and approval at the wonderful joke radio had played on their ears!

At the death of Marlin Hurt in 1947, those in power in radio were still not ready to give up what they considered a surefire way of getting laughs. So they hired Bob Corley, another white man.

Corley was 22 when he took over the role, and he soon found out that the vocal demands of imitating Beulah were too much of a strain and left the show.

His replacement? An honest-to-goodness woman of color: the marvelous actress Hattie McDaniel.

In addition to Miss McDaniel, there were other blacks cast in the show. Vivian and Dorothy Dandridge, Nicodemus Stewart, Amanda Randolph, and, returning to radio from her picture-stealing performance in *Gone with the Wind*, Butterfly McQueen.

You Don't Sound Jewish

Jack Benny (born Benjamin Kabosky), along with other members of the Jewish faith, knew all about prejudices. Weren't they barred from all WASP (white Anglo-Saxon Protestant) country clubs?

One time, Phil Baker had been invited as a guest to play at a fashionable Westchester County golf course. As he was about to tee off, he was approached by an embarrassed assistant manager. With no doubt some discomfort, the distressed fellow managed, "*Ahem* ... Sorry, Mr. Baker; we're restricted."

Baker, hiding his anger, resorted to his stock in trade, humor. Facing the man, he fixed his face with a stage smile and responded: "Can't I at least play nine holes ... my wife is a gentile."

This no-Jews-allowed condition became so intolerable that Baker, along with George Burns, Milton Berle and others, built Hillcrest Golf Club and opened it to all faiths and colors.

Listener prejudices, then, weren't limited to blacks, or people from the South, or to those of us who spoke a glottal Brooklynese. So how did Jews escape the "sorry, we're restricted" mantra so prevalent in many private clubs and industries? Simple—they changed their names. At least most of them did.

People bent on being prejudiced had a number of ways of identifying their targets. Someone's looks, voice, and name were perhaps the easiest and earliest characteristics scrutinized. Those that had only a name problem were the luckiest. And that included most of the members of the radio acting community. As a result, "strange" sounding Polish, Russian, German, French, Rumanian, Italian and Hebrew ethnic names were discarded for fear of offending the studio heads, the networks, the casting agencies, or the listening public at large.

If, however, a Jewish radio actor insisted on keeping his ethnic name, he risked loss of work on certain types of programs. Westerns for instance. Producers felt that names that sounded Jewish (you see, you didn't even have to be Jewish, you just had to *sound* Jewish) weren't appropriate for a pioneer, or a two-gun gunfighter in the Old West tradition. Their excuse was that "It wasn't historically accurate and hurt the believability of the show."

One of the early violators of these taboos was Molly Goldberg. Not only did she have an ethnic name, she used her own voice and sprinkled it with the vernacular of her Jewish background. Although the *Molly Goldberg Show* was extremely popular with the people that enjoyed Goldberg's honest approach to an ethnic theme, it didn't please everyone. Many Jews hated it. They felt it was demeaning and reinforced stereotypes.

Not on My Show You Don't!

Breaking into radio as an actor, announcer or sound-effects artist was a cinch compared to becoming a star and representing a sponsor's product.

When a nationally known company sponsored a show, they were not only paying the bills, they were putting their image and reputation on the line. Especially if the show bore the name of the company. For instance, *The Happiness Boys* was sponsored by the Happiness Candy Stores; *A&P Gypsies*, sponsored by the Atlantic and Pacific Food Markets; *Cliquot Club Eskimos*, sponsored by Cliquot Club Soda; *Ma Perkins* by Oxydol; *Jack Armstrong* by Wheaties; *Little Orphan Annie* by Ovaltine; *Jack Benny* by Jell-O; *Bob Hope* by Pepsodent Toothpaste; *Philip Morris Playhouse* by Philip Morris cigarettes. So if there was any hanky-panky going on with the stars or with anyone connected with the show, it was a direct reflection of the prestige and image of the sponsoring product. Not only that—it hurt sales.

If, for instance, the Shadow decided to stop "clouding people's minds" and come out of the closet, or if the Lone Ranger took off his mask and his face wasn't lily white, or if Ma Perkins was caught in her chair doing more than just rocking—well! The panic on Wall Street caused by the 1929 stock market crash would have been nothing but a slight market correction compared to the effect such moves would have had on Madison Avenue!

Another Couple of Words from Our Sponsor

And those words are *advertising agencies*. They too had a hand in picking who got into radio and who didn't. Although thousands of commercials came out of the radio each day, the advertising agencies that controlled them were relatively few. Not only did the agencies make the commercials for their clients, they very often controlled the shows where their commercials were used.

Even if you worked for a network, as those of us in sound effects did, the agencies could dictate to the networks who they did and didn't want on their show. Usually, this had nothing to do with your work. If an agency representative didn't like your attitude, or even the cigarettes you smoked, you were off the show—period!

When I temporarily replaced Jack Amrhein on the *Philip Morris Playhouse*, I found that everyone was given a carton of cigarettes, whether you smoked or not. I happened to smoke, but not Philip Morris, Chesterfields. Thinking I was doing the honest thing, I politely refused the offered carton, saying they weren't my brand.

The agency man smiled his acknowledgment of my honesty and remarked that he didn't give a shit what I smoked, just as long as it was Philip Morris! Since he put it that way, and since I saw him edging toward the phone to have me replaced, I thanked him and Philip Morris for their generosity and dumped my Chesterfields, which hadn't done anything for me except give me a dry, hacking cough.

This tremendous power worked two ways. If an agency representative wanted a certain sound-effects artist on their show, they got them. Period. They even paid these chosen artists a fee. But supposing two shows wanted the same artist? Because the networks had little to say, the artist usually figured out a way to go with the highest bidder.

Little wonder why one network vice president, infuriated at this practice and his inability to stop it, labeled his sound-effects department "a bunch of damn prima donnas!"

Breaking into Sound Effects

As difficult as it was to break into radio as an actor, it was even more difficult to get a job at one of the networks in sound effects. After all, how do you apply for a job in sound effects when the networks were reluctant to admit that there even was such a thing as sound effects in radio?

Despite all the noise sound effects made in radio, networks discouraged publicizing its importance. They rarely if ever allowed giving the soundmen name credits at the end of the show. Their thinking was "If kids found out the hoofbeats heard on the *Lone Ranger* weren't done by the great horse Silver, it would damage the credibility of the program."

How I Broke into Sound Effects

I apologize for this autobiographical interruption. But because everyone I spoke to broke into sound effects a different way, I thought it best if I wrote about what I was most familiar with—me.

In 1951, only CBS, NBC, WOR (Mutual) and ABC had a sound-effects department in New York. This meant that in a city that totaled over seven million people, fewer than one hundred were doing sound effects. There were, then, fewer people doing sound effects in radio when I broke in than there are quarterbacks in pro football today.

My big break of getting into sound effects came about because of World War II. The war lasted just long enough for me to serve three years in the Marine Corps and become eligible for the school benefits provided by the G.I. Bill of Rights.

Briefly stated, veterans that qualified could head back to school to receive the college education that the war either interrupted or preempted. All government bills since that time should be so beneficial to so many.

Critics of the government's largesse were given a rather grim alternative. Would they as taxpayers rather foot the bill for educating the veterans for future jobs or have an army of jobless ex-servicemen walking the streets? And when they factored into the equation the fact that the only civilian-friendly skills most of the veterans had was the art of shooting enemy snipers out of palm trees, well, few governmental choices have ever been easier.

School Days

Ever since I was young I had been fascinated with radio. Now, when the government offered me an opportunity to go to New York University and study radio writing, I jumped at the opportunity.

The first thing I learned about studying writing for radio was that it entailed more than just studying writing for radio. New York University had taken a page out of World War II. At that time, in order for a tavern owner to get a case of Scotch, he was forced to buy six cases of the less desirable wine. Colleges decided to do the same kind of thing. My six cases of wine came in the form of classes in radio acting and announcing.

Although I had no desire to become an actor or announcer, it came as a shock to learn that I had a speaking problem. Instead of pronouncing *bottle* with two distinctive *t* sounds, I took a short cut by way of Brooklyn and pronounced it "but'uhl." I had the same problem with all glottals.

Battle came out sounding like "bat'uhl," *rattle* came out "rat'uhl." As a result, I was told that unless I corrected this regional speech problem, I could never hope to become a network announcer. My speech was identified with New York City's teeming millions in general, and the gangster element of Brooklyn in particular.

I received the same type of criticism from my acting instructor. He too strongly recommended that I hastily seek serious remedial speech therapy. Although I had no career aspirations of becoming an announcer or an actor, no one likes being told they can't talk right.

With acting and announcing out of the way, the final requirement of the Radio Production Course was doing the sound effects for the acting class. Since this had nothing to do with talking, I was asked if I'd like to go first. I accepted, deciding that, unless I intended to spend my acting career waiting for a role as a Brooklyn cab driver or mobster, I might as well try doing something temporarily that might help me with my writing.

This is week seven of my not acting in my acting class. Here the class performs its weekly broadcast over WGYN. That's me way in the back wearing the sound effects headset (author's collection).

When I first started doing sound effects for the class, I looked on it as an excellent way of learning a craft that would help me with my writing. But creating even the limited amount of effects required of me soon showed me how difficult and engaging the art of sound effects could be.

The first requirement of sound effects was timing. Knowing when to do the Fibber McGee closet crash, and for how long to do it, plus the all-important tinkle of a bell at the end of the crash, all took a great deal of timing.

The second important sound-effect requirement was to be ambidextrous enough to be able to move your hands independently of each other. Having been a drummer for a number of years helped me with both demands.

Trying to Get Started

After graduating from NYU, I had little thought of doing sound effects for a living. Instead, I concentrated all my efforts on writing. Most of those efforts came back rejected; the others, unread in their unopened envelopes.

The author, an aspiring young Buddy Rich, mans the drums in 1940 (author's collection).

It was then I learned how fortunate it was for me that I had that glottal speech disorder that renders all my *bottles* "but'uhls."

Al Schaefer, an occasional guest speaker at the NYU production class, was a sound-effects engineer at WOR. Schaefer did the sounds on *Quiet Please*, *The Mysterious Traveler*, and *The Doctor Fights*. His partner, Barney Beck, who also worked at WOR, did the sounds on *Bobby Benson*, *The Sea Hound*, *I Love a Mystery* and *True Detective*. Then the two paired up and did the sounds for *The Shadow*.

In addition to doing sounds at the Mutual Network, they had a busy little freelance sound-effect company and asked me if I'd help them out by doing some of the freelance sound effects. I jumped at the opportunity. Now, I would be paid for doing sound effects, and I could still write. Does my life get any sweeter?

My luck lasted two years. And during that time I had hit gongs on *Radio Free Europe*, killed a pioneer with a bow and arrow on *Voice of America* and did horses' hooves on *So Proudly We Hail*. I felt it was time for me to make a change.

My Big Day

As I neared 485 Madison Avenue, the home of the Columbia Broadcasting System, I still had 20 minutes before the employment office opened. Just enough time for yet another cigarette. As I reached for my pack, a terrible thought hit me. Supposing CBS hired me and didn't allow smoking in their studios! Impossible. Radio's bread and butter was cigarettes and black coffee.

Before I could dwell too long on this disturbing thought, a cab pulled up and a smiling uniformed doorman materialized from out of the revolving doors. As he opened the cab door, a tall, strange looking man got out wearing a huge cowboy hat and boots!

I had only seen a hat and boots like that in the movies on the famous cowboy movie star Tom Mix. But to see a cowboy hat now, here in the middle of New York, and on fashionable Madison Avenue!

If there had been any doubt in my mind of how badly I wanted to work in radio, it was immediately dispensed. Standing in the boots and under the ten gallon Stetson hat was an in-the-flesh cowboy movie star, Joel McCrea!

I tried not to let him see me watching him, but as he passed, he gave me a small smile and disappeared through the revolving door. If I hadn't been nervous before, I was now. CBS not only had *Gangbusters* and *Inner Sanctum*, it even had real live movie stars! Maybe even Betty Grable!

As I stepped out of the revolving doors into the lobby, a pleasant voice with an Irish brogue called out:

"Can I help you sir?"

It was the same doorman who had just escorted Joel McCrea to the elevators, and he was calling me "sir" with the same smile and tone of voice he used for a big-time movie star! Damn! Was CBS big time, or what! I had to get a job here! But first I had to find the employment office.

"Pardon me, I'm looking for the employment office…?"

The doorman (Mike Donovan) smiled and pointed to a bank of elevators. "It's on the third floor, sir." He then smiled and this time his voice was thick with an Irish brogue, "And the luck of the Irish be with you sir!"

Again he called me "sir"! Damn! As I walked to the elevators, CBS had not disappointed me. There was energy and excitement in the air—and class—right from the time you were greeted by Mike Donovan, to the polished brass on the bank of elevators! None of those ricky-ticky self-service kinds for CBS!

I was about to enter one of the elevators when a smartly uniformed operator motioned me back to let a 1936 Chevrolet gray car door get off. The door, and the large frame it was in, had "CBS Sound Effects 5" stenciled on it in neat blue letters. My God, not only did they have *this* beautiful door for the sound effect of a car door, but they had four more!

Even the pay at CBS was not to be believed. If I was lucky enough to be hired by the network, my salary would immediately improve from the $5.00 a week I was now getting for each show I did, to a steady $85 a week—each and every week! If I lasted the three-month probationary period and passed the Union's written and oral exam, my salary would even scale to the incredible heights of $117 a week!

To put this salary business into perspective, in 1951, I was paying $19 a month for a cold-water flat up on 86th Street in the heart of Yorkville. Although the rent was reasonable, the apartment came with a price.

In addition to providing shelter for my wife, and six-month-old baby girl, Susan, there were a few inconveniences. We had to walk up five flights of stairs, provide kerosene for a small heater to heat our unheated apartment, and order ice for a small icebox that served as a refrigerator. The good news is, because our closet-sized bedroom was so frigid in the winter, we were able to move the icebox in there and cut the cost of ice in half.

Some of the other apartment amenities were that the bathtub was in the kitchen, and so was the toilet. The tub was next to the sink, and the toilet was in a broom-sized closet that allowed just enough room to stand, or sit.

Because of the closet's limited space, any of our guests over six feet, male or female, were at a decided disadvantage. Once you sat down, you'd soon discover that it was impossible to gather in both legs far enough to accommodate closing the door. So if someone wanted to use our tiny water closet, they had to make certain that everyone was aware of this fact. This meant that the kitchen was now off limits until the person using our little facility gave the all-clear signal.

Despite these minor inconveniences, the apartment was not without its positive points. It was, for one, located in a nice section of New York called Yorkville. And because of the large population of Germans that had made Yorkville their home over the years, the restaurants that lined East 86th Street reflected this German influence with names like "The Old Berlin," and "Edelweiss."

Despite its convenient location, Yorkville, because of its reputation for being predominantly German, was not a place to live during World War II. Neither signs written in German nor the German tongue were very popular, especially in a bar populated with American servicemen.

Even if you weren't German or of German descent, if your neighbor got a whiff of sauerkraut cooking in your apartment, you risked being thought of as a Nazi spy and could expect a prompt visit from the FBI.

While most Americans found these stories of neighbors spying on neighbors to be ridiculous, the nationwide sale of canned sauerkraut fell like a ton of bricks.

Warmth Goes Just So Far

The CBS Employment Office was on the third floor. As I walked in, a young, attractive receptionist looked up from her typing and gave me a warm smile.

"May I help you, sir?"

Despite my nervousness, I somehow conveyed that I wanted to work at CBS. Again she smiled warmly, handed me an application and resumed her typing.

When I finished filling in all the blanks, the application looked impressive even to me. I handed it to her and tried my best to imitate her warm smile.

I watched her closely for any sign of encouragement, but if it was there, she kept it well hidden behind that warm and friendly smile.

At last she glanced up, and seemed impressed with my background and experience, but they weren't hiring anyone in sound effects just this moment. Maybe if I were to try in six months…?

I did better than that. I tried twice in the six-month period and again three months after that. Still they weren't hiring anyone in sound effects at CBS.

At this point, I don't know whether it was because I was lucky, or because they felt guilty for having kept silent, but Beck and Schaefer, the two WOR soundmen I worked for, finally told me of the errors of my ways in inquiring at CBS.

It seems the warm and smiling secretary was either knowingly or unknowingly screwing me. The truth was, she didn't have a clue what "sound effects" was and, worse still, couldn't have cared less to find out. Her department had nothing to do with hiring engineers—only clerical help.

When I finally did get to see the person I should have been seeing all along, I was hired, and three weeks later I was the third man on—are you ready?—*Gangbusters!*

Earlier I mentioned the part that luck might have played with my getting hired by CBS. During my job interview, I was told I would be only the second sound-effects person they had hired in ten years!

The point is, if I had become discouraged, or if I hadn't known someone in the business who finally told me of the correct person to see, chances are I never would have gotten into radio.

Today when we talk about all the many things that barred people from working in radio—the speech defects, the regional accents, having "too Jewish" a name, or being black—I had them all beat. I was almost kept out of live radio by a CBS secretary's warm, sweet and friendly smile.

CHAPTER 3

Behind the Picture Tube

Before Ed Sullivan ever made his familiar Sunday night boast of "a reeeeely big show!" there had to be people making certain his microphones and cameras were in the right position. People to comb his hair, powder his nose, straighten his tie and tell him where and how to stand. There were, and Sullivan, along with the thousands of other performers in live television, not only trusted these people to make them look and sound good, they virtually trusted them with their careers.

Whether you watched early television in black and white on your own small screen or followed the crowds down to your local appliance store and gawked through the store window at the antics of "Uncle Miltie," just about everyone in America was marveling at this magical medium. It wasn't long before having an antenna on your roof was as much of a status symbol as having a Cadillac in your garage. Even those who couldn't afford a television set sometimes did the next best thing: they put up a bogus antenna that wasn't connected to anything but their egos.

Milton Berle's television show began on June 8, 1948, and television was never the same again. When his show started, there were only 500,000 hearty souls who owned television sets. In a matter of weeks, his popularity was such that the number doubled. But despite Berle's talents, he would be the first to admit he could never have done it without the help of the people behind the picture tube.

In the Beginning

What was this thing called "television"? Was it simply an entertainment curiosity? A toy with no practical use? Or was it a serious threat to both radio and the film industry?

Hollywood decided to sit on the sidelines and wait and see how the public was going to accept television. If the medium caught on, the film moguls had the money, the studios, the experience and the stars to jump on the bandwagon. But at the moment, Hollywood couldn't see how the public, accustomed to watching their big-screen entertainment, in living color, with glamorous stars, could possibly accept a puny, seven-inch picture in black and white, with no other redeeming features other than you didn't have to buy a ticket to watch it.

Hollywood's gloomy appraisal of television's future was just what the diehards of radio wanted to hear. Unfortunately, both Hollywood and radio were captivated by their own blind hopes and desperate wishes.

Getting Started

Early television was a hodgepodge of technical and production talent. Not surprisingly, veterans from the film industry were not those among either the hodge or the podge; they just stayed away in large numbers. The few that did make the switch were soon to learn that working in films didn't prepare them for the demands of live television.

Films used one camera; television used a lot of them. Films had time; television didn't. Films had money; television was supported by radio. Films had postproduction; television was live.

While most of the experienced production and technical people in Hollywood turned their backs on television, the United States government didn't. Veterans of the U.S. Army Signal Corps and Propaganda Units, with experience in radio and film, were especially welcome.

As valuable as these returning army veterans were to early television, their numbers weren't nearly enough. People with all types of theatrical skills were needed immediately. But as many of the makeup artists from the Broadway stage soon found out, television had unique requirements. The performer wearing the amount of lipstick applied to a stage actor appeared clown-like to the probing eye of the television camera. It would take time for the craft people and artists from other fields to adapt to the demands of live television.

But while all this was going on, the one thing that television needed right away were cameras, and people to operate them.

The Camera

To be a camera operator at CBS you had to have one of two qualifications: a background in electronics or experience with either a moving or still camera.

Bob Holmes, who later became an award-winning technical director at NBC-Hollywood, was one of those rare television cameramen with experience. He

RADIO AND SOUND CREW-JUNE 3, 43
U. S. NAVAL TRAINING STATION-GREAT LAKES ILL

This picture was taken in 1943 at the Great Lakes Naval Station. Shown is a mobile unit of the Sound and Motion Picture Unit. Because of the many remote (off-base) radio shows they did without the proper technical facilities, they packed everything they needed in the pictured truck. Pictured from left to right: Bud Pritchet, an unidentified sailor, Lt. Swan, Gerry Peterson, Bob Engdal. All of these men went into broadcasting after World War II (photograph courtesy of Gerry Peterson).

received some experience while doing camera work in the Air Force, while even more came from his love of photography.

In addition to the basic requirement of some type of camera experience, network camera operators were often asked to put in 20-hour days and work weeks without a day off. If that wasn't enough to discourage potential camera operators with stars in their eyes, you had to be young, strong, have a very high threshold to stress, and not mind getting filthy dirty.

If you qualified in all of these areas, you were given the job title of assistant technician. The networks would then give you a six-week course in learning how to operate the all-important television camera.

After the basic camera training, you would then be assigned to a technical crew. These crews were headed by a technical director, who, among other jobs,

Bob Holmes films movie star Ella Raines. Although filming a film star makes the life of a camera operator seem very appealing, doing camera in live television was an entirely different story (photograph courtesy of Bob Holmes).

was responsible for the work and behavior of their camera operators, boom operators, video operators, the audio mixer, and a number of assistant technicians.

It was the job of the assistant technicians to help the camera and boom operators in any way possible. This is where the hard work and getting filthy came in.

Although you had training with a camera and you aspired to become a camera operator, this did not mean it was a done deal. First you had to do whatever was asked of you by your TD (technical director).

This included (but wasn't limited to) pulling camera cables, affectionately known as "snakes."

Each camera had a cable that was connected to the control room. These camera cables were long, heavy, and the diameter of the small end of a baseball bat. They also were as efficient as a vacuum cleaner in getting studio dirt to cling to them.

That was the good news. The bad news was, if the assistant tech wasn't constantly alert, they would get snarled, tangled or wrapped around everything, or anyone, that could impede the camera's free movement.

In addition to the cables, there was another disaster waiting for the unwary: cigarette butts. Yes, in those days, most of us smoked. And although putting a cigarette butt out on the studio floor was forbidden, it wasn't forbidden *enough*. And if one of those little suckers got stuck on a camera's wheel, it was like a woman trying to walk in only one high-heel shoe: Each time the wheel turned to where the cigarette was, it would bump the camera slightly and jar the picture. If this happened to the camera an assistant tech was responsible for on air, it wasn't likely that this technician would soon be given his own camera to operate.

During rehearsals, the studio personnel and actors were given five-minute breaks each hour to go to the bathroom, drink coffee or smoke a cigarette. But if you were an eager, ambitious assistant tech and you did all your cable work without whimpering, you'd forgo going to the bathroom, drinking coffee, smoking a cigarette or anything else! This was your opportunity to get your hands on a camera and show the people in the control room what a good camera operator you'd make!

This interest and practice was extremely important if the assistant technician ever hoped to move up in the CBS studio engineering hierarchy. It also gave the assistant technician an opportunity to work with the tricky multiple camera lenses.

Cameras were equipped with four lenses mounted on a wheel-type lens holder that could be rotated to whatever lens a camera shot required.

The four most versatile lenses were the 50mm lens and the 90mm lens, used for wide angle shots when dollying (moving), while the 135mm and the eight-inch lenses were used for closeups. The problem with these lenses was the camera had to remain stationary or it would lose its focus.

The important thing to remember about these lenses is that they were all used for specific purposes. One lens would include the actor from head to toe, another from just the waist up. A third could show the whole studio, but the fourth could only focus on one small object, like the sparkle of an engagement ring.

Becoming a full-fledged camera operator at CBS was the dream of all assistant technicians. Not only did it mean an increase in job security and money, it also meant the pride you felt when half the country was watching Jackie Gleason, Ed Sullivan or Garry Moore, through the lenses of *your* camera.

Not a bad way to make a living. Unless of course it was your first time on camera.

Keep Your Eye on the Damn Ball!

One of the most prestigious, most looked-at camera shots in all of television occurs just once a year. But when it does, it makes the camera operator the center of attraction for millions upon millions of revelers on New Year's Eve. If you haven't guessed by now, it's the camera showing the lighted ball in Times Square making its slow descent and heralding in another joyous New Year.

The one drawback to this special assignment has always been the fact that it was impossible to rehearse this exciting and dramatic event prior to the midnight hour.

What if the hundreds of thousands of celebrants, pressed together in claustrophobic delirium in Times Square, confused the rehearsal for the real thing and thought it was midnight?

They would scream and holler and blow funny horns and then it would be over. Then, having thought they had already welcomed in the New Year, they'd return home, leaving television audiences that were still thirsty for fun, with nothing more exciting to watch than the street cleaners sweeping up confetti and funny little paper hats.

It was for these reasons that the camera shot of the ball making its slow descent eclipsed all other camera shots in television on New Year's Eve.

Perhaps you're wondering why, if this shot was so important, it was given to an assistant technician (we'll call him Roy), who had never done camera on air?

A good question. But because each camera crew is limited to a certain number of technicians and the camera operator that was assigned to this camera left with a high fever, Roy was given the job.

Despite its being the recorder of such high drama, it was a camera shot nobody wanted. Not the least of the reasons why was the camera's location: You were on top of a tall building, unprotected from the cold and damp wind blowing off the Hudson River. You shivered your butt off, drank gallons of hot black coffee, and hoped the building's rest rooms were still open and not too far away.

Among the experienced camera operators that were delegated to work on New Year's Eve (yes, you worked all holidays too), being assigned the camera with the ball shot was considered an insult.

It required no technical know-how or camera experience. And if you could find a 10-year-old child that was dumb enough to want to do it, they would have no problem, unless they fell asleep from boredom. In short, no one could possibly screw it up, no matter how hard they tried.

But now, as the big hand on the clock ticked away the old year, the excitement from Times Square became deafening. It also signaled that it was Roy's moment to shine! Roy clenched his teeth in gritty determination. He kept the big, brilliantly glowing orange ball in the center of his viewfinder and waited for it to make its descent.

Meanwhile, the roar from the celebrants in the street below became increasingly louder. Suddenly a frantic voice on his headset began screaming, "Roy! Pan down with the ball—pan down with the goddamn ball!"

Due to the screams of the crowd and blaring noise from the party horns, it was difficult for Roy to make out what the director was saying. So instead, he focused his eyes more intently on the big orange ball in the center of his viewfinder.

Again the director screamed, "Roy! Pan down with the goddamn ball!" This time he heard him and screamed back indignantly, "I am on the goddamn ball and it ain't moving!"

"Of course it ain't, you stupid asshole! Your camera is on the goddamn *moon!*"

Identical—But Not the Same

Being a camera operator at CBS was not the same as being a camera operator at NBC or ABC. The work was the same (mostly, anyway) but the unions were different.

At NBC and ABC, the technical union was (and is) NABET (National Association of Broadcasting Engineers and Technicians). The directors were required by NABET to give each camera operator a written "shot sheet." A shot sheet, as the name implies, is a detailed list of the camera shots and angles the director required of a particular camera during a show.

At CBS, the technical union was (and is) IBEW (International Brotherhood of Electrical Workers). There, the camera operators didn't want the distraction of looking at a shot sheet. Their system was to have the assistant director give them their camera instructions over their headset. These instructions consisted of reminders and "readies" (alerts to the operator that his or her camera was about to become the hot camera). The job of actually calling the various camera shots belonged to the show's director.

Neither system of cueing cameras was a problem if you were accustomed to it. But if you weren't, it could be a very big problem. Especially when you consider the way the control rooms were laid out.

Each camera had its own monitor in the control room. In addition, there was the on-air monitor, which showed which of the cameras was being "taken"

This is a view of the monitors that the director watched when calling a camera shot (author's collection).

(on-air), and a preview monitor. This preview monitor indicated what camera was about to be taken next.

The names of operators were attached to these control room monitors, and in rehearsals, the assistant director often used the names of the various camera operators, but once the show went on the air, names were dropped and the number of their camera was used instead. On a busy show, it would be too difficult and time-consuming for the director to have to say the operator's name, let alone remember it.

Because of the radical difference between the two systems, some directors, accustomed to working at only one network, had difficulty adjusting to the other. I recall one rehearsal at CBS where the camera operator, working under a director who was new to the network, did what was pretty much standard at CBS. Instead of shooting a camera shot in the exact manner he had in the previous rehearsal, the operator felt he was improving the shot by slightly changing his camera's angle.

At CBS, directors were accustomed to, and most often appreciative of this help on the part of their camera people. Sidney Lumet, for one, depended on his camera people to do just that. Jerry McCarty recalls that when Lumet directed *Danger* and *Studio One*, he often ignored his script and would just ad-lib many of his camera shots.

In the case of a new director to CBS' system, however, having the camera operators making changes on their own could be interpreted as both threatening and disruptive. As a result, when the aforementioned new director saw one of his cameras getting a shot on his own, he let him hear about it.

"Camera Two, who told you to get that damn shot?! Just do the shots I give you and we'll get along fine!"

The camera operator bristled. His innocent attempt to help had been misinterpreted, but he kept his cool. He knew his time to teach the director a lesson about working in live television would soon come.

When the rebuffed cameraman's next shot came up, his time came. When the director told the operator to dolly (move) the camera in on an actor sitting in a chair reading, the operator responded in an appropriate fashion. What the director didn't say was when to stop. As a result, the camera kept moving in until it knocked over the actor's reading lamp and was in the process of knocking over the set's wall before the director screamed for the operator to stop.

Needless to say, the director learned a hard lesson about the intense teamwork needed to work in live television.

The Technical Director

A technical director was the head of the technical crew. It didn't matter what network you were at, it was their responsibility both to see that all audio and camera requirements of a show were met and to do the actual switching of cameras ordered by the show's director.

Technical directors were selected on the basis of excellence demonstrated in one, or all, of the technical job functions of a television technical crew: camera, audio, boom, or video operator. In addition, they had to be diplomatic in dealing with the directors who lose it in the heat of a live-air show, especially when the director knows little or nothing about the workings of a camera.

These neophyte directors start out fine. "Camera One, get me a cross shot of the actor. Camera Two, get a shot of the picture on the wall. Camera Three, get a wide shot of the actor's hands. Now, super Camera Two over Camera One and ... Holy shit! Get me out of this mess!"

Bob Finch, a technical director at NBC in Hollywood, began his career as the audio man on the *Colgate Comedy Hour*. When he became a technical director, he found that life at the top didn't make it any easier.

After working 30 hours without sleep on this one show, he collapsed from exhaustion. The show's director, alarmed at seeing Finch slumped on the floor, immediately responded by shouting, "Somebody get an ambulance!"

Meanwhile, the more practical-minded producer, seeing the possibility of his live show having to go off the air and the potential loss of sponsors' revenue, called out, "But first, get a replacement for Finch!"

The Video Portion of Television

One of the least publicized technical contributions made by the early technicians was that of the video personnel. No matter how competent the camera operators were in getting pictures the director wanted, it was the video people who made the shots technically acceptable for television.

Each camera had a video operator. They brightened a picture if it was too dark, or darkened a picture if it was too bright. But most importantly, they protected those expensive and sensitive black and white cameras from being ruined.

The primary job of the video operator was to keep a constant vigil on the electronic bleepings on his video screen. If a bleep dared to exceed a prescribed video level, the culprit was tweaked back into compliance.

Perhaps the most important job for the video operator, though, required a great deal of grousing and yelling. If a camera, by accident, neglect or carelessness, was focused on a bright light too long an operator would scream, "Get it off! Get it off! You're ruining my camera!"

Men in front of the camera weren't allowed to wear white shirts; it made their faces "bloom," said the operators. Neither men nor women were allowed to wear eyeglasses, no matter how myopic they were. If, like Phil Silvers, eyeglasses were a part of your persona, you were allowed to wear the frames but under no circumstances the vital lenses that were supposed to be in them.

Women, of course, suffered the most. Both from the video people and the sharp eyes of the network censors. No shiny earrings, necklaces, bracelets, diamond rings or any other flashy adornments. They were not allowed to wear spangled or beaded gowns, and were absolutely forbidden from wearing low-cut gowns that showed cleavage. And even if one eensy-teensy nipple-bulge showed, it was buried behind a Band-Aid!

As one distraught actress put it, "If a director wasn't worrying about the boom shadows on my face, or on the back walls, or the noise the cameras make flipping from one lens to another, or seeing me sweat, or losing a camera, or an overhead light, I would think with all these distractions they would welcome the only two things about live television that were honest and real—my tits!"

The Sound Portion of Television

In live television, an audio mixer does what the movie's "sound designers" do: ensure that the actors, music and sound effects come together in one homogeneous sound. The difference is, sound designers today have the convenience of post-production; audio mixers back then didn't. Nor did they have the luxury of having the performers use R.F. (radio frequency) microphones. These microphones are attached to the performers' bodies and allow them the freedom of movement.

In live television, all stage audio was done with either a hand mike or boom mikes.

The number of mikes a show required often depended on the type of show being done. For instance, in live radio, one audio man I spoke with used only one microphone for a large symphonic orchestra containing strings, percussionists, woodwinds and brass.

In those days, for an audio mixer to suggest that an instrument or instruments in a symphony orchestra be moved, or that additional microphones were needed to improve sound, would be unthinkable. Each musician, he would doubtless be told, was capable of controlling his own loudness or softness.

Doing audio in a crowded television studio was a different matter. "It's difficult getting a good, distinctive sound from a violinist when she's afraid that any minute a sliding trombone is going to goose her."

The Audio Man's Best Friend

Unlike radio, where the actors moved to where the microphones were, in television, the microphones followed the actors with a boom mike. A boom mike

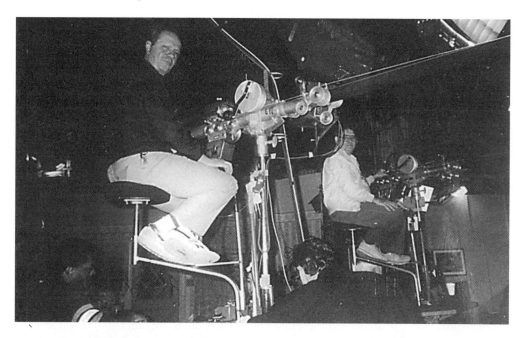

Ernie Dellutri, in the foreground, and Manny Ferrara can be seen relaxing before **Laugh-In.** *Although this show was taped, it was often more hectic than a live show because of its lack of rehearsals and the lunacy of the cast, which included Goldie Hawn and Robin Williams (photograph courtesy of Helen Ferrara).*

The crowded conditions of an early live television studio. The technician in the center is pushing a crane camera similar to those used in films (photograph courtesy of Malachy Wienges).

consists of a microphone attached to a long retractable arm mounted on a high three-wheeled movable pedestal. The boom operators can either telescope the mike out relatively long distances, swing the microphone in horizontal arcs, raise or lower it, or swivel the microphone from side to side to cover two people talking.

By the time a live television show finished its final rehearsal and was ready to go on the air, the studio took on the appearance of a steaming hot electronic jungle.

Vine-like cables were everywhere. Some hung down from the lights, and others snaked in and out and around equipment or slithered across the studio floor, hoping to trap whatever got in their path.

The camera cables were fat, and so were the lighting cables. The boom mike cables were thin, so were the monitor and P.L. (private line) cables. Each one presented a formidable blockade for any piece of equipment needing to roll over them.

Despite all the precautions taken in rehearsal to see that each camera and boom had a clear path to operate in, one actor or one boom mike or one camera in the wrong position could mean serious trouble. As it did on *Lux Video Theater*.

After one of the boom mikes finished with the announcer's opening introduction, the boom had only seconds to get in position to mike the actors at the other end of the studio. Unfortunately, a camera had to make a similar move. In all of the rehearsals, the boom had always crossed in front of the camera. But on air the camera moved too fast and crossed in front of the boom mike, leaving in its wake, a large, fat camera cable. The boom pusher, unaware of the camera's cable, hit it at top speed, causing the top-heavy boom to tip over and send the boom operator flying through the air!

Because of the control room's location, none of this was seen by the director, the technical director, or the audio man. As the cameras came up on the bewildered actors wondering where their microphone was, the equally bewildered audio man, Harold Flood, began screaming to his fallen boom man, Dave Yoder. "Yoder, where the hell are you!?"

Manny Ferrara, having witnessed the accident, had his boom hurriedly pushed in to cover for the stricken Yoder. But because of the cables and his location at a different end of the set, the closest he could get his boom mike to the actors was on top of a wall. As a result, the whole scene was played with the actors sounding as if they were talking at the bottom of a well.

When the director demanded to know why the actors sounded so terrible, Manny Ferrara, not wishing to cause any further undue noise from the set, clicked his P.L. on and responded in a hushed whisper: "Because the regular boom man is flat on his ass."

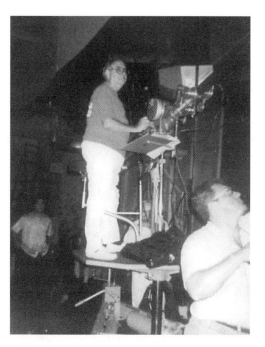

Whether seated or standing, as Manny Ferrara is here, being so close to the lights was a hell of a hot way to make a living (photograph courtesy of Helen Ferrara).

May I Have Quiet, Please—Dammit!

The two biggest problems of live television were the unwanted off-camera noises and the sauna-like heat of the studios. Noise, no matter how seemingly insignificant, was either eliminated or muffled. Men weren't allowed to wear leather-heeled shoes, while women's high-heels were silenced with tape. Studio heat was a more frustrating problem because it involved both heat and noise. Although air conditioners were used extensively during rehearsals, the loud humming noise they produced made them unusable for the air show.

This lack of cool air to offset the suffocating heat was difficult on everyone. But no one suffered more than the boom operators. Standing six feet off the studio floor on the boom's platform brought them six feet closer to the intense heat of the overhead klieg lights.

On a one-hour show, the heat reached such a high temperature, the boom operator passed out. He was immediately replaced by the technician pushing the boom. Fortunately, the boom operator needed only a short rest and some water. And, yes, the show did continue uninterrupted.

Not Now, Captain!

One of the most important functions of the boom operator on the *Captain Kangaroo Show* was to keep his microphone out of the televised picture. This was tricky because in order for the actor or singer to be heard properly, the mike had to be a matter of inches above his head. This distance was called "headroom."

If the boom was too close to the speaker, it would be in the picture; if the boom was too high, it was difficult to hear the speaker. As a result, the boom operator had to constantly adjust the height of the boom microphone to compensate for the speakers' movements and the proper level of their voices.

Finding the correct headroom was particularly difficult if the actor was either making a number of quick moves or if he was simply sitting down. In television, an actor rarely sits forever. The trick is to know when he's going to get up so that you adjust the mike without giving him a concussion.

Because the *Captain Kangaroo Show* was virtually unrehearsed, Bob Keeshan, the kindly old Captain, had his own method of giving signals to the boom operators. If he were seated and talking, his cue to the boom operators to take the boom mike up was to slap his thighs. He would then wait a beat and stand up.

During one episode, however, a personal emergency called the boom man away from his post, and since all the replacement people familiar with the show were doing a political convention in Chicago, Keeshan was given a new boom operator unfamiliar with the ways of the Treasure House.

As the Captain read a story from a book to the children at home, the new boom operator had his microphone skillfully poised inches away from the Captain's gray, well-coiffed wig, so as not to miss a word. Then, as the Captain finished reading, the Captain did the obligatory thigh-slap and stood up. Unfortunately, the microphone didn't. Instead, it hit Keeshan in the center of his wig.

Suddenly, the show's director, Peter Birch, informed Keeshan over the studio speaker that he had stopped the tape. Keeshan, not having suffered any physical harm, demanded to know why Birch had stopped the tape! No one had that authority but Keeshan himself!

Then the boom operator gave Keeshan his answer. As he lowered in the boom mike responsible for hitting Keeshan, there, caught on the mike, and dangling from it like a gray, hairy shroud, was Keeshan's wig.

The Makeup Artists

One of the most difficult jobs back in those early days was trying to make the performers' faces appear natural to the viewers at home. Because of the harsh overhead lighting this took a lot of skill and luck.

Part of the skill was in getting the actress' makeup on without making her look like a hooker, while it took luck for the studio's suffocating heat not to sweat it off.

In the movies this was never a problem. The lighting was better, the studios were cooler and the director had the luxury of time to do a scene over if anything should go wrong.

In live television, once you were on the air, that was it. And no one suffered more than the makeup people. Even after they had done their job of making up the performers, they had to hover next to the camera with a powder puff in one hand, and a box of Kleenex in the other, scrutinizing the actors for a droplet of sweat.

Makeup artists weren't the only ones on perspiration patrol. If a director so much as spotted a molecule of moisture forming on his star's face he'd shout, "Get read to mop her off!"

The next series of events was a picture of fluid efficiency: the stage manager would get the attention of the makeup artist; the director would cut to another camera; the floor manager would cue the makeup artist; the makeup artist would race in, wipe with tissue, pat with powder, and race back to her post.

The Magic of Makeup

Tom Buchanan, a CBS sound-effects artist, was assigned to do the effects on a CBS spectacular entitled *Mame*, starring Rosalind Russell. Because of the difficulty factor of the role and the technical problems of trying to do a show of this magnitude, Tom wasn't at all surprised to see a stand-in doing Ms. Russell's part during the early rehearsals.

What did surprise Tom was how seriously this stand-in was taking her moment in the sun. She complained that this prop wasn't in the correct position, that chair wasn't where it was supposed to be. Although the director put up with her whinings the first day, Tom felt sure she would be replaced.

The second day, it was the same woman and the same complaining. As yet Ms. Russell hadn't made an appearance. Tom could only guess that if this is the way that they did it in films, Ms. Russell was in for a big surprise when she tried to do the upcoming dress rehearsal without any prior rehearsals.

As the moment arrived for Ms. Russell to make her appearance, she did the show from top to bottom without a mistake, miscue, or a flubbed line!

Tom couldn't believe it. For a Hollywood actress, accustomed to the safety net of film, Russell's performance was flawless. Added to that was the fact she didn't have five minutes of on-camera rehearsal! She left all the rehearsing to her stand-in!

When the director heard Tom's comments, he turned and gave him a funny look and replied, "Stand-in? Stand-in? Stand-in hell! That was Rosalind Russell before she put on her Rosalind Russell face!"

The problem with live television is that one moment may find you receiving kudos for your work and the next moment, looking for a place to hide.

One of the nicest actors Buchanan ever worked with was Boris Karloff. In a live performance of *Man of La Mancha*, the script called for Karloff to be wounded in a sword fight. As he lay on the ground dying, he slowly turned to the camera to give his final impassioned speech. And as the camera moved in for a closeup on his face, all America saw that the Man of La Mancha had somehow lost half of his mustache.

As funny as it appeared, no one on the crew laughed. Instead everyone felt heartsick that such a gentle, polite man should be made to look so foolish. And no one felt the pain more that night than the makeup artist who had glued the mustache.

The Stage Managers

Stage managers were the eyes and ears of the director in a television studio. They cued the performers, signaling them when to talk, when to enter, when to exit; they told the performers when to go to lunch, when to come back, when to go to makeup, when to go to wardrobe and even if and when they could go to the bathroom.

Despite early television's requirement that their stage managers have experience as stage managers on Broadway, Ted Baker's experience as a singer, dancer and actor on Broadway in such shows as *Carousel*, *Make Mine Manhattan*, and *Call Me Madam*, more than made up for any lack of actual experience as a stage manager.

Clint Eastwood—Make My Day!

Baker recalled his worst moment in television came during an early Oscar telecast.

A live telecast such as the Oscars is, at best, a mob scene of some of the biggest stars in Hollywood, each one accustomed to being pampered with special treatment. Therefore, unlike the theater with its half-hour call prior to a

In addition to being up for all the normal jobs that went along with being a stage manager, you had to have the ability to get along with people. Your salary may have been paid by NBC, but the stars were your real boss. Being available to make the stars as comfortable as possible under the stress of live television was part of a stage manager's many valuable functions. And yes, the empty glass in Baker's hand once contained Dean Martin's Scotch (photograph courtesy of Ted Baker).

performance, a show like the Oscars depends on each star being at the right place at the right time. And normally they are. But on this night, the next presenter was Charlton Heston—and he was no place in sight! (Heston's limo was stuck in traffic.)

To make matters worse, the director, Marty Parsetta, was in no mood for last-minute surprises. I had worked with Parsetta, and his reputation for being demanding and difficult was well justified.

"Get ready with Charlton Heston!" cried Parsetta.

"There is no Heston!" Baker cried back.

"I don't want to hear there is no Heston!" Parsetta retaliated. "Get Heston out!"

Baker, himself apoplectic, saw a tuxedo out of the corner of his eye and started pushing it out on the stage. When a baffled Clint Eastwood protested that this was Charlton Heston's presentation spot, Baker kept pushing Eastwood and told him, "You're an actor—go out and *act* like Charlton Heston."

CHAPTER 4

Television's Early Risk Takers: Ed Sullivan and Garry Moore

Nineteen forty-eight dawned over 485 Madison Avenue and found Bill Paley, chairman and founder of CBS, desperately searching for new talent to keep up with the ratings of his more well-heeled, deep-pocketed arch-rival over at NBC, David Sarnoff.

Although television had been around since 1927, it was Milton Berle, with all his outlandish vaudeville schtick, that made everyone along Madison Avenue get their noses out of their martinis and take notice of the medium's commercial potential.

Back in the 1920s and 1930s, it was next to impossible to walk down a street on a hot summer's night without hearing the radio voices of Amos and Andy coming from open windows.

In 1948, it was next to impossible to walk past an appliance store without seeing crowds watching the outrageous lunacy of Milton Berle, television's "Mr. Tuesday Night."

To combat this show business phenomenon, William Paley decided to gamble with a newspaper man whose only experience in television was a radio gossip show. His name? Ed Sullivan. If Milton Berle was "Mr. Television" and ruled the airwaves on Tuesday night, Sullivan would soon be "Mr. Sunday Night."

The Ed Sullivan Show

Nothing ever prepared anyone for *The Ed Sullivan Show.* Not the comedians, singers, musicians, bands, magicians, acrobats, jugglers, animal trainers, dancers, and certainly not the long list of celebrities who were victims to Sullivan's own inimitable way of handling introductions.

Appearing on the Sullivan show was a double-edged sword. It could mean national exposure and immediate stardom, or something quite different and certainly unexpected. For instance, if you were Roberta Peters, the renowned Metropolitan Opera singer, would you like to hear yourself introduced as Roberta Sherwood, the pop singer? If you were Shelley Winters, the famous actress, would you like to be introduced as Shelley Berman, the comedian?

Who, of all the performers to feel the sting of Sullivan's often disastrous introductions, received the strangest welcome? José Feliciano, the blind singer and guitar virtuoso, deserves the questionable distinction.

In fairness to Sullivan, because of José's blindness, he was afraid the young man would come off looking awkward. What if he fell? To avoid this embarrassment to the singer, Sullivan wanted José to make his entrance with a seeing-eye dog. When José assured Sullivan he didn't need any assistance, Sullivan wasn't so sure.

When it came time to introduce José Feliciano, what Sullivan said reflected those fears. "And now ladies and gentlemen, next on our stage is the talented young singer, José Feliciano. Not only is this young man blind, he's also Puerto Rican."

Why Sullivan felt compelled to couple blindness and nationality was known only to Ed Sullivan.

And yet, how can you hate someone who at the close of his show wishes his studio and home audience "Happy New Year" in August? Or wants to wish his own hospitalized son-in-law a speedy recovery and can't remember his name? (It was Bob Precht, Ed.)

Sullivan Before There Was Sullivan

Ed Sullivan started out in the newspaper business. His popular *New York Daily News* column, *The Toast of the Town*, was a chatty account of the goings-on in and around Broadway, show business and the sports world.

In addition to writing about show business, Sullivan began talking about it over his own radio show, heard on CBS in 1931. Some of the stars that he lured (without pay) from the theatrical and musical world were Irving Berlin, Jack Pearl, George M. Cohan, Flo Ziegfeld and, on May 2, 1931, a young violinist from Waukegan, Illinois, named Jack Benny.

Sullivan never let Benny forget that he was the one who gave Benny his first radio exposure. In fact, he'd make a point of taking credit for his prize discovery every chance he got. Finally, Benny, tired of hearing it, told one interviewer, "Allowing me to appear on his radio show hardly puts Ed up in the same class with a Columbus, Moses or Einstein."

Although Sullivan had the radio show and was master of ceremonies of the immensely popular Harvest Moon Dance contests sponsored annually by his newspaper, he could neither sing, dance, tell jokes or juggle. Then again, he didn't have to. He had something far better, a widely read newspaper column.

Since the beginning of broadcasting, radio executives recognized the influence these gossip writers had over the often naïve public. The words of Walter Winchell, Louella Parsons, Hedda Hopper, Jimmy Fidler and Dorothy Kilgallen were read in the paper and heard on the radio every day by millions of readers and listeners. Each gossip journalist, then, exerted some control over the public's perception of a celebrity's life and work. And any one of these gossips had it in their typewriters to radically alter the image of an idol.

The power the gossip columnists had to make or break people was frightening. One of these columnists could give a movie "three yawns" in their newspaper and it was enough to cause it to bomb at the box office.

The importance of the power these columnists wielded can best be illustrated by the treatment allegedly given to Walter Winchell by 20th Century–Fox's Darryl Zanuck. Winchell was given a private home, complete with food, drink and a limo on the studio grounds for his own self-indulgence. No strings attached!

It was therefore not an accident, nor was Sullivan's name drawn from a hat, when it was decided to give him a chance to make good on television.

Sullivan Takes the Leap

When Sullivan went into television on June 20, 1948, his total budget was a hefty $1,373! With $375 left to pay for talent that included Dean Martin and Jerry Lewis. Their payment? A whopping $200. This left $175 to be split up among the rest of the performers, including concert pianist Eugene List, Richard Rodgers, Oscar Hammerstein II and the Toastettes, made up of the six original June Taylor Dancers.

Despite Sullivan's clout, some performers still demanded money. In 1956, eight years after Sullivan could only afford $375 for all the performers that appeared on his show, just one performer demanded the unheard sum of $7,500! His name? Elvis.

The only regulars on the Sullivan show were the Ray Bloch Orchestra, Art Hannah (the announcer), and the June Taylor Dancers. Because the early Sullivan show was referred to as *The Toast of the Town* (after his newspaper column), the June Taylor Dancers were referred to as the Toastettes. Later in their career, these dancers would glamorize the stage of *The Jackie Gleason Show*.

It was on the Sullivan show, however, that one of the Toastettes became more than just a pretty face. Because as this young dancer tapped her little heart out, one of her breasts did too. No, it didn't tap; it just came out. As the young lady, unaware that more than her smiling face was showing, continued to smile brilliantly, a national audience of appreciative males smiled back.

Ed Sullivan, as much as he always tried, was not a performer. Fred Allen, the marvelous radio comedian, once said, "Sullivan could be replaced by an Irish setter. Not only would it be cheaper, but if the performers could be made to smell like ducks, they'd make better pointers."

Sullivan was first, second and always a newspaper man. This was reflected in the format of his show. He made certain there was something of interest for the millions of families that watched every Sunday at eight.

It was this huge Sullivan audience that made it one of the most important television shows for a performer to showcase his talents. But being booked to do the show and actually *appearing* on the show were two different matters.

Sullivan rarely took part in rehearsals. Instead, he'd sit off to the side of the stage on a high stool, making notes on a legal pad and watching with a critical eye. An eye that seemed to instinctively know what his audience wanted. When dress rehearsal was over, Sullivan would go up to his dressing room and decide who would, or wouldn't, be seen that night.

It didn't matter what newspapers or *TV Guide* advertised would be on the show that night, it was Ed who had the final say. Even the headliners, the stars, weren't exempt.

Bobby Darin had gotten a reputation of being a pain in the butt. He wasn't; he was a perfectionist. The problem was, being a perfectionist during the days of live television could very well earn you a reputation of being a pain in the butt.

On this particular night, Darin wasn't happy with the way the band was playing his arrangement. He kept insisting on doing it over until they got it right. In live television, no one was more important than the clock on the wall, and as the hands began moving perilously close to show time, Darin was told he had to stop rehearsing. When Darin refused, saying if he didn't get another rehearsal he wouldn't do the show, Sullivan countered with, "Yes, you're not getting another rehearsal, and no, you're not doing the show!"

The Rolling Stones

When my daughter heard the Rolling Stones were going to be on the Sullivan show, she insisted I take her and her girlfriend to see the performance. Having never heard of the Rolling Stones, I wondered why she was so excited, but I agreed.

Because the part of the show that involved sound effects didn't happen until after the Rolling Stones rehearsal, the three of us found seats in the back of the house, and began watching a juggling act rehearsing.

Suddenly my daughter shook me excitedly, "Daddy, that's Mick Jagger sitting over there! … Don't look!" Without looking, I whispered, "Who is Mick Jagger?" My daughter answered with a half-moan, half-sigh.

While she was doing that, I glanced over and saw a very thin, pale young man who, like the Beatles and Three Dog Night, wore his hair long and ragged.

"Do you want to meet him?"

For an answer my daughter only squealed a "Please don't; I'll die!"

So what's a father to do? But if this Mick Jagger was so important to my daughter, what else could I do? I called across the aisle, "Say, Mick, I'd like you to meet my daughter Gail and her friend Lynn." Again my daughter squealed. And as we got up to go over and see him, Mick was on his feet, smiling, with his hand extended. "What a pleasure it is to meet you, Gail and Lynn." Was that class or what?

That same night, I had an occasion to run into Jagger by myself. He was sitting backstage with his thin legs crossed under each other and was smoking a cigarette. I was about to thank him again for his kindness but decided he was being bothered enough by people asking for his autograph.

One man especially stood out. He was one of the huge, bearded Scottish bagpipers who were on the show that night. He wore a kilt and a leopard skin sash across his thick, broad shoulders. As he gruffly asked Jagger for his autograph, I couldn't help wonder who it would be for. Perhaps he too had a daughter.

Ten minutes later he was back. And ten minutes after that he was back. This time I couldn't help watching him as he left. He went directly to the stage door, and as he opened it, a group of teenagers held up money, waving excitedly at him for autographs.

Controversy still rages over who was the most popular rock group to appear on the Sullivan show. All I can say is that the members of the CBS page staff had it down to a science before there were computers.

It all started with the Beatles. The overwhelmingly teenage audience not only screamed and yelled—most of them peed in their pants. And from that day on, the staff CBS pages judged a rock group not by the noise the teenage girls made but by the enthusiasm, excitement and dampness of their seats.

The winner? The Beatles! And to this day, my daughter insists they never counted her seat for Mick Jagger and the Rolling Stones!

The Good with the Bad

Early in Dick Van Dyke's career, he was booked on the *Ed Sullivan Show*. As Van Dyke's writer I was ecstatic, but as an Ed Sullivan sound-effects man, I was scared shitless. Because nothing about the Sullivan show was a certainty. Not even Ed Sullivan.

Whether it was cheapness, a lack of organization or a combination of both, when the Sullivan show needed to have sound effects for one of their acts, they always waited until Sunday, and even then it was the last possible second. It was always, "Get in a cab and get right down with the sound effect of the World Blowing Up!"

Even if it wasn't a request for a sound effect that dramatic, the need for a simple phone ring on the Sullivan show could send your blood pressure soaring.

The first thing you noticed when you arrived at the Sullivan show was the noise. If it wasn't the lighting man screaming last minute adjustments to someone up a tall ladder moving lights, it was the cameraman yelling at anyone that walked in front of his camera while it was on a test pattern.

And there were plenty of people to walk in front of the test patterns. There were the jugglers, the plate spinners, the singers, the seal acts—all trying to cram in some last minute rehearsal before they let the audience in.

Although this gave the appearance of a three-ring circus, it was more like an ant hill that had just been kicked over. And in the midst of it all, here you stood with your phone bell box, wondering who the hell your phone ring was for, and where and when it was to be done!

Sharing the madness of the Sullivan show were his guests. Unlike a dramatic show where scripts were involved, the Sullivan show was a variety show where the only thing resembling a script was a rundown sheet indicating when the acts were supposed to be on, and this often created more confusion since only God and Sullivan knew when—or if—the acts were actually going to be on.

Adding to the chaos were the performers themselves. Most of them spoke little if any English. And old-timers like Buster Keaton hadn't used a script since 1922. The best sound effect cue you could get out of these old-timers was "Ring the telephone when I break the fiddle over my wife's ass!"

Sharing Sullivan's responsibility for the show's bedlam was Marlo Lewis, the show's co-creator and executive producer. Since he was one of the few who knew, in an uncertain short of way, what was going on, I looked for him.

When I found Lewis, he was backstage, surrounded by a troupe of angry Italian jugglers. After Lewis finally fought his way free of them, he was about to be accosted by a tuxedoed animal trainer being trailed by his three seals, who were boisterously honking for more fish.

With time running out, I decided to get Marlo's attention in the only desperate way I knew how—I started ringing my telephone.

Even the seals stopped honking at the sound of the phone ringing. And as I walked up to Lewis, he looked at me, and then at the prop sound-effect phone.

"What the hell is this!?"

"That's what I'd like to know. I got a call to do the sound effect of a phone ringing and no one knows anything about it."

He quickly shrugged, told me to see Ray Bloch, the orchestra leader, and went back to telling the seal trainer that Sullivan wants them to cut 15 seconds out of the seals' playing "God Bless America" on their horns and to go right to the big finish!

The last outburst I heard from the trainer was, "It isn't enough I teach my seals to play an American song—now I have to teach them to tell time!"

I found Bloch in the basement playing cards. I waited for a break in the game, introduced myself and asked him if he knew where the phone ring occurred. Without bothering to look up, he told me it was all taken care of musically.

I looked down at the top of his bald head and told him he was mistaken and that I was the designated ringer of the phone. This time he did look up.

"No, you're mistaken. Specs Powell in rehearsal, used his drummer's cowbell for the phone ring, and he'll do it on the air."

Now it was my turn to get huffy.

"Not unless you want a lot of union trouble. Hitting a cowbell ain't a phone ring. One is part of a drummer's traps, and the other is a sound effect. And unless Specs Powell has a piece of music with that cue written on it, I ring the phone."

Hearing the heat in our voices, the musicians in the game laid down their cards to listen. But it was over. I turned and went up to the box seat where the sound effect area was and waited until air—and to find out who would ring the phone.

On air, I ignored what was happening on stage and kept my attention focused on Bloch. It got so I felt like part of the old vaudeville routine where a monkey is told to keep his eye on a banana so no one steals it.

At last, my banana looked up at me with an extended finger. Then it pointed at me and I rang the phone. Although I was relieved to have the nasty business over, it wasn't over. After all this, because we hadn't rehearsed, the audio man forgot to open my microphone! But it turned out fine; Ray Bloch forgot to tell Specs Powell his cue was cut, and he made the phone sound with his cowbell!

Writing on the Sullivan Show Was Just as Difficult

The pantomime sketch I wrote for Dick Van Dyke to do on the Sullivan show involved Van Dyke coming home from a late-night party a little tipsy. After a series of mishaps, he finds to his horror that he's in the wrong house.

Getting in the wrong house was the surprise payoff to the whole sketch. And in comedy, the payoff is designed to get the biggest laughs. And perhaps it would have, if Sullivan didn't think a pantomime was too highbrow for his audience.

As Van Dyke and I both stood offstage waiting for Sullivan to introduce him, Sullivan ignored the brief introduction I had written, and instead ad-libbed:

"And next on our stage is a young, new comedian named Dickie Van Dyke. Tonight, Dickie is going to do a pantomime. And as we all know, a pantomime doesn't have any spoken words. This is a little pantomime about Dickie coming home to one of those houses on a street that all look alike—"

The color went out of Van Dyke's face, and I felt sick. One of us said—or maybe we said it together:

"Now all he has to do is tell what the payoff is!"

"—and so poor Dickie gets in the wrong house!"

Sullivan didn't have a clue what live television, or any television, was all about. He would walk away from the boom mike over his head and wonder why the audience couldn't hear him. He'd walk out of camera range and wonder why people couldn't see him. Or even worse, at the last minute, change the sequence of when an animal act was supposed to be on.

I'll Sleeet Your Throat!

No one on the show suffered more than Eddie Brinkman, the stage manager. Compared to the problems sound effects and Van Dyke had on the show, it was like comparing a hangnail to a nervous breakdown.

It was Brinkman's responsibility to get the acts on and off the stage. To do this in an orderly fashion, he had a rundown sheet he had used in rehearsal indicating where an act was to appear in the show. I can only say this rundown sheet was more of a hindrance than a help. What act went on, or didn't go on, and in what order it went on, was totally up to Ed.

On this particular night, the production song number was to be a desert scene. And to give the tent and plastic palm tree more of an authentic look, Sullivan thought it would be a nice touch to have a camel walk past the tent at the opening.

The problem the show always had with animals as large as a camel or elephant was the lack of space backstage. As a result, the animals were kept out on the street.

The first problem with this outside location was that it was colder than hell out there. And as Sullivan should have known, camels aren't accustomed to cold, nor was their Arabic trainer.

That night, after an uncomfortable day out on the street, the camel's moment had arrived. It was time for his desert number. As the trainer led him on stage behind the curtain, Brinkman got word that Sullivan wanted to delay the desert number and put the German plate spinner on instead.

Brinkman, through frantic gestures to the trainer, waved the camel offstage and back out to the street.

As the plate spinner concluded his act, Brinkman was notified: "Sullivan wants the song number!" Brinkman made a dive for the street and signaled for the camel. The camel had no sooner squeezed its way through the stage door, when again Brinkman heard, "No, wait! Sullivan wants to jump ahead to the balloon clown!"

Again, the camel was ushered out into the cold, and the clown into the warm spotlight.

As the show neared the end, Brinkman heard the voice from hell saying, "Bring in the camel!" Eddie quickly pushed his way through the crowded backstage, and out into the now-frigid air. This time the Arab trainer spoke what must have been the only English he knew.

"Theees time, my camel goes on, or I sleeet your fucking throat!"

The good news is, Brinkman didn't get his throat slit, and the camel finally did get on the stage, and when he did, he made the most of it. Right in front of the tent, the tenor and the millions of Sullivan viewers at home! The *Sullivan Show*—there would never be another like it!

On June 6, 1971, after 23 years on CBS, the *Ed Sullivan Show* went off the air. How popular was this show that critics said couldn't last? In a list of the 100 most popular shows in the history of television, the *Ed Sullivan Show* finished seventh. One can only wonder how high the show could have finished if Sullivan could have sung, or told jokes, or juggled or had at least *some* sort of talent.

The Garry Moore Show

As crazy as the Sullivan show was, that's how organized and sane *The Garry Moore Show* was. And it was all due to Garry, who, of the early risk takers, was perhaps given the least credit for his contributions to early television.

What can you say about a man that only got angry twice in the eight years I did his show? And even then it wasn't at me or anyone else directly connected with the show; it was at agency representatives.

What can you say about a man—really a television star—who wouldn't allow any sponsors on his show unless he personally approved of their products? Or, what can you say about a man who never had a scandalous word printed, or even said, about him?

Perhaps Durward Kirby, Garry's announcer and longtime friend, said it all when Garry was being honored with a roast by the Friars Club. The Friars Club is a fraternal organization composed of people in the entertainment business. Periodically they "roast" one of their members with a dinner and a lot of good-natured kidding.

When it came time for Durward to speak, he had this to say: "People often ask me what it's like working on television with Garry five days a week, fifty-two weeks a year. All I can say is—" At this point Durward paused and looked solemnly over at Garry and continued in a voice fighting to hold back the tears, "If you're familiar with St. Joseph—" an audible and somewhat angry moan rippled through the crowd of merrymakers. If Durward wanted to kissass with Garry, this was not the appropriate place or time to do it.

Durward waited for the crowd to settle down, and continued, "or even if you aren't familiar with St. Joseph, then you know [*looks affectionately over at Garry*] what a dirty, filthy little city it is!"

The crowd screamed, applauded and stamped their feet; it was the biggest laugh of the evening. And the one that laughed the hardest and loudest was Garry Moore.

Garry Moore was born in Baltimore on January 31, 1918. In 1934 he left high school to accept a job as a writer and announcer at WBAL, Baltimore. This lasted until 1938, when he left to take a job in St. Louis at KWK. While there, his talents were soon recognized by NBC, and in 1939 he moved on to be the writer and star of the immensely popular radio show *Club Matinee.*

Up until the time he starred on *Club Matinee,* Garry Moore was really Thomas Garrison Morfit. But once his name was being heard on network radio, he decided he needed a shorter and simpler name for audiences to remember.

Most celebrities have their press agents come up with a new name; not Garry—he held a contest. A contest open to all his listeners. And if their name was selected, they would win $50.

After receiving an avalanche of mail, the winning name came from a lady in Pittsburgh. And from that time on, Thomas Morfit became (but only professionally) Garry Moore.

Garry did the *Club Matinee* show for four years. He then left Chicago and signed to be the co-star of the *Jimmy Durante–Garry Moore Show.* Although that *was* the formal name, because of Durante's celebrated bulbous nose and Garry's short haircut, the show was affectionately referred to as "The Haircut and the Schnoz."

Durante was a master at malapropisms and mispronouncing words in his hoarse, raspy, often perplexed sounding voice. Moore, on the other hand, had a smooth and effortless delivery.

This contrast of styles was a comedy writer's dream. Each week they gave Garry a torrent of *tongue-twisting-text-to-tease-titillate-tantalize-trip-and-trap* Garry, upon the successful completion of which Durante, sounding amazed, would shout one of the show's catchphrases, "That's my boy!"

What perhaps even Durante didn't know was that Garry as a boy hadn't always been on such friendly terms with words, especially speaking on the telephone. His stuttering became so debilitating and embarrassing to him that he covered it with humor by telling his friends, "If you call me on the telephone and no one answers, don't hang up; it's me."

The Water's Fine

When Garry Moore accepted Bill Paley's offer "to test the waters" of early television, he told his agent that he would like to accompany him when the latter negotiated with the CBS Business Affairs people.

His agent gave Garry a gentle smile but wisely declined his request. "No, Garry. To those people you're just a commodity." Garry, however, was insistent. "I'd still like to see how it's done."

Garry and his agent arrived at CBS and met with Zack Becker, Paley's money man. After a few moments of politeness, Garry's agent pushed across the desk the show's budget proposal, already cut to the bone by Garry and his staff after many hours of haggling, soul searching and nit-picking.

Zack picked it up, took one quick glance at the figure and exploded, "What! You want this much for *him*!"

Garry picked up his hat and left the rest of the negotiations to his agent.

The first member of the cast to be recruited was an old friend and colleague of *Club Matinee*, Durward Kirby. Although Durward was an excellent and highly respected radio announcer, this was to be his television debut.

Garry couldn't have made a better choice. The contrast between Durward's height of 6'4" and Garry's 5'6" would be put to use in the hundreds of sketches that they were to play together.

In addition to Garry and Durward, Ken Carson and Denise Lor were hired as the show's two singers. Again Garry struck pure gold. In addition to singing, both Ken and Denise appeared in comedy sketches and helped out with the desk talk between Garry and Durward.

This is the way the people in the CBS Publicity Department saw their four new stars: Ken Carson and Durward Kirby—top row; Garry Moore and Denise Lor—bottom row (photograph courtesy of Durward Kirby).

When I joined the show in 1951, I was extremely impressed with how quiet everything was. No camels out on the street, no fights with the orchestra leader over who would ring the phone, and yet Ivan Sanderson, a noted English zoologist, did bring in live animals without threatening to "sleeet" anyone's throat.

Garry's guests varied from an 80-year-old former buffalo hunter to the eminent architect Frank Lloyd Wright. He also interviewed the Trapp Family about their harrowing experiences during World War II and listened to them sing. Perhaps because of this exposure, the exploits of the Trapp Family served as the inspiration for both the musical and the movie *The Sound of Music*.

Where Moore Discovered Much of His Talent

Because Garry couldn't compete with Sullivan in luring the big-money stars to his show, he did welcome the talents of future stars. Some of the young talent that appeared on the show were Don Knotts, Don Adams, Jonathan Winters, Carol Burnett, Steve Allen, Phil Foster and Harry Belafonte. These are just a few who were given an early career boost. Unfortunately, not all of them were hits.

A shot of the four stars after a quick wardrobe change—Durward, Garry, Denise and Ken. On one occasion, the beautiful Denise Lor made a costume change a little too rapidly. The song she was doing required that she dress as a tramp. And she did, well almost. Where else but on live television do you get applause for forgetting to button your fly? (Photograph courtesy of Durward Kirby.)

One comedian from the West Coast had been highly recommended. Unfortunately, his performance fell far short of the praise he had been given.

His routine focused on the problems of trying to hang up your clothes with the wire coat hangers supplied by most motels.

"There's always a bunch of them. And they're always tangled up … or bent … or … or…," and so on for six excruciatingly long minutes.

Six minutes without one single laugh. Those of us on the show died with him. You hated to see a comedian, or any young performer, go through such a horrible ordeal. To his credit, he didn't let this experience destroy him or his confidence. His name? Johnny Carson.

Rising stars weren't the only people that Garry helped. When Garry found out that Marshall, the theater's black janitor, had been fired for moonlighting, Garry was furious.

First he petitioned the company to reconsider and give the elderly Marshall another chance. When the finally did, Marshall went to Garry and thanked him for getting his job back at the theater.

"Cause you know, Mr. Moore, show business is my life."

The number of people it took to bring **The Garry Moore Show** *into the homes of 2,000,000 Americans daily. This includes everyone from Garry to the production people, technical personnel, writers, wardrobe and makeup people, stage hands and page staff. Standing to the right of Garry (second from left, first row) is Herb Sandford, the producer. On Garry's left is the director, Clarence Schimmel (photograph courtesy of Durward Kirby).*

Some Other Live Television Problems

Although the Moore show lacked the chaos of the Sullivan show, it wasn't without controversial issues of a more serious nature. This occurred in the winter of 1957. Garry was invited by the Florida Citrus Commission to be their guest for a week and do his show out of Winter Haven, Florida. Garry, anxious for a change of scenery for his show, agreed ... provided certain conditions could be met.

Two of Garry's staff were black: Alfreda Diggs, Garry's production assistant; and Blanche Hunter, his wardrobe mistress. Because of Alfreda's light color, she could "pass" for white; Blanche couldn't. Although in 1957 color wasn't a problem in New York City, it *was* in Florida. To make certain there wouldn't be any problems during the show's one-week stay, Garry phoned the show's Winter Haven host, Bob Eastman, and made it clear that everyone on the show—especially Alfreda and Blanche—would be given the same privileges.

This was a gutsy phone call for Garry to make. It would be three years before

Martin Luther King, Jr., and 52 of his black supporters would stage a sit-down demonstration in an Atlanta department store. Most national entertainers wouldn't have made the call. Arthur Godfrey didn't when his show went to Florida. As a result, because the Mariners Quartet had two members in the group who were black, the group was left behind.

Alfreda and Blanche recalled later, "In and around the hotel there was no segregation problem as long as we ate in a designated place. Although it was difficult accepting the fact that we were only first-class citizens in our 'compound,' I must admit being fearful straying off for fear of an accident."

Does It Really Pay to Be Honest?

One of the features on the Moore show was something called a "Public Service." These were the moments Garry would share something with his audience he felt important. Like the time he related a problem he had with hotels.

In checking out of a posh resort hotel, Garry made the unthinkable tourist faux pas. In an effort to be honest, he actually told the checkout clerk he was "stealing" a towel! Not a big one, just a small hand towel with the logo of the hotel tastefully emblazoned in the center. Garry explained that his wife had started a collection of hotel towels for their guest bathroom and asked him to get one at this particular hotel.

At first the clerk was startled, then perplexed and finally excited as he recognized the honest thief to be in reality a television celebrity who made his living making people smile. Perhaps that was what this was all about, the clerk doubtless concluded—some sort of television hijinks. Or better still, perhaps both he and Mr. Moore were on *Candid Camera* and that umbrella Mr. Moore was carrying was really a microphone!

Quickly running his hand over his head smoothing out any errant strands of hair, he flashed Garry his toothiest of smiles and waited for further developments in his sudden thrust into the glaring spotlight of show business.

When it finally struck home that Garry Moore was really telling the truth and there wasn't an Allen Funt hiding behind a potted palm, it put the clerk in an embarrassing position.

Garry Moore, a big television star, had just confessed that he had stolen a towel. No, that's not quite accurate. He didn't say he *stole* it. He simply said that he had *taken* a towel and that he wanted the cost of the towel put on his bill. A hotel clerk's accounting nightmare. Never in the history of innkeeping had this ever been done. There was nothing in the hotel's billing manual that covered unvarnished, blatant honesty. So what was a clerk to do?

After a moment of hesitation, he decided to take a drastic step into uncharted hotel waters by being as honest as his celebrated guest. Casting fearful eyes over the lobby lest the hotel manager be lurking within hearing, the clerk leaned over the counter, almost crushing his coronation boutonniere, and conspiratorially whispered, "To be perfectly honest, Mr. Moore—and telling you this is against the hotel association's code of things not to reveal to guests—but you have already paid for the towel. At the end of the year we compute the money lost through guests"—again the clerk gave a deferential smile—"accidentally *removing* such items as towels, silverware, sheets, blankets, bedspreads, you know, little forget-me-nots of their stay here. So, please, Mr. Moore, accept your little memento with the compliments of the hotel."

Garry, who by now was running late for his plane connection, rushed across the hotel lobby wondering how something could be considered "complimentary" if you've already paid for it.

After relating the story on the air, the response from the viewers was overwhelming. The amount of mail tripled. Unfortunately, all of it was from irate hotel chains wishing the next time Garry felt like being honest, television wasn't the place to do it!

The True Christmas Spirit

During the height of the Christmas shopping madness, Garry wondered whether parents were really and truly buying toys their children wanted or were overly influenced by what a present cost. Should a child love and appreciate a toy simply because the parents took out a second mortgage to buy it? Garry decided to find out.

It was two weeks before Christmas and Garry, prior to the show, had his staff pick out a young boy and girl from the studio audience. He then had them taken to a dressing room backstage so they couldn't hear what was being said onstage.

When the time for the little test came, the curtains opened, revealing a stage filled with toys. The audience, made up almost entirely of adults, *oooh*'d and *aaa-ah*'d their delight at the dazzling sight.

Garry then took a tour of the toys. They ranged from an inexpensive stuffed doll to a dollhouse from Fifth Avenue's fashionable—and expensive—F.A.O. Schwarz.

The dollhouse had a dozen rooms, fully furnished, right down to tiny satin pillows on the beds. It was even electrically wired so that all the lamps and ceiling lights could be lit. It was magnificent. And the cost? A month's salary for a 1953 office worker. The *oooh*s that greeted this announcement fairly shook the theater.

As the children were brought on the stage, their little 8-year-old mouths dropped open nearly as wide as their disbelieving eyes. At first all they did was stare. Then as Garry invited them each to pick out one gift—without revealing what any of the toys cost—including the dollhouse, the children's quest for a toy began.

Of course, all the women in the audience, from ages 20 to 80, wanted to shout out to the little girl, "Honey, pick the dollhouse!" But all they could do was sit on the edges of their seats in agonizing silence as the girl paused at the dollhouse and then continued on to the array of toys on display.

The boy also had his pricey temptations. But, as yet untouched by the more mercenary aspects of this most joyous season, he walked past a cowboy suit that featured a fleece-skin vest and leather chaps, to get to a Roy Rogers BB gun. But after looking down the sights at some imagined, unshaven varmint, he put the gun down and moved on.

At last, after what seemed to the audience unspeakable hours, the children had made their decisions. The boy went first. And without hesitation, he went for the Flexible Flyer snow sled.

Then came the big decision for the little girl. She too had made up her mind. As she walked towards the dollhouse the women in the audience squealed their delight and approval. But horror of all horrors—the girl didn't stop at the dollhouse! Heavens no! The child, instead, made a beeline for an inexpensive stuffed doll that couldn't have cost more than a buck and a half!

The audience moaned and groaned. How could the child have been so foolish! Would the poor little thing ever amount to anything in this world making decisions like that? The little girl's response to Garry put the audience's mind at ease. "I picked my doll because she looked so lonely."

When the boy was asked why he had selected the sled, his eyes lit up with excitement. "I've always wanted to go sleigh riding!"

When Garry asked the boy if it was snowing now where he lived, the child answered brightly, "No, I live in Florida."

Garry paused a moment and then asked gently, "Has it ever snowed where you live in Florida?"

The boy, undaunted by the question, shook his head and smiled, "No, but this year I'm hoping it will."

From my sound-effects position up in the box seat overlooking the stage, I could see by Garry's eyes, and the tenderness on the faces of the audience, that if wishes could come true, this Christmas, Florida would be getting one hell of a blizzard!

I could never characterize Garry as a great comedian. He wasn't. No one knew this better than Garry. He never lied to himself. No, his greatness was his ability to communicate an honesty and genuine respect for his audience. And despite the huge successes he had with his daytime show, *I've Got a Secret*, and the nighttime *Garry Moore Show*, he refused to attribute it to anything he personally did. "An awful lot of talented people made the wheels go around," he'd say.

Not only was Thomas Garrison Morfit an early risk taker, he was a remarkable man.

CHAPTER 5

Not All the Days Were Golden

If many of the top studio engineers in live television had the same free agent's clause that the star sports figures have with their clubs today, live television would have been a bloody battleground of broken bodies and careers.

The networks foresaw this problem, and, to prevent it, they had an unwritten agreement among themselves stating that there would be no raiding one another's key technical personnel. This worked out fine for the rival networks. But what the networks didn't have control over was the intrigue that went on among some of the technical people working for the same network, especially regarding shows that paid substantial fees to their audio mixers.

Although the Godfrey show never used sound effects, I was sent over to play a recorded commercial on the show.

As I entered the control room, the first person I saw was the already legendary, and controversial, Arthur Godfrey. The entertainer simply had a presence that could be felt.

Famous for his ingenuous, friendly way of speaking on radio, he added a boyish and disarming smile for television and raised sincerity to an art form.

At the moment I walked in, he had his jacket off and was neither friendly nor smiling. His already ruddy face was rapidly approaching the redness of his silk suspenders. He had one knee up on the audio console and was talking over the studio "talkback" (P.A. system) to his orchestra leader.

"Damn it, Archie, the music sounds awful! What's wrong?"

Blyer shrugged and looked helplessly at his musicians. "I don't know, Arthur. It sounds good out here."

"Well, it sounds like hell in here!"

Before Arthur could go any further, the audio man spoke up. "It's over-orchestrated, Arthur."

Godfrey, anxious to solve the problem, called out to Blyer, "It's over-orchestrated."

Blyer seemed stumped by the word *over-orchestrated*, so he simply echoed, "Over-orchestrated, Arthur?"

At this point the audio man spoke up with a jaunty air of confidence. "I can fix it, Arthur. Just give me a moment."

It was at that moment that I recognized there was another audio mixer in the control room listening and carefully watching both Godfrey and the other audio mixer. This was not uncommon. The scheduling department often assigned their engineers to observe other shows in case the regular got sick or went on vacation. But just by the way this audio man hung back in the shadows, I doubt if that's why he was here.

As the Godfrey audio man twisted a number of dials and rearranged a number of patch cords, he finally said, "Tell Archie to try it now, Arthur."

Arthur did, and the music sounded great. Even Godfrey was impressed. He pounded the audio man on the shoulders for doing a great job, then turned and began talking to his producer about other pressing matters.

As soon as Godfrey's slight confrontation with Blyer was over, the visiting audio man, without bothering to say as much as hello or goodbye to anyone, quietly slipped out of the control room and went offstage to talk to Blyer.

"Archie, the audio man is screwing you. There was nothing wrong with the orchestra's sound. That was all bullshit to impress the old man. He didn't fix anything! He had the mikes closed to the string section! Then when he told Godfrey he could fix it, he simply opened the mikes to the string section! The audio man is screwing you, Archie, to make himself look good!"

Archie Blyer turned to his informant and smiled, "So? What else is new?"

It's All in the Ears of the Beholder

Despite the madness of working the Sullivan show, the technical crew was the envy of all the engineers at CBS. Although the show offered ample overtime, the allure had less to do with the money than with the prestige of being associated with one of CBS' top-rated shows. A number of envious engineers tried their damndest to get on the show by using some rather bizarre tactics.

Vacation time was often backstabbing time at the networks. And the backs most often targeted by audio mixers belonged to their colleagues who worked for *Studio One, Playhouse 90, Jackie Gleason, Garry Moore*, and especially the *Ed Sullivan Show.*

Because doing the audio on Sullivan was such a difficult and stressful job, Sullivan gave the audio man some special perks. In addition to the extra overtime, the show picked up his check whenever he went out on the town with his family, presumably for the purpose of scouting possible acts for the show. But whether he did or didn't scout, and instead just enjoyed himself, the show always picked up the tab.

On one vacation break, the replacement saw an easy way of getting rid of the regular audio man. During the prior week, when he was observing the regular audio man, he noticed the man was making his job look especially difficult by having an enormous number of mike patch cords that didn't connect to mikes. And just to even things out, the regular had set up dozens of mikes throughout the theater that didn't connect to patch cords. Armed with this juicy information, the replacement couldn't wait to reveal what it was like to have an honest audio man doing the Sullivan show.

When his turn in the hot seat arrived, the audio man was proud of the amount of mikes and patch cords he had eliminated. And more important, he thought, he had reduced hours of padded overtime the regular audio always put in for.

As the producer came into the control room, he went into the audio booth to introduce himself. As he did, he became curious at the half-empty patch board. When the audio man shrugged and told him the story of the bogus mikes and cords, the producer thanked him for his alertness and for bringing it to his attention.

The next week, even though there were four weeks remaining before the regular man returned, the relief man was kicked off the show. The reason?

"The music, the singers, Ed's voice, everything sounded lousy!" complained the producer, "just because that sonofabitch of a relief man was too lazy to connect the proper amount of mikes!"

You Want a Tiger to Do What!

One of my early television shows was a popular thriller called *The Web*. Many future stars appeared on the show. One I remember in particular was an actor who came out of the then-popular "Actors Studio" mold. His appearance, the way he gestured, and the mumblings of his words were a direct imitation of another young and talented actor appearing on Broadway, Marlon Brando. I couldn't help thinking, that's just what the world needs, two Marlon Brandos! Well, the world didn't get two Brandos; his early imitator turned out to be Paul Newman.

On this particular night, the *Web* script was loaded with sound effects. The story involved a circus that had somehow foolishly misplaced its huge, ferocious Bengal tiger—a tiger that was now terrorizing a town and looking for a few people to snack on!

The suspense as to the whereabouts of this fearsome beast kept building and building till just before the middle commercial, and then all hell broke loose! Then, the air fairly exploded with sound effects: tiger roars, police sirens screaming, police cars screeching to a halt, gunshots, ricochets—all the sounds that four turntables could carry! But was the producer satisfied? No! He wanted to hear the sound of the tiger running across the roof!

The sound of the tiger running would take only a brief three seconds, maybe less. And with all the other sounds I had going, the audience would never hear it. In addition, I didn't have anything for that effect. You just couldn't come up with as complicated an effect as a tiger pawing his way over a roof in a matter of a few minutes, or even a few hours, and make it sound realistic.

At first I tried talking the producer out of doing the effect. We had just done the dress rehearsal! There wasn't enough time before the air show to experiment with effects! The sound was too soft to be heard over the other, louder sounds! He insisted. I then told him the tiger sound was such an ambiguous one that the audience wouldn't understand! He demanded I do it. I then resorted to a sound man's argument of last resort with balky producers. I pointed out I would have to get a *second* man.

The sound of the dreaded words "second man" and the extra money they suggested was enough to strike fear in the hearts of any self-respecting, money-pinching producer. But to my surprise, Herb Hirshman's voice never flinched: "So get him."

I fired my last hope at him. "He won't have time to rehearse before air time, and he'll have to *ad-lib* something!"

"So get him."

That did it! I went to the phone, called the office and made my request.

The man they sent couldn't have been a worse choice. He didn't have any great love for me because I skipped over the traditional apprenticeship program and started right out doing shows. He cared even less about television. The old-timers from radio called it "the damned Mickey Mouse medium."

Although I hadn't served an apprenticeship period, I had done sound effects freelance for more than two years. But that didn't count with Al Binnie. He was of the old school, which held that in order to learn how to do sound effects the *right* way you had to be an apprentice first! And like I said, he hated television and everyone in it with a burning passion.

When I told Binnie the effect the producer wanted, Binnie exploded.

"What! You got me away from a poker game when I was winning to come here to do *WHAT*!"

"A tiger running across the roof," I reminded him.

"You got me down here for one lousy effect!"

"No, Al," I corrected, "the producer got you down here for one lousy effect."

It should be of interest that Al Binnie was the sound-effects artist who coined this phrase back in radio: "They'll never hear it in Canarsie."

Canarsie, for those of you who don't live in the New York City area, is a section of Brooklyn. And because the Canarsie section of Brooklyn was only a moderately long subway ride from the CBS transmitter located in Manhattan, if a sound effect (or surface noise of a record) couldn't be heard in a neighborhood as close as Canarsie, it couldn't be heard anywhere. The inference being, don't sweat the small stuff. And because the sound of a tiger running across the roof would most likely not be heard under all the other sounds—including music—this was, in Binnie's opinion, definitely sweating the small stuff.

As a result, for the next few moments Al just stared at me with disdain. Then a wicked and cruel smile began to play around the corners of his mouth, and a cold gleam came to his eyes. This time his voice was calm, and his words deliberate.

"If they want the sound of a tiger running across the roof, I'll give them the sound of a tiger running across the roof."

With that, Al picked up a large rubber mallet and by way of demonstration, walked over to the back wall that contained our large-sound effects. Effects like a large house door, a screen door, a closet door, cupboard doors, and a huge 1935 Ford car door. Al, of course, passed over anything made of wood, which in my mind would have best simulated the sound of a log cabin's roof, and instead, stood poised at the metal car door.

"I just hope the roof is made of tin," Al sneered gleefully. He then proceeded to bang the mallet across the length and width of the metal car door.

It made a terrible racket. Nothing like the sound that the padded paws of a lithe tiger would make—more like that of an elephant trampling down on empty beer cans.

Vic Rhubei, CBS–New York, doing sound effects out of Studio One. And what Vic has his right hand on also served as the roof that Al Binnie's tiger scampered across on **The Web** *(photograph courtesy of Malachy Wienges).*

This photo shows Al Binnie more in his element—radio. He's the one in the center of the picture who isn't smiling. Others are (from left to right) Jim Rogan, doing manual effects on the floor, Walt Pierson, two unidentified production assistants, Jack Amrhein (in back of Al) and, seated next to the tympanies, Vic Rhubei (photograph courtesy of Malachy Wienges).

"Is that what those Mickey Mouse producers want?"

Again, Al flashed that look of contempt, half for me and half for television.

Being the junior man in the department, I decided I had reasoned with Al enough. If he wanted to make a horse's ass of himself just to show up the inexperience of a television producer, let him; I had enough to do with my sirens, screeches, ricochets and gunshots.

When I asked Al if he was going to give the audio man a sound level check for his tiger effect, he simply shook his head and smirked fiendishly.

"Why? And spoil the surprise of the tiger effect I had spent so much time creating?"

In radio, this would have never happened. Everything was carefully rehearsed and the mere thought of changing an effect after dress rehearsal, without the producer hearing the effect, was unthinkable. Suddenly I had a disturbing thought! Although Binnie had been called down to do the tiger effect, the producer had no way of knowing this. I had simply said I needed a second man. So by Binnie screwing up the effect, he might be trying to get me kicked off the show! If he was, at least he wasn't doing it behind my back.

As the show went on the air, Binnie sat to the side, idly tossing the rubber mallet from hand to hand in street-gang fashion as if it were a switchblade knife.

As the conclusion to Act One drew near, Binnie rose, ground his cigarette out, and walked over to his 1935 Ford Bengal tiger.

Suddenly, we heard over our headsets "Ready with all the sounds, including the new tiger effect. Take it on the camera cut to Camera Two. Ready Camera Two. Take it!—sound effects!!!"

I sent all four records spinning at once! The sirens, the car screeches, the gunshots, the ricochets, and then as I winced I heard Binnie's tiger banging across the tinny car door!

I was grateful when we went to black and into the commercial. It would give me time to whip off my headset so I wouldn't have to listen to the angry tirade from the producer. But fast as I was, I wasn't fast enough. It was Herb's loud voice.

I turned to see if Al had his headset on. He did. Good! Let him hear it too! Herb was talking again, this time even louder.

"Bob, that was the best damn effect of the show! I could actually see the tiger running across the roof! Keep up the good work!"

As Al tossed the mallet on the table, he turned to me and flashed a scornful smile, "And this is what's going to replace radio? Not on the coldest day in hell!"

Live television—was there anything ever like it?

You're Allowed Just One Phone Call, Buddy!

One of the Sullivan boom operators was noted for his practical jokes. To get even, or more likely, get him replaced with one of his own buddies, one of the cameramen decided to play a little trick of his own.

First he went to a military store and bought several dummy hand grenades. He then placed them in the boom man's car trunk. And because the boom man lived in New Jersey, he called the George Washington Bridge authorities, stating that a man threatening to blow up one of the toll booths would be coming through around twelve o'clock that night. Then, after giving the mad bomber's license plate number, he hung up.

Not everyone who heard of this serious prank thought it was funny. And that Sunday during rehearsal, the boom man was alerted as to what was being planned. The boom man thanked his informant and, remembering that one of the featured acts on the show involved elephants, figured out a way of having the cameraman's prank blow up in his face.

During a rehearsal break, he hustled out to the street and gathered up a half dozen of the huge elephant droppings. He then took the hand grenades out of the trunk and replaced them with the elephant droppings.

At the stroke of midnight, as his car approached one of the toll booths, he was met by armed guards. After being ordered from the car, he was told to open the trunk. He refused, saying there was nothing in there but a bunch of elephant dung.

"Oh, nothing but elephant poop, huh?"

"No sir, I said elephant dung. You said poop."

"And you wouldn't be wanting to use that *dung* to blow up a toll booth, would you?"

"No sir, just to help my daffodils grow."

"Open the goddamn trunk—*now!*"

As the boom man opened the trunk, the guard ripped open the large paper bag. Not believing his eyes, he began suspiciously sniffing what he saw.

"Well, I'll be a sonofabitch, it *is* elephant shit!"

As the triumphant boom operator smiled at how he outwitted the trap, one of the other armed guards noted in a concerned voice:

"On the other hand, maybe it just looks and smells like elephant shit. We better have the bomb squad examine it. Okay, buddy, come with us."

Ah yes, live television. Was there ever anything like it?

CHAPTER 6

Radio SFX and Television Face Off

Although live television had been a reality since Farnsworth transmitted the first picture on September 7, 1927, many radio diehards firmly believed as late as 1951 that television would never become the dominant force that radio was.

For instance, how could live television with its hot, crowded little studios have the Lone Ranger chase a band of ruffians out of Dodge City like radio could? Or could Buck Rogers pursue the dastardly Killer Kane to the outer reaches of the solar system?

And what about the bread and butter of radio, the beloved soaps? For God's sake, what housewife had the time to watch them and *still* cook, mind the kids *and* do the housework?

As arguments raged for and against television, those of us in sound effects crossed our fingers, lit candles, and prayed TV would never catch on. But, of course, it not only did, but radio supported its growth during the lean years.

It might not have been so bad if our role in radio hadn't been so important. But it was. In radio no one made a move without us. No one so much as walked to a door, washed a dish, or shot off a gun unless we did the walking, washing and pulling the trigger!

Walt Gustafson, ABC–New York, even received kudos for his sound-effect work from the highly respected author, S. J. Perelman, who praised the sound man for being able to "ring like a telephone, crash like a chair, and slither like fog. Gee, what a man!"

Walter Kerr, *The New York Times* theater critic, had this to say about Gustafson's demanding work in the hit Broadway comedy, *Children from Their Games*, starring a young Gene Hackman:

> The comedy revolves around an embittered man who, whenever he needs rein-
> forcement to incite his apoplexy against modern times, turns on a tape recorder he
> has transformed into an instrument of self-torture. Including "every single sound

that goes through the ear of contemporary man." It is a symphony of toilet flushes, vacuum cleaners, demolition squads, fire sirens and television programs!

After ringing like a telephone, crashing like a chair and slithering like fog on radio and the Broadway stage, Gustafson somehow found time to supply the effects for Gene Autry's classic Christmas song "Rudolph the Red-Nosed Reindeer"!

And what television show would entrust their sound-effects artist with $100,000 in jewelry? Radio did.

And how funny would Jack Benny's trips to his basement money vault look on television without the accompanying sound effects? Why, shoot, Benny might just as well have electronic depositing!

And what about the most famous of all sounds in radio, the Fibber McGee closet crash? Would television take the time and allow the space the way radio did? No! Or even provide instructions as to the proper procedure to follow? Radio did!

Robert J. Graham, a sound-effects artist for NBC and one of the originators of the famous crash, had this to say:

> I did Fibber McGee and Molly in 1938 and '39 when it was still coming out of Chicago. The show came out of Studio A of the Merchandise Mart.
>
> The crash set-up for Fibber's closet was always staged for studio audience appeal. The control room was in the back wall behind the top riser and also on the audience left—hence we operated with our backs to the audience facing the booth and the performers.
>
> The studio seated about 350 people and the performing area was built up on three permanent risers about 70 feet across (width of studio). Each riser was about 12 feet deep, with the band on the top two risers and the players on the first riser above the audience. Our sound-effect setup was on the audience level as we couldn't raise our heavy turntable consoles up on the risers. We were on the audience's left and were quite an attraction, especially on the comedy shows such as Fibber's.

What Graham doesn't mention is the amount of time, stuff and planning that went into making this the most famous of all radio comedy crashes! Would television do it? No!

It mattered little what the sound artists used for the crash; the ending was always the same: either a small spoon dropped on a slab of marble, or the tiny tinkle of a bell.

That's how important sound effects were to radio. But it didn't start out that way. The Fibber crash, the *Gangbuster* opening, *Inner Sanctum*'s squeaky door—those sounds all came about when radio finally learned there was a better way of describing action than by just talking about it.

That was sound effects original reason for being. We supplied the movement that helped the radio listener "see" what was going on. Then, as the writers became more accustomed to writing for radio, they saw the many other advantages sounds offered.

Television hadn't arrived at that point. It was still riding on its success of being

This photograph shows the pains that radio went through to keep their sound-effects artist Walt Gustafson happy. If the script called for the sound of expensive jewelry, radio saw to it they got expensive jewelry! It even provided two uniformed guards! (Photograph courtesy of Anne Gustafson.)

Monty Fraser, NBC–Hollywood, is shown starting his version of the Fibber crash that includes everything from a guitar to an enameled bedpan (photograph courtesy of Opal Fraser).

able to bring a visual medium into the home for free. And because it was young and struggling for its own identity, it certainly didn't want to be identified with that other in-home, free entertainment, radio.

Perhaps that was the problem. Because of live television's fear of being accused of being nothing more than radio with pictures, they wanted nothing to do with anything as identifiable with radio as sound effects.

Ironically, to those of us in sound effects, that's exactly what television was— radio with pictures. We still did the same effects, with the same equipment we had used in radio. The only difference now was, to those in television, radio was the past, and the quicker they got it out of the public's mind the better! And that held for that other old radio remembrance—sound effects!

TV's Race for Space

While many of the people in radio were still hoping television would go away, the networks on both coasts were frantically searching for theaters to accommodate their television shows. One of the problems they ran into was that radio had beaten them to it.

Bud Tollefson, NBC–Hollywood, preparing to open the famous McGee hall closet door. The resulting sound, recognized as the Fibber crash, delighted listeners across America (photograph courtesy of the National Broadcasting Company).

At a time when radio was beginning to boom, the Great Depression was causing the legitimate theater to go bust. As a result, empty, dark theaters did little to brighten Broadway's Great White Way.

Fortunately for radio and the theaters, they both had what the other wanted. And so the stage where the melancholy Dane once trod the boards became the new home for many of radio's top shows.

But by the early 1950s, radio's popularity began to fade. Despite this, there were still some radio shows with leases in theaters at some of the most desirable locations. This left television with a problem. Of the few theaters they did manage to obtain, what shows would get them?

Even the **Red Skelton Radio Show** *got in the act! Shown are NBC sound artists Jack Robinson (top right) and Fred Cole (bottom). With stuff that took hours to select and pile to the ceiling, the two artists wait nervously for Red to throw the cue before a California earthquake beats him to it (photograph courtesy of the National Broadcasting Company).*

Monty Fraser ringing the coup de grâce for all Fibber crashes. It's one thing to get your laughs with the junk falling, but knowing when to ring the bell separated the doctors from the patients (photograph courtesy of Opal Fraser).

First crack at the premier theaters went, understandably, to the Milton Berles and Garry Moores. But one not-so-premier theater also went to Rod Brown of the Rocket Rangers.

Perhaps it was because neither Rod Brown nor any of his Rocket Rangers sang, danced, juggled, told jokes, or had lovely legs. Or perhaps it was because this was primarily a children's show. Whatever the reason, CBS sure picked out a dump.

Most of the legitimate Broadway theaters the networks were snatching up still had a faint lingering smell of colognes and expensive perfumes. The place that CBS stuck Rod Brown in must have been a converted movie theater that had once shown pornos. The only smells that lingered there were of decay and sweatiness—smells that even the sickly sweet smell of buttered popcorn couldn't overcome.

But it wasn't just the smells or depressing atmospheres that made any of these renovated theaters the pits. It was their locations.

Now, there are good locations, not-so-good locations, and the location that CBS picked up on 109th Street for Rod Brown. Not only was it difficult getting to that location, after you got there you wondered why you did. Especially at four o'clock in the morning. At that hour the only people on the street were either drunks, muggers or painted ladies asking if you wanted to top off your coffee and donut with a good time.

The show was no *Star Trek*, and neither was its budget. But whatever they did was done with imagination. The sets and costumes were creative and convincing, it had a great cast and it even starred a young future movie star in the role of Rod Brown, Cliff Robertson.

But if you think it's difficult getting a cab in New York when it's raining, try to get one to go up to a battle zone like 109th Street at four o'clock in the morning! Even if you were crazy enough to take your car, and by some miracle found a parking space on the street, you had to worry whether it would still be there after the show. And if it was, what sort of condition would it be in? Would it still have four tires, or even four wheels?

In spite of these drawbacks, both Ham O'Hara and I thought the show was great. It was young, innovative and needed the help of sound effects badly. Because it had none of the advantages of films or video tape, all the action had to be done in the confines of a few sets—the most important set being, of course, their spaceship.

The ship was made of plywood, plastic and paper, none of which made any sounds that would convince an audience that it was capable of zooming around in outer space at the speed of light. But zoom it did! And the plywood doors clanged when they were opened and shut! And the spaceship realistically blasted off to Mars! And the equipment hummed, beeped and crackled every time it was turned on! All created by good old, reliable sound effects!

So where did the CBS engineers stick us? At the very top of the balcony, in front of the double exit doors. Every time we'd open our microphone to help old Rod get out of the ship for a stroll in space, we could hear the more earthly sounds of horns, sirens, and the screeching of brakes from the street outside the theater—just the sort of convincing sounds you would expect to hear in a *Star Wars* movie.

But despite the honking horns and early morning hookers, the one thing the show had that early live television needed so badly was—imagination.

More Bad News

This seeming inability on the part of CBS engineering to place the sound-effects artists in an area that at least gave us a fighting chance at doing a good job always mystified me.

When the *Captain Kangaroo Show* moved from Liederkranz Hall (a former German beer hall) to an old theater at 53rd Street and Broadway, I was delighted. Then I learned that the new area for the sound-effects room was going to be in the basement that abutted—so to speak—the theater's only ladies' room.

That in itself should have been enough, but it wasn't. The fact that I was in

The sound-effect location for the **Captain Kangaroo Show** *at the* CBS *Liederkranz Hall Studios. Because of the lack of space, the sound-effect turntables are practically onstage. This wasn't the Kangaroo studio exclusively. On the weekends, there might be a half dozen shows in here (photograph courtesy of Malachy Wienges).*

the basement of the theater brought me that much closer to the Eighth Avenue Subway that ran beneath me. Every time I cued up a record, the vibrations of the subway would knock the needle off the cue mark. So between the rumbling of the subway and the flushing of the toilets, my room was an acoustical time bomb.

Asking the city of New York to inconvenience millions of subway riders to accommodate my sound effects was asking a tad too much. Besides, I at least knew when the subway was coming when the floor began to shake. Not so with the toilet flushes. They came at random without the slightest warning.

Now there are toilet flushes and there are toilet flushes, but I had never heard one with the power, exuberance and yes, the joie de vivre of this toilet flush! It was awesome! But as royal as this flush was, it had no place on the *Kangaroo Show*. Especially if the Captain heard the flushing sound coming from my microphone!

When I appealed to CBS regarding my problems, I was told it would cost a fortune to relocate either me or the potty emporium. And secondly, they couldn't shut down the studio to make the extensive alterations.

I finally came up with a solution I felt was both economical for CBS and ingenious on my part. I made up a simple, handwritten sign, and just before air time I'd hang it on the ladies' room door: REST ROOM BRIEFLY OUT OF ORDER.

As I returned to my room, I couldn't help thinking what an ingenious idea this was. Not only had I saved CBS money, but now my potty problems were over!

But as I should have known, nothing in this world is infallible. On this memorable occasion, after dutifully racing out and posting my out-of-order sign, I filled my two hands with the Popsicle sticks I used for carrot crunches and waited for my cue to open my microphone. And for once I didn't have to worry about the unwanted sound of toilet flushes.

As Bunny Rabbit grabbed yet another carrot from the Captain, I opened my mike just in time to hear the sound of a distressed female's voice through the paper-thin wall screeching loudly: "Out of *order*! Oh, *fuck*!"

Keeping the Peace

As you might imagine, early television and sound effects were not getting along. Even on one of CBS' most prestigious television shows, we weren't getting along.

Studio One came out of the studios CBS leased at Grand Central Station. Yes, the train place. This time they stuck our sound-effects area high above the studio floor on the lighting bridge. The only way up to this eagle's nest was to climb a narrow, 75-foot iron ladder that went straight up.

This ladder was particularly hard on any of the new young female production assistants. It was their job to bring the Sound Effects department any new pages that might have been added. Not that these young ladies weren't in good shape—perhaps they were in too good shape.

Back in the early 1950s, proper attire for the working girls was dresses. It was also before open admiration for the feminine figure could be construed as sexual harassment. Therefore, when one of these brave young ladies got halfway up the ladder, her feminine intuition told her she was not alone on the ladder. Well, she was alone *on* the ladder, but she had also attracted an admiring audience *beneath* the ladder.

Of course all the men at the bottom had a perfectly legitimate reason for being there. Cables needed straightening, a set needed shoring up—all legitimate reasons, none of which the young lady bought. She therefore scrambled back down, gave them all a dirty look that sent them scattering, cupped her hands to her mouth and called up, "Sound Effects! Your script changes are down here!"

This ladder arrangement wasn't just hazardous to females, though; it posed serious problems for the "board men" (lighting electricians) of advanced ages.

These lighting technicians controlled all the lights in a studio. When an actor made a move to turn a lamp on or off, it was these electricians who actually threw the switch that operated the lamp.

Because this job required little physical labor, the electricians were usually older members of the union. Therefore, those killer climbs up the ladder (or down it) were made only when they came to work, when they visited the bathroom (when it didn't require the use of a pee can) and when they went home at night. If they wanted coffee or cigarettes, they lowered the rope with a small open box at the end.

Even the young lighting director in the control room refused to make the climb. If he had any changes for his board man, he would call him on the phone. As a courtesy to Sound Effects, instead of having the board man's phone ring, a light would flicker. This precaution took care of the problem of their phone ringing being confused with the phone ringing from Sound Effects. It didn't, however, take care of the board man's snoring.

In those early live television days, studio space was at such a premium that no sooner did one show fade to black than another show was waiting to load in. This back-to-back show pressure often required that the stage crew work around the clock.

These long hours weren't limited to the stage crew, either. Tom Buchanon, in doing the sound effects for a John Frankenheimer special, worked 126 hours straight!

As a result of these torturous hours, crews that worked the shows grabbed catnaps whenever and wherever they could. And in the case of the lighting man who shared the area with Sound Effects in Studio One, his naps, and his loud and insistent snoring were known to whoever worked in that studio.

This was the case the night that I did *Danger* out of Studio One. I was told that whenever I had to open my microphone, I was first to run over and make certain he was awake before hustling back to ring the phone, knock, do punches, or even do a gunshot.

One thing you never did in live television was to get the dues-paying members of the stagehand's unions pissed off. They practically lived in the studios where they worked. And because so many things could go wrong with your equipment naturally, the last thing you wanted was problems with another union that understood some of the *unnatural* things that could go wrong with your equipment.

To add to the problem, my friend not only snored, but was also an avid reader. Therefore, when he was quiet for a long period of time, it meant one of two things: he was awake and reading, or asleep and perhaps getting ready to snore. I therefore adopted a habit of double checking his state of consciousness.

One memorable night on the show *Danger*, my headset went dead right before air time. And because this was the only communication I had with the control room, I climbed down the ladder, raced to the maintenance room, grabbed another headset, and climbed back to the sound-effects area just in time for the show to go on the air.

The cue for the gunshot was right at the beginning of the show. I just had time to dig the two guns out from my briefcase and open the mike. Suddenly a dreadful thought struck me! Was he awake and reading or, God forbid, sleeping? I quickly glanced over and he had the back of his chair to me. It looked empty! Oh how I hoped he had simply had to go to the rest room!

Suddenly the voice of the assistant director was on my headset: "Stand by with the gunshot!"

My fingers tightened slightly on both triggers. "Cue the gunshot!"

I pulled the trigger and the gun responded with a loud *BANG*! Unfortunately, my gun wasn't the only one that responded! The gunfire brought life to the seemingly empty chair. His gray head jerked up suddenly, and as he whirled around his mouth opened and his lips began forming the big "F"word.

It didn't take a lip-reading genius to know what was coming next! Because of the two guns, I couldn't throw the mike switch, so I did the next best thing! I fired off another gunshot and prayed it would cover the soon-to-be-voiced television no-no!

Again the assistant director was on the headset.

"Sound? That ad-libbed gunshot worked great!"

In live television, compliments were so rare, you took them where you could get them and kept your mouth shut.

Sound Effects Strikes Back

By now, those of us who worked in radio were getting fairly used to the locations live television was assigning to us. It wasn't what we were used to in radio, but that had been radio and this, well, wasn't.

We even became resigned to the fact that the CBS Engineering department was having its hands full just trying to renovate these new locations to accommodate the demands of the cameras. All this we began to understand; however, the churlish attitude of some of the people working in live television was something else.

As one producer so brainlessly put it: Didn't sound effects ride out in the sunset with radio?

It was the job of the production assistant in live radio to time the show. One week, Art Strand, the sound-effects artist on Studio One, went into the control room before rehearsal to get a revised script.

As he walked in, he saw a new, attractive young lady he had never seen before on the show. After introducing himself, she told him she was replacing the other production assistant for the next three weeks and asked what could she do for him.

Strand then made the mistake of asking for the new sound-effects script. The young lady looked at him as if he were joking.

"Sound effects? Are you joking? You must have the wrong studio; we're doing live television here, not radio."

She said it to the wrong man. Strand, regarded as one of the more capable sound-effects artists, also had a sense of humor that could best be described as bizarre. Take, for instance, the time he enraged Nila Mack, the director of the wonderfully imaginative children's radio show *Let's Pretend*.

The script called for the hooting of a owl. Although the owl sound was on record on *Let's Pretend*, all the vocal effects on the show were done by Strand's partner, George O'Donnell.

George was a distinguished, older man who in vaudeville had taught a young Mae West a number of dance routines. In addition to being a dancer, George was an excellent animal imitator. The only thing that kept him from doing it exclusively was his shyness in front of audiences.

On that particular *Let's Pretend*, George was going to do the mournful hooting of an owl vocally. As the cue came on air, when George bent over to make the sounds of the owl, Strand goosed him!

As I said, the production assistant at Studio One picked on the wrong sound-effects man. She further went on to tell Strand, "Besides, this is television, the viewers can see the actors making their own noises."

That did it! "Make their own noises, indeed!"

It wasn't the PA's (production assistant) youthfulness or her inexperience that rankled Strand; it was her overbearing arrogance. Even arrogance is sometimes acceptable, if there is something about the person that backs it up, but this lady used her arrogance and rudeness to camouflage ignorance.

Normally the sounds required on Studio One were varied and many. But this night the show required only the one sound of Strand doing the ringing sound for a prop alarm clock that could be seen on camera. Because of this, Strand felt it was the ideal time to test just how much this young PA had learned about the difference between "radio" sounds and television sounds. Make that *live* television sound effects.

There were two types of props in live television. One was a "practical prop," which meant it did what it was supposed to do. For instance, when someone turned the water on in a kitchen sink you saw water coming out of the faucet. It also requires the expensive services of Special Effects to supply the portable water tanks to make certain the water does come out. The less expensive way was not to show the faucet, and have Sound Effects supply only the sound of water.

In regard to the alarm clock, this was not a practical prop. If it were, the ticking sound under the dialogue would have been too distracting. Secondly, no alarm clock in the world is made to ring at a specific second—certainly not when a group of actors on national television are standing around waiting and hoping it will ring.

Before putting his devious plan into effect, Strand let the prop man handling the clock, the executive producer, the director and the technical director in on it. They too must have seen the error in her overbearing way because they all whole-heartedly agreed to the idea.

At the conclusion of dress rehearsal, Strand went to the young production assistant and explained a family emergency had just come up and he was needed at home right away. And since there was only the one sound of the alarm clock ringing on the stage—done by the clock on stage, of course—could he be excused?

The PA, thinking if she let Strand go early, she could let the producer know about all the money she saved him, seemed inclined to give her blessing. But one thing bothered her. Didn't that mean the setting of the alarm clock to ring and the timing of the show had to be crucial?

Strand quickly pointed out the alarm had always happened at the right time in all the rehearsals, so why shouldn't it happen on air? All that was needed for this to happen on the live-air show was precise timing. At this point Strand paused and frowned questioningly at the young PA, "Your times for the rehearsal are accurate, aren't they?"

The young PA straightened back her shoulders and threw out her shapely chest indignantly and flared, "Of course they are!"

The desire to make a perhaps higher name for herself prompted the young PA to make up her mind. She'd do it! She then hustled off to talk to the prop man about getting the alarm clock and her stopwatch coordinated.

That night on air, Strand remained hidden at his sound-effects area listening to the voices in the control room over his headset. As the show neared the end, the young producer's voice started getting shakier and shakier. At one point she shrieked, "Give the actors a speedup, we're ten seconds behind the time for the damn alarm clock!"

As the time came closer and closer, Strand could actually hear the young producer holding her breath. Then as the cue came and Strand rang the alarm clock, she let out an exultant scream. "I did it! I did it!"

The next week, Strand wanted to see how much the "ringing alarm clock caper" had accomplished. This time when he saw her, he gave her a warm, friendly smile and said, "Congratulations on the fine job you did with the timing of the alarm clock ring."

The young production assistant's smile was even warmer and friendlier as she replied, "Would you please go fuck yourself?"

In that brief moment, Strand knew this lady would go far in television.

CHAPTER 7

On the Road Again

One of the problems with doing sound effects for a living, besides the locations CBS put us in, was the locations we put ourselves in. Even on vacation, the sound-effect artist's obsessive search for new sounds was endless. No mountain was too high, no canyon too deep, and no desert too hot or dangerous.

Jim Rogan, in addition to being an excellent sound-effects man on such shows as *Gangbusters* and *Grand Central Station*, was also an accomplished songwriter. (If you've ever eaten in a Hungarian restaurant in New York City and been serenaded by a violinist playing "When a Gypsy Makes His Violin Cry," you have been more than serenaded by an emotional Gypsy's violin, you have just heard one of Jim Rogan's songs.)

But even hit songwriters and sound-effects men need a vacation. And this was the year that Jim, a long-time resident of New Jersey, decided to fulfill a lifetime dream by driving cross-country to California. What wasn't part of Jim's dream was the fact that wherever Jim and his wife went, Jim's mother-in-law was sure to go.

Everything was going fine until the threesome was crossing a particularly arid stretch of desert in Arizona. Although the desert was void of anything that would make the average tourist want to stop, that's exactly what Jim did. Not only that, but he did it with an air of eagerness and unbridled excitement.

His mother-in-law wasted no time in pointing out her surprise. "What the blazes are you stopping here for?"

Jim, even though he was on vacation, was still a sound-effects man. And nowhere on earth would he find a quieter place to record the sound of *presence*.

Presence is the movement of air particles in an environment. It's what we hear around us when there are no specific sounds. The fact we're not hearing sounds is not to be confused with silence. True silence only exists in a vacuum. If you ever have your hearing tested by an audiologist, you will be placed in a small booth that is devoid of sound, much like a vacuum. This, again, is silence. Although we are always craving a "little peace and quiet," there would be very little peace connected with true silence. In fact it would be eerie.

This photograph shows the extremes that today's Foley artists go to record the sound of silence (photograph courtesy of Dane Film Studios).

Jim's mother-in-law, seeing her son-in-law checking his tape recorder, could only wonder at what her daughter had married and at what had kept them together these past 30 years. Glaring at Jim, she demanded, "What are you going to do with that thing in this godforsaken desert? There's nothing out there!"

Jim's professionally trained ears bristled at the word *nothing*. *Nothing*? *Nothing* existed only in a vacuum. God hadn't forsaken this desert; he made it beautiful to those who appreciated silence. *Silence*, the most evasive of all sounds. No jets roaring overhead, no cars racing by, no dogs barking, no chain saws, no hundreds of other unwanted sounds when you wanted to record an ambient background presence that didn't intrude. *Silence* imbued the setting with a palpable new expression of life.

But Jim didn't say any of this. Instead, his fingers trembled with uncontrollable anticipation as he unloaded some of his other priceless taped treasures. The sound of that coyote howling outside their Tucson motel; the squeaks of a windmill when he changed the flat tire next to a farm outside Denver; the herd of lowing cattle that refused to get out of that country road; the exquisite sound of a griddle full of hamburgers sizzling in that small diner where his mother-in-law got a touch of food poisoning—all these sounds were now safely residing on Jim's tape.

Jim Rogan (background) and Frank Mellow in action on **Grand Central Station** *(photograph courtesy of Walter Pierson).*

As Jim opened the car door and stepped out into the noonday desert, a wave of fiery heat engulfed him.

"Do you feel that?" his mother-in-law screamed. "It's like an oven out there!"

Did Jim "feel it?" Hell, he couldn't even breathe.

"You'd be a fool to go out there! If the sun doesn't keel you over with a sunstroke, it's just the place to be crawling with deadly, diamondback rattlesnakes!"

Did that woman never stop? "Sunstrokes and rattlesnakes"—that's all she had on her mind ever since they crossed the border into Arizona. But just to keep peace in the car, Jim forced a smile and answered, "I have my sunscreen on. I'll wear my hat and watch where I step."

Jim moved quickly into the desert and away from the car's intrusive motor sounds, so necessary for the operation of the air conditioning. As he did so, his mother-in-law's taunting admonishments were almost as annoying as the furnace-like heat.

Sunstrokes and diamondback rattlesnakes! Did that woman think he had never been out of New Jersey?

At that moment, just as Jim was about to record the delicious, elusive sound of silence, his unbelieving ears heard the even more unbelievable sound of a car coming to a screeching stop. Turning angrily around, Jim saw the screeching sound came from a car that had "Arizona Highway Patrol" emblazoned on its side.

As the uniformed officer stepped out of his vehicle, he shaded his eyes with his left hand, while with his right hand he pressed the switch on his bullhorn. And in a loud voice that echoed and reechoed across the vast desert, boomed out, "You sir! Don't you know you can get sunstroke, and this place is crawling with deadly, poisonous rattlesnakes!"

CHAPTER 8

Juggling Two Hats

The excess of anything has never been enough in the entertainment business. Take job titles for instance. When you ask someone outside of show business what they do for a living, most can answer in one word. If they have the talent to make something disappear, they are most likely to be a magician or, perhaps in too many cases, your stockbroker.

In show business, however, they created a term for people presumably capable of wearing two job hats at the same time. These people are called "hyphenates."

A hyphenate may be a writer-producer, or an actor-director. And the ones who are really hyphenated have this ambitious title: "actor-writer-director-producer."

The problem isn't so much with the amount of hats you wear, but what the hats represent. Writers, in show business circles, are considered artistic and referred to as "talent." Whereas sound-effects artists, perhaps because you knew which end of a microphone cable went into the wall and which end went into the microphone, were deemed "technical."

Mixing technical and artistic together is more volatile than mixing oil and water, or apples and oranges. Artistic people are considered warm and creative, whereas technical people are cold and analytical. In show business, the schism is even more pronounced.

In live television, writing was at best a tenuous form of earning a living. It also represented the popular notion of personal deprivation and mental suffering in an unfurnished garret.

Sound effects, on the other hand, represented the safety and security of a technical job. You know the type. They go to work, punch a time clock, do as little as possible, go home to a hot meal, take the little woman out for a beer and a movie, go to bed, and when they wake up they're 65.

These were the traditional show business myths forged from hundreds of B movies. If you wanted to be known as an artist, the last thing you wanted tainting your image was the fact that you had any technical ability whatsoever.

But before you could become a hyphenated anything, before you could espouse the cause of the artistic or ply the trade of the technical enablers, you first had to figure out a way to get into live television. Because of the lack of both technical schools and colleges, live television was pretty much a mystery. So while you figured out a way to solve this mystery, you had to support yourself with some sort of day job.

For those trying to break into acting, the day job most often picked was working in a restaurant as a waiter or waitress. Because so many successful actors and actresses started out this way, there was no blemish attached to restaurant work. And perhaps most importantly, your work schedule waiting on tables allowed you to knock on the doors of live television.

My day job was nothing as temporary as restaurant work. I had a rock-solid job doing sound effects—a job that left me little time to pursue what I hoped to be my real job, comedy writing.

My big break came because I was the newest member in the Sound Effects department. Although I had proved my abilities by doing whatever radio show I was assigned to, when the opportunity to get rid of me came up, they jumped at it. When I say getting "rid" of me, I mean that since I had the least department seniority, I was sent to the Devil's Island of radio, live television.

With the fees and camaraderie that radio still offered, it was little wonder I was sent to television. Although I was not too happy about being sacrificed to television, as it turned out, dumping me on the daytime *Garry Moore Show* was the best thing that could have happened to my career.

Garry Moore, in addition to being one of the finest men I ever worked with, was kind enough to buy my very first comedy sketch for $25, an amount that today will hardly cover the costs of two pastrami sandwiches at New York's Stage Delicatessen. Yet if you had seen the look on my face when Garry said he wanted to use what I wrote, it was all the payment I needed.

Dick Van Dyke

Of all the young, talented comedians that the *Garry Moore Show* introduced to television, one of the most outstanding was Dick Van Dyke. His first time on the show he did a routine about the disappointment that the highway historical signs must feel when no one ever bothers to slow their cars down long enough to read them.

On the first run-through, Van Dyke just talked the piece through. Although it was moderately funny, Garry thought by adding the sound effect of speeding cars whizzing by, it would give Van Dyke movement and something to react to. Garry was right. For all his talent, Van Dyke's weakness was talking. He seemed uncomfortable and constrained. Having the sounds to react to improved the sketch's laughs considerably.

After the show, Van Dyke came to me with another sketch he had written, about an amusement park. He asked me if I could add sound effects to this sketch as well. I read it and told him I could, and even made a few writing suggestions that he seemed to like.

These casual meetings lasted for the next three years, as I wrote all of his comedy material. But despite our success together on most major television shows and one Broadway show, I continued working at CBS. Why? I wasn't quite certain I was ready to lose the security of sound effects.

In the short time I was at CBS, I had proven to myself that I was capable of meeting the challenges that sound effects demanded. With writing, I wasn't quite so sure. Although writing offered many advantages that sound effects didn't, both satisfied my creative desires.

Although both jobs were creative, one was easier to explain to people. Especially when you tried to explain what doing sound effects entailed. With writing, everyone knew. Especially big-chested bleached blondes.

End of Mister Nice Guy

The major Hollywood film studios became rich and famous doing films about the downtrodden chorus girl who finally gets her big break on Broadway. I believe the movie *42nd Street* led the big box office parade of hits. All I can say to this genre is—baloney! It ain't true! Not in the real world, anyway. And here is my reason why.

Aaron Rubin, a gifted producer of such shows as *Sanford and Son* and *Gomer Pyle*, once produced a comedy pilot involving Van Dyke. In one of the sketches, Van Dyke played a bachelor with a Jekyll-and-Hyde type personality who attended a swinging singles party. While there, he meets a gorgeous Amazonian woman. Outwardly he's very polite, shy and inhibited. Inwardly his Hyde personality is lasciviously urging him to "stop being a wimp—grab her!"

At the end of the sketch, the Hyde personality becomes more and more dominant until, finally, when it again orders Van Dyke to "grab her!" Van Dyke gives in. Taking the woman in his arms with a licentious leer, he throws her over his shoulder and carries her off.

The problem was, where were they going to get this gorgeous, well-stacked Amazon? Funny they should ask ... I knew one. And after doing a selling job to both Aaron and Van Dyke about her, I told them I would deliver the perfect, big-bosomed, bleached blonde.

As I left them and made my way to a phone, a sense of warmth and goodwill came over me. Rarely are you given an opportunity to make someone's dreams come true. But that was exactly what was going to happen to an unsuspecting secretary. Just like in the movies!

The girl I had in mind worked at Olmsteads, a popular New York commercial recording studio where I did a lot of freelance sound effects. One evening while there, the commercial I was scheduled to do some sounds on was delayed, so I had an opportunity to talk with her. She told me she was only doing secretarial work until she got her big acting break. As I nodded politely, a dark voice deep inside me said, "Grab her!" But, instead, I shyly nodded. Later in our little talk, I happened to let it drop that in addition to doing sound effects, I was also a comedy writer. At the mention of the word *writer*, her big, blue eyes got bluer and bigger. She pursed her full lips and purred, "If you ever need an actress, I'll do anything—*anything*—all you have to do is put your lips togther and I'll blow." Although her Lauren Bacall quote didn't sound quite right, it was close enough. As I looked deeply into the big-busted bleached blonde's blue eyes, I made a mental note to chalk one advantage up to being a writer over doing hoofbeats with coconut shells. I replied, "I certainly will," not thinking that I ever would—or could. After all, didn't a secretary getting an acting break only happen in the movies?

Now as I began dialing the Olmsteads' number, I couldn't help but admire myself. Here I was giving a little girl her first big break, and I didn't expect anything in return. Nothing! If all the men in the world were being as darn nice as I was, the world would never have heard of sexual harassment.

My first indication that things would not turn out exactly as they had in the movies was when the Amazonian secretary didn't remember who the hell I was. Finally, after a lengthy explanation, she remembered me. "Oh yeah, you're that sound-effects guy. What's sound effects got to do with 'auditioning' for a television pilot?"

I didn't like the tone she used when she said "auditioning." I tried to immediately quell her suspicions by saying I wasn't doing this as a "sound-effects guy," but as a writer. Then, hoping to impress her, I added, "I write for Van Dyke."

She countered with "Van Dyke? I thought a Van Dyke was a chin beard." Then she added suspiciously, "So if you are a writer, how come you still knock coconut shells together and do other sound-effect stuff at Olmsteads?

Having two jobs and trying to be a good Samaritan wasn't as easy as it looked. Her next question was even more suspicious. "Auditioning *where*?" When I told her the name of the hotel and the room number, I almost lost her. "A television audition in a sleazy hotel room? Ya gotta be kidding!"

Where she got "sleazy" from I don't know. But I was getting desperate. Perhaps I shouldn't have been so cocky when I promised Rubin and Van Dyke not to worry and that I'd deliver them the perfect Amazon!

Now she was demanding to know how many lines she'd have! Was this the same blonde secretary who was so desperate for a break into television? The one that would do "anything—*anything*?" All I had to do is put my lips together and whistle? Now she was demanding to know how many lines?

When I had to explain that she didn't have any lines but that the eyes of all America would be on her, she interrupted me in a very unladylike manner.

"Cut the bullshit. Is this a gag?"

By the tone of her voice what she meant was "Is this a porno?"

"For God's sake no!" Now my voice was getting panicky. Right there I swore I'd never be a good Samaritan or mention I was a writer again! Not only was I going to have to disappoint Rubin and Van Dyke, but after this woman got through telling everyone what a horny letch I was and that I was the head of a show biz porno ring, I'd never be able to freelance at Olmsteads—or any other recording studio again!

If only either Van Dyke or I were famous! Or the name Aaron Rubin meant anything to her! And why did I ever get into this damn nice guy business anyway?

I used every ounce of sales savvy I knew. Finally she agreed to come to the hotel. But if there was any funny business, I'd not only never work at Olmsteads again ... she had a boyfriend who was bigger than she was who would see that I never did horses' hooves again—with or without the coconut shells.

The minute I hung up, I raced back to the room and told Van Dyke, "When you grab her, be careful what you grab, or how long you grab it, or I'm dead!"

As it turned out she didn't even get the part. Van Dyke, even soaking wet with all his clothes on, weighed about 147 pounds. In fact, Fat Jack Leonard, a very funny, rotund nightclub comedian used to tell Van Dyke: "The weight I lost last week would make two of you!"

On the other hand, the big bleached blonde was as tall and statuesque as she was femininely unsuited for a junior-miss bra. Later when I called Van Dyke to find out if she got the part he answered, "I couldn't lift her off the floor. Then when I did, I couldn't get all of her over my shoulder—but the part that I did, made up for the part that I didn't!"

Things Began to Heat Up

To illustrate how confusing my double identity had become, this career mix-up happened on a Garry Moore nighttime show involving Carol Burnett. I had written a sketch for Carol, Marion Lorne and Durward Kirby. On a lunch break from the *Captain Kangaroo Show* (that's when I put on my writing hat), I took a cab to the theater just in time for them to rehearse the sketch I had written.

Although it was only a rehearsal, the director was shooting it all wrong. In my capacity as a writer (even though I wasn't a Garry Moore staff writer), I wouldn't be too far out of line if I got the director aside and mentioned this fact. For a sound-effects man who had just done the show a scant two weeks ago, however, such a stunt would be unheard of. And yet, he was screwing up my sketch.

As I sat there wondering what I should do, the staff writers came down the aisle and sat a few rows away from me. Now there is a big difference between *staff* and *freelance* writers. Basically the staff writers looked upon freelance writers as pains in the ass who are looking to take their jobs. But inasmuch as I had a job, they hated me even more for being a freelance writer who had the security of a job. Comedy writers didn't have that luxury. Theirs was an insecure existence where only the funniest survived, which is why it was difficult tossing my sound-effect hat into the writing ring. What would happen to me if I ran out of funny ideas?

I glanced at my watch to see how much time I had to get back to the Kangaroo show. I still had some time, so I waited for Vinnie Bogert, Garry's head writer, whom I knew from the daytime show, to stop joking with his staff so that I could ask him for some guidance. Bogert had started out in radio writing the popular *Duffy's Tavern* series. We had worked together for eight years on the daytime Garry Moore show; he had worked as a writer, while I did the sound effects and on two occasions sold Garry comedy sketches.

As I left the safety of the darkened part of the theater, I couldn't help noticing his writing staff. Arnie Rosen had been one of Jackie Gleason's early writers and would later become the head writer for Carol Burnett. Seated next to him was Buck Henry, the co-writer of the movie *The Graduate*. To his right was Doc Simon, of Sid Caesar's *Your Show of Shows* fame. Doc would soon drop his sobriquet "Doc" to become the incredibly successful Neil Simon of Broadway and movie fame. And finally, a writer who was better known as a standup comedian, Woody Allen.

As I started to go over to Vinnie, he got up and went on stage to talk with Garry. Again I looked at my watch. Why the hell was I putting myself through all this? Why didn't I make the break and chuck the Kangaroo show and sound effects and just be a writer and the hell with the Great Depression and my mother's constant reminder: "Never throw away your dirty dishwater until you're sure you can get fresh."

Today there are experts who make handsome livings explaining the bright and dark sides of life's most agonizing moments. During the Great Depression, such analysis was part of the territory that came with being a mother.

Once during a chilling rain storm, I worried about walking the three miles to school. It wasn't the rain, or the amount of rain, or getting my cap or sweater or knickers soaking wet; they would dry on me in school. It was my shoes. They wouldn't dry in school. Especially not with the amount of water that would come sloshing through the gaping holes in the soles.

Normally my parents were able to put aside enough money for new school shoes. But this had been a scorcher of a summer and our chickens weren't laying eggs the way they should. Selling our eggs had become as hard to do for us as laying them had been for the hens. Besides, the country was in the midst of the Depression and, as everyone knew, money didn't grow on trees—or under chickens that weren't laying eggs.

The accepted manner of home-patching your shoes was to cover the holes with a piece of double-folded cover from a Sears and Roebuck catalog. But not for this rainstorm. It would take the whole Sears book to block out the water.

When I finally posed the problem to my mother, asking her how I was supposed to walk the three miles to school with holes in my shoes the size of half dollars, she just wagged her wise head at my youthful ignorance and responded in a sort of deprecating tone: "What's the matter, you can't walk on your heels?"

Those were the good old Depression moms. They sewed, patched and made do until they were absolutely certain they could get something better. Because, as they loved to say, it was always better to "have a bird in hand, than a bird in the bush." And most certainly, you never "threw away the dirty dishwater until you had clean dishwater." To tell you how tough those times were, people with jobs in the post office were the envy of the people who had once lived on Park Avenue.

Money was in short supply for everyone. As a result, insurance companies, realizing how difficult it was for people to scrape up enough money for monthly payment on their policies, would send their agents to your door weekly to collect the 10¢ or 25¢ policy premiums that insured you at least got buried.

Heating was another problem. The coal company didn't pour the shiny black nuggets down the metal slide into your cellar until you paid the $10 first. To save heating costs, most homes let their coal fires die out at night. And if the night was only moderately cold and you couldn't afford extra blankets, you put a coat on the bed to keep warm. If the night was really cold, you put two coats on the bed. And if the temperature sank below freezing, you fought over who would get the third coat. As a result, during the Depression, there was no need for a meteorologist to tell you how cold the night was. All you had to do was count the coats.

Just as I checked my watch again, Vinnie came off the stage and I told him what I thought was wrong with the way the sketch was being shot by the director

Vinnie was cordial and sympathetic with my plight. He too said he wouldn't sit still and let them ruin a sketch *he* wrote! As I walked toward the control room that housed the director, I couldn't be certain but I thought I heard snickering coming from Arnie, Vinnie, Buck, Doc and Woody.

Once before I had taken Vinnie's advice. I had written a sketch that the show had given to Ford and Hines, a husband and wife comedy team. The sketch was subtle; Phil Ford and Mimi Hines weren't. When I saw it in rehearsal it was terrible. I told Vinnie so and he agreed. His words to me were, "Don't worry; they'll kill it."

On my break between the morning and afternoon Kangaroo show, I raced the three blocks over to the Moore show (a cab might get caught in time-consuming traffic), and to my dismay—horror—they were still doing the sketch! Again Vinnie assured me it would be killed.

Arriving at the theater after finishing ten hours with the kindly old Captain Kangaroo, I found the sketch was still in the show! Before Vinnie could assure me it wouldn't be done I had a sickening feeling it would be done. Vinnie assured me again that it wouldn't. The problem was, both Mimi and her husband were ruining the subtlety of the humor by doing too much mugging. As a result, it wasn't just unfunny, it was embarrassing.

Vinnie was sympathetic—perhaps a shade too sympathetic—and suggested I talk with Mimi. After all, she was a nice lady and, who knows, it might even turn the sketch around and make it hilarious. Vinnie's use of the word *hilarious* struck me as a case of overkill. And I should have been suspicious when a staff comedy writer was kind and thoughtful to a freelancer who had just gotten a script accepted over the writing efforts of his five experienced writers.

As I introduced myself to Mimi, her husband wasn't with her. Trying to be as tactful as I could, I gently hinted that she might just be using a tad too much energy, hilarious though it may have been. If she could just tone it down a tad, it would make Garry's part a tad more amusing.

At that point she turned to me, smiled and responded sweetly: "No, I disagree. I like the way I'm doing it. Besides, I don't give a fuck about you, your sketch, or Garry Moore!"

I thanked her for her openness, and as I got up to leave, I could have sworn I heard the faint sound of giggling coming from where the writers were seated. Was this a case of writer's revenge against a two-hatted writer/sound-effects man? Would they possibly put a sketch on that was lousy just to make a point? No, they wouldn't. They *couldn't*. If Vinnie said it was going to be killed, surely it would be killed!

That night the sketch wasn't killed, it simply died from the lack of laughter. Yes, this was the days before canned laughter. No, adding laughs wouldn't have made the sketch any funnier. It just would have made the five minutes not seem so long and, well, quiet.

The curious thing about being a freelance writer on a live show was, your name was rarely if ever listed with those of the staff writers on the credits. Unless, of course, your sketch was a huge success. Then it was added to the end of the staff writer's credits so that an interested party taking note of the credits would assume the sketch was written by anyone of the listed writers.

On the other hand, if you wrote a bomb (like I just had), you were given special treatment. Then the announcer gave you a voice credit at the end of the entire list of all show credits. Somewhere between the name of the limousine company that chauffeured the guests, and the salami sandwiches that came from the catering Stage Delicatessen. But your name would be in the clear. And loud.

This was done, of course, to ensure that there wasn't a soul in all of America from the age of three on up who wasn't made aware of who wrote that terribly unfunny sketch. And to make it perfectly clear that everyone understood that, the announcer would boom out in stentorian tones, "The Ford and Hines sketch was written by [PAUSE] ... **BOB MOTT!**

The Other Hat Gets in Trouble

When a sound-effects man went on vacation, or had a scheduling conflict where he was unable to do a show he normally did, it was customary for the regular sound-effects man to tell his replacement something about the show's likes and dislikes.

For instance, some shows liked the soundman to break up the tedium of rehearsing by adding an occasional ad-lib. Other shows hated it.

This particular show was a CBS special titled *Calamity Jane* and starred Carol Burnett. Although I had worked on several occasions with Carol on the *Garry Moore Morning Show*, this would be the first time I worked with her in several years. As a result, one of the things the regular sound-effects man impressed upon me was how much Carol loved ad-libs from sound effects. This helped her in breaking up the tedium that came from the often grueling rehearsals. And one of her favorite all-time ad-libs was the sound of an old-fashioned toilet flush.

During the rehearsal I cued the record up on the turntable and waited for just the right moment. It came towards the end of an exhausting day when in doing a sketch, Carol had to make an exit out the door. After rehearsing it a dozen times, everyone was getting on edge. Now was the time for the old-fashioned tension breaker. As Carol made her exit, I waited a beat and played the toilet flush. As promised, Carol, and just about everyone else thought it was funny except Joe Hamilton, who was her husband and, more importantly to me, the producer.

He stormed up into the balcony where the sound-effects area was and didn't mince words. "Give me that fucking record!" He broke it in half. "And if I ever hear that goddamn toilet flush again, you'll be the one getting flushed!"

Yes, they could talk to you like that in the days of live television.

Who Is That Guy?

We now cut to a different time and show. This time I had written a pantomime for Garry that he was doing on his nighttime show. The camera shots of Garry were dreadful. And since everything in this particular sketch depended on the camera angles of Garry, I felt I had to say something to the director (Norman Jewison).

Telling a director that he or she didn't have a clue what was and what wasn't funny was never an enjoyable experience. But if it was done with a careful choice of words and just the proper tone of voice, it could be done. All I had to do was take the director aside, be tactful, and everything would be fine. After all, when you've been told by Mimi Hines she didn't care who the fuck you were, you learn a valuable lesson.

The control room was in semidarkness. Along with the regular Garry Moore technical crew was the producer, Joe Hamilton. Yes, the same Joe Hamilton you recall who broke my record of the toilet flush and used the big *F* word.

As I entered the control room to do battle with the director over the destiny of my ill-fated sketch, this same Joe Hamilton frowned when he saw me. But since he couldn't put my face with the sound of a toilet flush, he had nothing to say to me.

When the director finally called a five-minute break, I took the director aside and in hushed tones explained my problem. The director smiled, nodded enthusiastically and said what I had seen was just a rough rehearsal for the actors, not the cameras. I was not to worry. I left the control room certain I had done the right thing. As it turned out I had. The director did a fine job.

A week later I ran into the show's technical director (T.D.). He told me that Hamilton had heard everything that I had said to the director. Because of my last unpleasant encounter with Hamilton, I was interested in knowing what he thought of me now.

"Did Hamilton agree with what I said?"

With that the man smiled. "Not exactly."

"Well, what did he say?"

"Now I can't remember the exact words…"

This was taking too long. Was the T.D. sparing my feelings or enjoying my torment?

"Just give me the gist of what Hamilton said about me."

Again the T.D. frowned. "As best I can remember, it went something like this: 'What the hell are you listening to *him* for, he's nothing but a goddamn sound-effects man!'"

CHAPTER 9

Which Was Funnier, Live Radio or Live TV?

To begin with, radio was an original; television wasn't. Radio depended solely on how funny it could sound. Television had the advantage of pictures as well as sound. And isn't a funny picture funnier than a thousand funny words? Groucho thought so.

Groucho Marx, the star of vaudeville, radio, films and television's *You Bet Your Life*, had this to say: "One of my rules of comedy is never let a spoken joke stand by itself; always combine it with some comic physical 'business.'"

To show that Groucho knew what he was talking about, F. E. Lange, in a study at Columbia University analyzing the different aspects of comedy and its effect on audiences, showed that costumes enhance the funniness by 100 percent and business by 400 percent!

So, if this seeming Goliath had such an overwhelming advantage over poor little sound-only David, you would think anyone that put their money on radio would be a fool, right? Don't kid yourself.

No other auditory form of entertainment that came before radio came close. Even the ancient storytellers around a fire had the benefit of facial expressions, gestures, and if that failed, they could drop their loincloth.

Radio had none of these visual advantages. All it had was the manipulation of sounds—voices, music and effects. And yet Orson Welles managed to put the three together and convince the country that it was being invaded by Martians! Something even Steven Spielberg couldn't do with a zillion dollars and a *Jurassic Park* overrun by velociraptors!

Live radio was the medium of sound. Comedians such as jugglers, magicians, prop comedians, tap dancers, pantomimists and ventriloquists need not apply. Unless of course you were Edgar Bergen.

In Edgar Bergen's case, radio was a blessing. Although Bergen had a wonderfully creative, comedic mind, as a ventriloquist very often his seeming inability to keep his lips from moving made radio the perfect medium.

100

Although Jack Benny was also a product of vaudeville, his style of humor was made for radio. His comedy didn't rely on anything physical; it was what he said, how he said it, and most importantly *why* he said it.

Benny's approach to comedy was to firmly establish his character in the minds of his audience. And the character that Benny chose to portray was cheap, stingy and vain. Seemingly unusual characteristics for getting laughs. Wasn't Charles Dickens' hateful villain Scrooge equally cheap and stingy? The difference is, Scrooge didn't have Benny's timing or comedy writers.

No one enjoys growing old. On radio, Jack Benny never aged a day. He got as far as 39 and stopped. In addition, the Benny radio personality was, plainly put, vain. When, for instance, he was asked his eye color, he, without hesitation, would reply, "Bluer than the waters of Lake Lucille."

An example of his stinginess is best illustrated in the following classic Jack Benny comedy sketch. The sketch was written over the years in part by George Balzer, a Benny comedy writer for more than 25 years, an incredible amount of time for a comedy writer to be associated with just one comedian. This is especially true when what you write has to get laughs in two different mediums, radio and television. And what were those 25 years with Benny like? Balzer smiled when asked. "They weren't long enough."

I met George after the Benny show finally went off the air and we were both writing the *Red Skelton Show* for television. Having been such a big fan of Jack Benny over the years, I couldn't wait to ask George a couple of questions. First of all, what was the funniest radio sketch Benny did? To my surprise, it wasn't the famous holdup sketch in which Benny walks down a lonely street and is suddenly accosted by a holdup man.

"Your money or your life?"

This ultimatum is followed by a long pause. Finally the hold-up man demands, "Well?"

Benny replies testily, "I'm thinking, I'm thinking!"

This sketch, according to George, received neither the longest nor the biggest laugh on the Benny show. The one that did involved a very dignified Ms. Dorothy Kirsten, a world-renowned opera star.

The sketch started by Benny introducing Ms. Kirsten to Mary Livingston (Benny's wife on radio, television and in real life).

When Ms. Kirsten finds out that Mary is a big fan of opera, they enthusiastically start discussing some classic operas. They begin:

DOROTHY   I just love Gioacchino Antonio Rossini's *The Barber of Seville*.
MARY   Oh, so do I, Dorothy. Almost as much as *The Beggar's Opera*, with words by John Gay and music by John Christopher Pepusch!

[At this point, Benny tries to join in the conversation by clearing his throat. The girls ignore him.]

DOROTHY   Oh, Mary, you're *so* right! And how about *The Bohemian Girl*, by Balfe, and text by Alfred Bunn!

[Again Benny clears his throat.]

MARY   Oh, I agree, Dorothy! But my all-time favorite is *Carmen*!

DOROTHY   Mary, did you know that when Carmen was first performed it was a failure?

[Benny, seeing a conversational opening, jumps in.]

JACK   *Really!*

[Both Dorothy and Mary respond angrily.]

DOROTHY/MARY   Aw, shut up!

Now you know what the biggest laugh on the *Jack Benny Show* was. Would it have done as well on his television show? Perhaps. But then again, the funniest thing about comedy is its uncertainty.

Most of us at one time or another hate to spend money. Jack Benny made being a cheapskate into an art form.

The following shortened Benny radio sketch was a group effort on the part of Benny's longtime staff of writers: Milt Josefsberg, George Balzar, Sam Perrin and John Tackaberry.

JACK   Wait here, I'll go down in the basement and get the money.

[*SOUND: Footsteps down a long flight of stairs on echo. Footsteps stop. Clanking of chains. Heavy iron door squeaks open, more footsteps down stone. More chains and heavier door creaks slowly open. More steps.*]

KERN   Halt! Who goes there? Friend or foe?

JACK   Friend.

KERN   What's the password?

JACK   A fool and his money are soon parted. Take out your gun, Ed. I'm going to open the safe.

KERN   Yes, sir.

JACK   Let's see ... the combination is right to forty-five ... (*light sound*) ... left to one-sixty ... (*light sound*) ... back to fifteen (*light sound*) ... then left to one-ten. There.

[*SOUND: Handle turns. Terrific steam whistles, bells, whistles, bells, gunshots, etc., ending with* beeeohhh *whistle.*]

JACK   I wonder if I need a louder burglar alarm. Let's see, this ought to be enough money.

[*SOUND: Vault door clanks shut and footsteps.*]

JACK   Say, Ed ... I've been thinking ... it must get pretty lonely down here.

KERN   No, no, I don't mind.

JACK   Well, nevertheless, I'm going to get you a radio.

KERN   A radio? ... What's that?

JACK   Well, ... it's something new that people enjoy.

KERN   Well, send it down. If I like it I'll eat it.

| JACK | No, no, Ed. It's nothing to eat. Well, so long. |
| KERN | So long, Mr. Benny. |

[*SOUND: Few footsteps and creaking door shut.*]

[*MUSIC: PLAYOFF.*]

Because of this sketch's huge popularity on radio, Benny couldn't wait to do it on television. The results were dismal. It was therefore with great reluctance that the visual medium of television forced Benny to drop one of his all-time biggest laugh-producing routines.

At the time the sketch was done on television, most of the viewers had heard the sketch done on radio. Was the televised vault as big as they imagined? What did the basement look like? Was it like a castle's dungeon? And what about Ed, who guarded the vault? How was he dressed? How old was he? Did he have a Rip Van Winkle beard? Did he look like the type that could be so dense as to think radio was something to be eaten like a Tootsie Roll?

Perhaps the Benny television set was accurate in regards to the way the set designer drew it in his blueprint. But was it the way the millions of listeners from radio imagined it?

Even the addition of alligators to a moat didn't help make it funny. Nothing the set designers came up with seemed to be as funny as what radio suggested with mere words and sounds.

To audiences, accustomed only to watching television, it might seem difficult to imagine how just listening to a radio could be so appealing. The answer is, radio was just as visual to the listeners as television is to the viewer. And no one knew this better than the Benny writers.

When I asked Balzer what it took to be a successful comedy writer in radio, he answered, "Writing for radio required words that formed pictures in the listener's imagination. Unlike writing books, in comedy we never described things in detail, we left that up to the listeners. So in a way, no two listeners ever laughed at the exact same thing. People of course, knew what Jack Benny looked like, but what about the guard? The basement? The vault? And that was the beauty part of radio.... It was such a personal medium for the listener."

George concluded by saying, "The only way those wonderful radio sketches could have succeeded on television is ... if radio hadn't done them first."

I agree with Balzer. Words that conjure up pictures are the ones an audience enjoys most and remembers longest. Early television, however, fearing that it would be compared to radio, leaned more to the Milton Berle, Buddy Lester, Sid Caesar, Imogene Coca, Jackie Gleason, Martin and Lewis type of physical comedy. Why bother to make your audiences think—wasn't that what television's four cameras were for?

The Sound-Effects Artists Give Their Opinions

In addition to the comedy writers and the comedians, some of the biggest laughs in radio were gotten by the sound-effects artists, who brought you, for instance, the closet crash on *The Fibber McGee and Molly Show*.

I therefore feel it only fair to give you the consensus of opinion from a group of these pioneer sound-effects artists: Their choice between radio and TV? *Radio*, of course!

Television is half sound and half picture. So is radio. However, whereas the television picture is electronically produced, radio's picture was the listener's imagination. It was, therefore, this difference that made radio sound effects so much easier and exciting to get laughs with.

When we did the Fibber crash on radio, it often lasted for over ten seconds, not including the laughs we got at the end of the crash with the tinkle bell. For the television viewer, that's about eight seconds too long to laugh without seeing a funny picture. For the radio listener, they got all the laughs they wanted from the pictures they saw in their imagination.

The Comedy Writers Speak Out

Hal Kanter, writer for radio's *Beulah* and an Emmy winner for *The George Gobel Show* voted for radio on the grounds that it allowed the writer more freedom.

Bob O'Brien, who wrote for Eddie Cantor in radio and Bob Hope on television, also voted for radio.

Providing yet another vote for the sound-based medium is one of the most successful and imaginative comedy writers I know, Gene Perret. Gene is also an author and producer, with this partial list of impressive credits: As a television comedy writer, he worked on *Welcome Back, Kotter*; *Three's Company*; *Laugh-In*; and the Bob Hope and Carol Burnett shows. He has written three books: *Comedy Writing Step by Step*, *Comedy Writing Workbook* and *Become a Richer Writer*. And, in addition, he received Emmy Awards in 1974, 1975 and 1978 and won the Writers Guild Award in 1974.

This then, is what Gene was kind enough to say:

> When I worked on the Carol Burnett show, I was stunned one day when two of the younger writers asked, "What was radio like?" It never occurred to me that there were people in the world, in the industry, who had never known radio.
>
> I never worked in radio, but it had a profound influence on me and my writing. I grew up with radio. Bob Hope, Red Skelton, Jack Benny, Burns and Allen,

Edgar Bergen and Charlie McCarthy, Fibber McGee and Molly—these were the characters I laughed at as a youngster. They're the ones who influenced my sense of humor.

As a craftsman, a comedy writer, I now feel that radio was superior to television for a couple of reasons. First, radio was constantly changing. Each year, the same show would change in subtle ways. The reason for that being that each listener supplied the cast, the sets, the panorama—almost everything except the dialogue.

When I heard Fibber McGee talk, I pictured how he looked. It probably wasn't how he actually looked, but in my mind, he appeared any way I wanted to see him. When he opened his closet and all the paraphernalia spilled out, I saw it in my head. His living room existed only in my mind. Jack Benny's vault and all the security around it looked whichever way I wanted it to look. The next year, I might redesign all the sets. Radio gave me that power.

With television, Archie Bunker's home always looked the same. Archie Bunker, in fact, looked like Archie Bunker. I couldn't change that on television. On radio I could. That kept the radio shows fresh in each listener's mind.

Second, as a gag-writer, I realize too, that the best writing was on radio because it needed no support. All that was going over the airwaves was the dialogue. The jokes had to be good.

Television has come to lean on many different factors to present the comedy— clothes, sets, funny faces, goofy costumes, wacky props. All of these take the burden of being funny away from the jokesmith. They allow it to be possible to get away with easier gags.

I miss radio. I also missed working in live television. In the modern technology, we can use editing techniques and camera tricks in producing our shows. Costume and makeup changes can be dramatic tricks in producing our shows because we have the time to permit them. In live television, you went on the air and you were there for an hour. You couldn't leisurely change costumes in your dressing room while a warm-up comedian talked with your audience. You had to change and get back on camera. The world was waiting for you.

Today, too, we have the luxury of redoing certain scenes, cutting back and forth between different takes. On one Carol Burnett show, we forgot to light the candles on the dining room table for the second taping of the show. On the air, as we cut back and forth between the dress rehearsal and the air show, the candles would mysteriously light and go out, light and go out....

The perfection of today's technology sometimes distracts from the fun. I've been in the control room where a performer would flub a line or make a mistake that would be hilarious. We'd laugh in the booth, the audience would howl, the actors would enjoy the blooper and the director would say, "That's OK. We can cut that mistake out in editing."...

Though I didn't work in radio and live television, I've been connected with many of the comics of those eras. I've worked with Bob Hope, George Burns, Jack Benny, Milton Berle, and others. People often ask me to compare the comics of that era with today's young talent.

To me, the comics of an older generation had a certain class that is missing nowadays. One reason, I feel, is that the older comics were raised with audiences.

Here the author gives a sound-effect demonstration at a local school and tries to keep up with two future Lucille Balls.

"Okay, now when I hit Ethel on the nose, give me a honk on your horn! And this time don't be late or you'll kill the laughs!" (Photograph courtesy of author.)

They knew how to entertain a live crowd. They struggled through many years of developing their craft and audiences were important to them. If the audience laughed, they got better gigs and more money. Many of the young comedians today look down on the audience. They don't want to impress them so much as they want to impress the television executives and their fellow comics.

That's a pity because it's the people out front that make comedy great. They put the fun in comedy. Actually, they're the reason for comedy, and us, the comedy writers.

Building the Better Mousetrap

Doing a radio show out of a theater presented no problem for radio audiences. The only technical equipment seen on the stage was several microphones and an area off to the side for Sound Effects. Nothing else was on stage to obscure the audience's view, or distract them from laughing.

Because of the cameras and the boom microphones, television audiences had a choice of craning their necks and watching the show on several monitors or counting all the rear ends of the people it took to put on a live television show.

Facing tough audiences, being hidden on a stage by cameras and booms, fast costume changes and overheated studios was only part of the uphill battle comedians had to face. Perhaps when Fred Allen, radio's nasal-voiced comedic and writing genius, once declared, "Technical equipment has taken over the business," he was right. Well, almost. He was wrong in one vital area: special effects—the Toys "Я" Us part of live television.

Today you can't watch a movie without seeing, at the very least, a car, bus, truck, train, subway, boat, bridge, tunnel, house, apartment, or building being blown sky high. In fact, the best way to sell a movie these days is to find the special-effects people a new place for them to stick their dynamite.

It wasn't always that way. On one Bob Hope show, the payoff of a comedy magic sketch involved a trained pigeon flying out of a cardboard tube. On air, as Houdini, Hope opened the tube; instead of a bird flying out, all the audience saw was tail feathers and kicking feet. The special-effects man had put the pigeon in the tube ass-backwards!

But all of the stuff television had—the funny costumes, outrageous makeup, scenery, props, and camera angles—came with a price.

Camera angles, for instance, were often a hit or miss proposition. Unlike the modern cameras, with their zoom lenses, the cameras in early live television were equipped with four lenses, each one designed for a particular function.

If a camera was on a closeup lens, it couldn't be moved without losing its focus. And if a camera was on a medium lens, it couldn't get a closeup. As a result, the camera operator had the job of moving the camera to accommodate the lens he was using, while it was the job of the actor or comedian to be certain he had hit his correct mark on the stage. If the performer missed the spot, there was a very good chance that on a closeup the camera would show only the actor's nose.

To make certain the performers were standing at the right place, the stage manager would make a mark with a yellow crayon pencil (yellow didn't show up on camera). In a scene or sketch with a lot of movement, this was both difficult on the camera operator trying to get the correct shot and the performer trying to hit the correct mark.

Some early comedians refused to play that game. At one rehearsal of a *Honeymooners* sketch, Jackie Gleason was doing a great deal of movement and ended up off to the side of the set. When the director complained (very, very mildly, I might add) that Gleason was not on his mark, Gleason responded, "Well pal [he called everyone 'pal' because it was easier than remembering names], since I'm the star of this show, and your camera has wheels, just who in the hell do you think is going to move their ass!"

Another problem that the live television writers faced was time. If a sketch required a quick costume change, this had to be carefully planned. If there wasn't time for it to be done offstage, the actor would have to underdress. And this need for performers to wear a costume under another article of clothing brought untold riches to trench coat and bathrobe manufacturers.

All of these technical problems added to the writing problems of getting laughs in live television. But they all pale in comparison to the comedy writer's live television nightmare of special effects.

My comedy-writing career started on the daytime Garry Moore television show. While doing the sound effects on that show, I thought of an idea for a comedy sketch. I wrote it down, gave it to Garry, and the next day he said he liked it and bought it. It was as simple as that. I didn't have to go through a dozen executive producers, five associate producers and four garden variety producers to get it done, either. All it took was an okay from Garry and it was a done deal.

Two days before we did the sketch, John Neukum (the unit manager in charge of the show's budget), came up to me and said, "In the script you wrote, is the door's peephole necessary?"

Not only was this my first professional script, I already was about to make my first compromise of many as a writer. "It helps Garry's move to the door."

"But it isn't absolutely necessary?"

"Well ... not absolutely. Why?"

"Good! Cause to rent a door with a peephole in it from Special Effects costs three hundred dollars!"

That did it! A compromise was one thing, this was rubbing it in! "Three hundred dollars! Hell, I'm only getting twenty-five for the whole script!"

He gave me a wicked smile and replied, "True. But then again, your script didn't come from Special Effects."

CHAPTER 10

Living on the Edge: Ad-libbing—Not for the Faint of Heart

The ability to think fast in a crisis is not an ability everyone has. Unfortunately, in live broadcasting thinking fast was a requirement. Like that night on the Jack Benny radio show when the sound-effects artist's telephone bell wouldn't ring. What would you have done? Sorry, your time is up.

The matter of seconds it took you to read that last line is approximately how much time Virgil Reimer, Benny's sound-effects artist, had to solve the problem. Of course he could have done nothing and then, after the show, apologized to Benny that the phone bell's battery went suddenly dead. But who would Benny have apologized to? The millions of listeners?

As it turned out, neither Reimer nor Benny had to apologize for anything. When Reimer pushed the button and the phone bell didn't respond, Benny, unaware of the problem, quickly repeated the cue line for the phone to ring. Reimer, in desperation, suddenly leaned into the mike and quickly ad-libbed: "Ding-a-ling-a-ling."

The audience's response was instantaneous! They roared and applauded in appreciation of Reimer's quick thinking. And as the laughs began to subside, Benny, not noted for his ad-libbing ability, matched Reimer's quick thinking by saying: "I'll get it, it sounds like a person-to-person call."

Although both Reimer's and Benny's ad-libs were highly unusual on a show as structured as Benny's, they also rank as one of the biggest laughs ever on the *Jack Benny Show*. What is even more unusual, in spite of the huge laughs this ad-lib received, Benny's ban on ad-libbing was never lifted.

Once, when Benny was recalling this incident with the phone to an interviewer, he was asked the obvious question.

"Weren't you, or your writers, ever tempted to fake these on-air miscues?"

Benny, without hesitation, answered, "No, because I'm not that good of an actor, and audiences aren't that dumb."

It's one thing for an actor or sound-effect artist to be fast on his feet, but unless it's accompanied by good taste, it's better to let the moment pass. Because simply being quick, without being appropriate, is simply being a smartass.

The Henry Morgan Show

On the *Here's Morgan* radio show starring Henry Morgan, his sound-effect artist was outstanding in creating funny sounds. But as Morgan recalled, "In the beginning it was challenging and fun. We were even getting mail from listeners saying how much they enjoyed the quick thinking on the part of the soundman. Evidently, that praise went to his head. Because now, instead of reacting with an ad-lib to what I was saying, he wanted me to contrive situations so he could do his funny sound effects!"

This is perhaps what the producers in both radio and television had against the art of ad-libbing. The laughs a successful ad-lib brought were addictive. And, as soundman Monty Fraser's experience on the *Tonight Show* demonstrates, succumbing to that temptation, even when things work out, can often have disastrous results.

The *Tonight Show* rarely spent a great deal of time rehearsing. The most you could hope for was that Carson would come down from his office and walk through the sketch. This meant there was literally no time for deviating from the written script. And ad-libbing? Don't even think about it.

This "no ad-libbing" policy was never challenged by the newer members of the sound department who had never worked in live radio or live television. But to Monty Fraser, ad-libbing was as much a part of his job as making certain the Fibber McGee closet crash got laughs.

For one episode, Fraser was assigned to the *Tonight Show* for the purpose of doing a single phone ring. Now to most of the newer members of the department this represented a good time to read or clean out their wallet. But not Monty. You could never tell when a comedy sketch might need help.

The sketch involved a heated battle of words between Carson and his wife over her love of stuffed animals, particularly a large, somber hound dog in the bedroom. As Carson casually rehearsed the various jokes, he came to one that got absolutely no reaction from the crew. To a comedian, no reaction from the crew to a joke in rehearsal sends up a red flag.

All comedians, whether they're the host of America's most watched nighttime talk show or a standup comic in a two-table comedy club, want laughs. Therefore, when Carson's joke didn't get one, he turned to the stuffed hound dog and jokingly ad-libbed, "It's all your fault!" and kicked the stuffed dog.

Normally, kicking any dog, stuffed or otherwise, is hardly the way to get laughs. And yet the response to this unexpected action on Carson's part brought howls of laughter from the crew.

If you asked Carson why he just suddenly kicked the stuffed dog, he most likely couldn't tell you. And that is the danger of ad-libbing. You never can predict or even think about what the reaction will be; something comes over you and you just do it.

Another interested party in Carson's ad-lib was Fraser. As he watched Carson struggling with the sketch, he too felt that irresistible "something" stirring within him and beginning to take hold of his better judgment.

That night, on air, Fraser dutifully rang his phone, closed his microphone and turned to his added piece of equipment, an audio tape cart machine capable of playing a recorded sound effect at the touch of a button.

As he waited, he idly wondered why he was about to take such a big risk with his career. The *Tonight Show* didn't take flaunting their show's policies lightly. And Fred De Cordova, the producer, had clout—big time. And yet here he was, the sound-effects David, taking on the *Tonight Show* Goliath with nothing more than a sound effect in his electronic sling shot.

With television turning to tape, much of the sound effects once done live were now laid in later in post-production with computers. As a result, the modern taped shows never considered sound effects or the folks who did them that important. But that night, the mighty *Tonight Show* was about the get a taste of just how valuable live sound effects could be before the machines took over.

As the sketch progressed, the feeling that Carson had in rehearsal was right on the money, the stuffed dog joke didn't get a laugh. But Carson, rather than just moving on to the next joke, did what he did in rehearsal and once again kicked the dog. As he did, the stuffed dog suddenly, and certainly unexpectedly, snarled viciously up at the startled Carson!

Mister nightly-cool-Carson literally leaped back from this suddenly vicious stuffed canine in shock and fear. The audience, sensing that this wasn't part of the prepared script, howled their approval. Up in the control room, Howie Quinn, the director, had other thoughts. And he screamed them over Monty's headset, "Stop fucking around, Sound Effects!"

Despite the screaming obscenities hurled at Monty, he didn't stop "fucking around," and neither did Carson. In fact Carson rose to Monty's ad-libbed challenge and between the two, the audience knew that what they were watching was not on the cue cards and they loved it!

And what was the price of Monty's ad-libbing? He had violated the producer's *Tonight Show* policy (which more than likely was kept from Carson) and was never accepted on the show again. Did this bother Monty? When asked, he just smiled and replied, "Not a bit. I never appreciated how funny Carson could be—until tonight."

There's a Fly on My Twinkie!

For all you stuffed-animal advocates that find nothing funny about kicking a dog, what do you think about having a dirty housefly as one of the regulars on a children's show?

You've already read how desperate the networks of early television were for locations. This time CBS outdid themselves, however, and renovated a building that had once housed horses. And this was to be the new home for Captain Kangaroo—and an awful lot of flies.

Every time the Captain did a food commercial, the flies were sure to follow. This of course required an expensive amount of time to get rid of the flies and do the commercial over. One time, I had used a small buzzer for the sound of a bee buzzing. And when I saw a fly making a beeline for one of the exposed Twinkies, I grabbed the buzzer and began making fly buzzes.

Peter Birch, the director, of course screamed, but the fly hadn't as yet flown in front of his commercial camera. But Bob Keeshan had noticed the pesky insect. And Bob, instead of screaming and stopping tape as he normally did when a fly invaded the Treasure House, went along with my ad-lib.

"Not now, Raymond, I don't have time to play."

And that, baby boomers, is how an ad-lib buzz effect created Raymond the Fly. It also saved the show stress and CBS money in wasted commercial time.

Although this may have seemed like quick thinking on my part, it was more like simply reacting as if the show were live. Had I never worked in live television, I probably would have said, "So we stop tape, what's the big deal? Isn't that why they invented tape?"

Ernie Kovacs

One show that wasn't taped was the *Ernie Kovacs Show*. Another name for the show could have been "How to Put on a Television Show Live Without Any Money."

It was because this extremely tight budget didn't allow for a writing staff that Kovacs encouraged his sound-effects man, Russ Gainor, to ad-lib whenever the spirit moved him, or more importantly, when Kovacs desperately needed him.

One memorable Kovacs moment occurred when CBS figured a way of cutting even more money out of Kovacs' already miserly budget. Instead of continuing to rent his background set, comprising pictures, curtains and windows, CBS would replace all these things and simply paint them on a set entirely made out of paper—even the windows,.

At the on-the-air inauguration of this house of paper, Kovacs took the home audience on a televised tour of the set, explaining the ingenuity—and cheapness—of CBS' skillful use of paper. As Kovacs ran out of things to say, he suddenly heard the unmistakable sound of knocking on glass coming from Sound Effects. As Kovacs walked toward the paper window, the glass knocking got louder. After making several unsuccessful attempts to find a way of opening the paper window, Kovacs finally smashed his fist through the paper. The sound of glass crash quickly followed.

Not satisfied with just breaking the "window," Kovacs went on to rip the rest of the flimsy paper set CBS had supplied him. It wasn't until after the show that Kovacs was to learn that the seemingly cheap paper set he had just destroyed had ended up costing CBS more than if they had used real furniture and windows. Despite this, it never cured Kovacs of his love of using television for his forum of doing the unexpected.

One of the difficulties Kovacs faced was getting legitimate guests on his show. Because of Kovacs' wild sense of humor, and his notorious on-the-air ad-libbing, the only guests he could get were people other shows either shunned or labeled undesirable. This was especially true of the guests who blatantly made outrageous claims for their products. For these hucksters, the apparent opportunity to plug their products on the Kovacs show for free often came with an expensive price.

If ever the popular phrase "Truth in Advertising" was put to the test, it was the day Kovacs came out wearing a suit that the guest manufacturer "guaranteed to maintain its creases and remain wrinkle-free even when caught in a driving rainstorm."

Kovacs registered doubt about these clothing claims, especially the one about rainstorms, which was his way of telling Russ Gainor to start getting his ad-libs ready.

Kovacs took a puff on his cigar, rose from his chair, and as the guest now nervously watched, Kovacs walked over and removed a sheet from a large laundry tub filled with water. Then, as the guest watched in shock, Kovacs, without so much as removing his shoes, stepped into the tub of water and sat down. He then looked up at the horrified clothing manufacturer and said, "Now I know this isn't a test like a real rainstorm…"

To the uninitiated in the fine art of ad-libbing, Kovacs' words may have sounded like a halfhearted apology to his now speechless guest, whereas in reality, they were a cue to anyone on the show to pitch in with the ad-libs.

The first to respond was a recorded clap of thunder from Sound Effects. Following was Eddie Hatrack, Kovacs' piano player, who came racing out armed with a bucket. Then, as the guest watched his dreams of riches go down the drain, Hatrack began dumping water over Kovacs to the accompaniment of thunder claps, while Kovacs hummed "Singin' in the Rain."

Captain Kangaroo

The sounds during the early days of the *Captain Kangaroo Show* were done live by Jerry Sullivan, ex–drummer with the internationally famous Paul Whiteman

Orchestra. This experience, plus his natural abilities, made him an excellent sound-effect artist. The problem was, nothing in his background prepared him for the shenanigans that go on in live television.

Bob Keeshan depended sorely on sound effects. Sounds for the Bunny Rabbit's carrot crunches, the Treasure House doorbells, Beepo's nose, the Hat Tree and the ticking of the Captain's pocket watch.

All of these various Treasure House regulars had their own special sound, some you did with your hands, some on records. The problem was, you never knew when or what sounds the kindly old Captain would suddenly demand.

At the time the show was live, it was coming out of Liederkranz Hall. The location of Sound Effects was in the studio squeezed behind the flat that contained the little clown with the big red nose, Beepo.

Beepo's nose required the sound of a bulb horn whenever Keeshan squeezed the nose. The problem was, because of our lousy location, the only way we knew what was happening on the other side of the flat was to watch our monitor.

Because of our blind location, Keeshan would wait until the conclusion of a commercial or cartoon and, when the camera came up on him, he would already have his hand on Beepo's red-rubber ball nose. And if he didn't hear a honk, he would turn to the camera and apologize to the boys and girls: "The funny little sound in Beepo's nose must be sleeping on the job. But he'll wake up—sooner or later."

Keeshan's reputation for trying to catch the soundman sleeping was known throughout the department. Therefore when the call came in for a replacement, Tom Buchanon and Jimmy Lynch decided to give Keeshan a few ad-libs of their own. When the two arrived at the studio, they introduced themselves to the director, Peter Birch, and told him they weren't familiar with the show.

Birch told them the show was pretty much ad-libbed and to do the best they could.

The best that Lynch and Buchanon could do happened two minutes into the show. As the Bunny Rabbit stole some carrots from the Captain and made his exit, it was accompanied by a whizz sound and a huge glass crash.

"What the hell are you doing!" Birch screamed. While the Captain, surprised at this uncharacteristic Treasure House sound, had to force a smile and call off-camera in a concerned voice, "Are you all right, Bunny?"

Inasmuch as the Bunny Rabbit was just a puppet, Gus Allegrhetti, the puppeteer, had to race Bunny back into the picture and vigorously nod.

Next was heard the off-camera voice of Mister Greenjeans (Lumpy Brannum) calling out reassuringly, "It's okay, Captain, I dropped my water glass but I'll sweep it up."

Next the Captain asked the boys and girls at home if they would like to see what he could find that was interesting in his pockets?

Then as the Captain was about to reach in he heard the sound of a cow mooing loudly, which brought forth another outburst of anger from Birch over the Sound Effects headset. But this time his voice was drowned out by a train whistle, a police siren, a factory whistle and a lion roar!

To the astonishment of Lynch and Buchanon, with each and every ad-lib sound that they threw at him, Keeshan responded as if it was all in a well-rehearsed, carefully written script. He not only didn't get angry or flustered, he actually enjoyed the challenge.

"Hear that? That's a train whistle, boys and girls. Do you find a train in a pocket? Noooooo! A train belongs on a track. I wonder if I can find a boat whistle somewhere way down deep in my pocket?"

By the middle of the show, Lynch and Buchanon realized they were fighting a losing battle. Keeshan, on occasions, may have been a pain in the butt, but he sure as hell was made for live television!

A few years later when I began doing the show, it was recorded on tape. The difference? If Buchanon and Lynch carried on like they did when it was live, Keeshan would have just stopped the tape and wanted to know what the hell was going on.

That's the difference between live and tape. And because there was no stopping a live show, you lived with the mistakes and did the best you could. And Keeshan was the best when he wanted to be, or, in the case of live television, when he had to be.

I recall one example vividly. Bob had just finished the show, undone his tie, given his wig to the hairdresser and was about to leave the studio when an unthinking CBS employee entered the studio with a dozen wide-eyed children. Bob, seeing the children before they saw him, literally dove behind the Treasure House desk so the children wouldn't be disillusioned seeing him without his familiar wig.

This is just one example of Keeshan's consideration for his young audience. During a commercial he never urged the children to "ask your mommy to buy…," nor did he ever do a playtime project that required special or expensive materials. He also did something that no other television celebrity I ever worked with did.

Television stars very often receive gifts from their adoring fans. This is especially true of soap opera addicts. At the drop of a hat they'll send their favorite soap character a cake. The problem is, most soap characters are on a strict diet, and the cakes either ended up in the trash or partially eaten by members of the crew.

Not so with Keeshan. Each month he'd buy a huge birthday cake to celebrate the birthdays of the children born in that month. Then, after the show, rather than have the crew ravage it, he'd have it sent to a New York City children's hospital.

Because so many young children almost reached puberty watching the kindly old Captain, it should come as no surprise that more than a few mothers got hooked on the show. This became embarrassingly evident years later when I was working at NBC.

I was doing sound effects at NBC, and Keeshan came to California to be a guest on the original *Hollywood Squares*. After the show, he was kind enough to look me up, and we went to a local bar to have a drink and talk about old times.

The bar we were seated at was dimly lit and circled a piano. And because no one wanted to disturb the sound of the soft piano music, everyone was talking in hushed tones. This of course included Bob and myself.

Now keep in mind Bob Keeshan was a television celebrity. However, no living soul, besides his wife and those of us that worked his show, had ever seen him without his costume, makeup, mustache and wig. And yet to show you the price of fame, a woman across the bar in the murky darkness cried out in a two-martinis voice louder than the piano music, "Jeesecrist! My kids are in college and I still keep hearing the voice of Captain Kangaroo!"

Jackie Gleason

Gleason, like many of the comedians in live television, earned their right to be on live television the hard way. Some came from vaudeville, some from nightclubs, and a few even from burlesque. Gleason came from them all—vaudeville, nightclubs, and, yes, burlesque.

Bob Keeshan, as a more sedate Captain Kangaroo, was one of live television's early risk takers (author's collection).

Burlesque taught Gleason a very quick lesson. Whatever was done on stage in burlesque that didn't pertain to a woman disrobing was a stage wait. So unless you were funny enough to distract the audience from their real purpose of attending the "girlie show," you were in for a very hot and sweaty time.

It was this type of rough and tumble background of getting laughs any way you could that Gleason brought to live television—a live television that had scripts and critical phrases to stand for the all-important cameras to see you.

Therefore, because of his healthy respect for the importance of audiences, he often ignored the more rigid requirements of a television show. To Gleason, it was the laughs that were important, and the hell with everything else, pal!

Every Man for Himself!

This literally meant "don't hold me to the lines in the script!" Of course this wasn't easy for Gleason to say. He had talent enough to pick up a script, look at it briefly and have a good grasp of its contents; however, a good grasp is not the same as knowing the script line for line, because he didn't. Nor did this seem to worry him. This was not only tough on Art Carney and Audrey Meadows, it was drinking time for sound effects.

On one show I did, the only sound effect I had was a phone ring. And because I had a script indicating where the phone ring occurred, I looked forward to a relaxing day and evening. And it was—right up to air time.

As the words in the script were spoken by Gleason, Carney and Meadows, with more or less faithfulness to the order they were written, it came time for the cue to ring the phone.

I held the bell box next to the mike, opened the microphone, put my finger on the bell button and—whoopseedaisy! Not only wasn't I given the proper word cue, Gleason wasn't even on the same page I was!

This was the nightmare of all sound-effect artists. Had the phone ring been cut and no one told me? After frantically going through the script, I found that Gleason had jumped two whole pages! Had he really jumped, or had both the pages and phone ring been cut?

My concern was mild compared to the panic in the control room. The director was screaming orders to the cameras and boom microphones to follow Gleason, while Carney and Meadows were desperately trying to get Gleason back on script!

In the meantime, no one in the control room was saying the magic words: "ring the phone." The only sound out of the assistant director was: "Holy shit! If we lose two whole pages, we will end the show two minutes early!"

During my early freelance days, one of my jobs was picking and furnishing the sound effects for Gleason's show *Cavalcade of Stars* (1950–1952) on the Dumont Network. I would take the effects to the theater and give them to the doorman, who in turn would give them to whoever was doing the sound effects for the show. This strange arrangement had to do with my not belonging to the stagehand's union.

Although I was not allowed to enter the theater with the effects, the doorman saw no reason why I couldn't watch the Gleason rehearsal. It was then that I often heard Gleason say to the cast, "Don't hold me to lines; it's every man for himself!"

Recalling Gleason's words that night on air, I thought, what the hell, let's see if he really meant "every man for himself!"

Suddenly I got cold feet. What if I'm wrong! My job was just to ring the phone. It was the director's job to tell me when. Is that what I was waiting for? Was that what doing sound effects was all about? To be nothing but a damn button pusher?

As I put my finger on the button to push it, I got cold feet again. The Gleason show was an important CBS show with an audience of millions. It had the sponsors and the network brass watching, maybe even Bill Paley, the head of CBS! Besides, I wasn't paid to make those decisions!

Now I was not only a damn button pusher, but I couldn't even make a decision. But why should I wait for a cue from someone who may just be out of college? Wasn't I the one that should know what to do in an emergency such as this? And then I got cold feet again.

All this thinking races through your mind making your hands sweat, and your mouth go dry. But then you finally say fuck it!—and you ring the phone. And Gleason, without breaking stride, goes to the phone, picks it up and ad-libs, "Well, pal, what took you so long to make up your mind to call?"

This was what live television was all about. Were all my concerns about doing the right thing worth the few ad-libbed words of thanks from Gleason? You bet your ass it was!

They Called Me a What?

Most comedians didn't have Gleason's enormous abilities. Certainly the physical comedians didn't. Their idea of a brilliant off-the-cuff remark was to drop their pants. Unfortunately, those kinds of ad-libs aren't acceptable on the *Tonight Show*.

The closest thing to live television is the *Tonight Show*. I can't think of any calamity that would cause the show to stop taping. When Jack Paar was the host in New York, Dick Van Dyke was asked to be the guest host for a week. Because Van Dyke didn't feel comfortable talking, the show promised him guests that had appeared on the show many times and would help him get over the rough spots. This was both a relief to Van Dyke and to myself, who at the time was writing for Van Dyke.

One of the first guests selected was the famed one-time burlesque stripper Gypsy Rose Lee. Although at the time of her appearance on the show, Miss Lee was more acclaimed for her way with words in writing best-selling books (*The G-String Murder*, for instance) than she was for shedding clothes.

Having myself been an occasional fan of burlesque, I had read where Miss Lee was a burlesque enigma. She had attained stardom not so much for what she took off, but what she kept on. But perhaps in spite of it, Miss Lee, at least in burlesque circles, was referred to as a "flash act."

When Van Dyke told me Gypsy Rose Lee was going to be on the show, I happened to mention what I had read at one time about her being a flash act.

That evening, during the taping of the show, the conversation began lagging, and Van Dyke, desperate for something to say, couldn't find the questions the regular *Tonight Show* writers had given him. Suddenly, out of the blue, he remembered what I had said several days ago.

"Tell us, Miss Lee, weren't you really one of the top flash acts in burlesque?"

This little gem of an ad-lib had no more than crossed the short distance between Van Dyke's desk and Miss Lee's ear when she whirled around, her face burning a flaming red through her ample makeup, and screamed, "What?! What idiot said that?!"

Van Dyke looked helplessly offstage at me.

"Not only wasn't I a flash act, I'll sue that person for character assassination!"

All I could think of was, Thank God the show was taped! All this embarrassment can be edited out! Right? Wrong!

Although the *Tonight Show* is taped, it would take a mistake of titanic proportions for the producers to stop the tape or edit the show's content. The show is taped to accommodate the various time zones around the country, not to offer a safety net for wrong information about a burlesque icon.

That night, the only thing that saved Van Dyke, and me, was a commercial. After the commercial, Miss Lee recovered beautifully and made a joke out of what a real "flash act" in burlesque was (a "flash act" bared it all) while Van Dyke just sat there wishing he could have thought of something clever to say—like dropping his pants.

On a comedy show, an ad-lib wasn't just "an unrehearsed anything"; it was a deadly form of Russian roulette. It didn't matter how many times you were successful; there was always a chance of dialing up the bullet.

Having said that, when these moments of madness strike, you either immediately react or forever wish you had. There is no time to think of the consequences or whether your ad-lib is funny or even appropriate. You just do it.

Because of the tremendous amount of uncertainty and risks involved in ad-libbing in comedy, I saved the worst until last.

The Garry Moore Show

In doing Garry's weekly daytime show, I was given free rein as far as ad-libbing was concerned. Much of this was due to the free and easy style of the show. Garry practically invented the talk show format. Although rehearsed, it wasn't rehearsed to the point that it precluded having fun.

It couldn't be. Doing the show five days a week, 52 weeks a year—live—Garry had to seize every scrap of entertainment offered him. Well, almost every scrap.

On one occasion, Garry and Durward Kirby, his extremely talented announcer and creative sidekick, were doing a sketch that was awful. After each and every joke the audience signaled their displeasure with an occasional embarrassed cough. Why I ever took it upon myself to think I could save this sinking ship, I have no idea. This is one time I should have kept my ad-libs to myself, but I just couldn't let my two buddies go down with the ship, could I?

In rehearsal, the reaction to the sketch was not encouraging. For one thing, no one in the band laughed, or even smiled. It might be pointed out that a band's reaction to comedy was not always reliable. They either laughed because something struck them as being genuinely funny, or they laughed because it struck them as being awful. This sketch fell somewhere in between and simply stunned them into disbelief. Assuming that Garry would kill the sketch, I didn't give it any more thought.

On air, however, Garry surprised me by going ahead with the sketch. Recalling that the sketch had one place I could ad-lib some sounds and perhaps help, I dug out what I needed and drove all doubt out of my mind as to whether or not what I was about to do was funny, or even appropriate.

Suddenly, I heard Garry say the line for my quick-witted ad-lib!

"Does the name, Harriette Hornswallow, ring a bell?"

In a flash, I executed the sounds that would save the day! First the wind whistle, then the gunshot, then the coup de grâce, the bell! Get it? Garry had asked, "Does that ring a bell?" And I ad-libbed a bell! Not just a bell, but a wind whistle, a gunshot, and then the bell! The magical three of comedy!

The reaction to my ad-lib was even more stunningly quiet than the silence Garry and Durward had been enduring. First Garry and Durward looked up at me with curious detachment and then the band. Then the members of the audience—all five hundred of them—looked up at me. But I had by now slunk down behind the protective covering of my box seat.

The only words I heard from the control room came in a stern voice over my headset from Herb Sanford, the producer. "Bob, I want to see you after the show."

Having already suffered the embarrassment that comes with an ill-advised ad-lib, I was now either going to be lectured to about deviating from the written word or summarily kicked off the show. As the show came to a close, I went backstage to wait for Herb and to receive my sentence.

As Herb and Garry started across the stage to their waiting cab, I couldn't help thinking that maybe Herb already forgot about my ill-fated ad-lib. Or maybe my fate had been already decided.

"Herb, you wanted to see me?"

Both Herb and Garry stopped. I could tell by the look on Herb's face my question had caught him off guard. Then, turning to Garry, he said, "Yes. I felt Bob's ill-advised ad-lib was not only totally uncalled for, but it was instrumental in ruining the sketch."

Garry paused a moment and I shall never forget his answer.

"Herb, if there was any way of predicting the reaction to an ad-lib, it wouldn't be an ad-lib."

Garry, I couldn't have said it better.

CHAPTER 11

One of TV's Finest Hours

Now that television was being accepted more as an entertainment medium rather than just a toy, it was still thought of as the movie's poor relative. After all, what had live television done that could challenge the magnitude of the movie's wide-screen, Technicolor pictures? For instance, could television's overcrowded and overheated small studios do a western?

It was for that reason and no doubt others, that television decided to challenge the movies by doing a western on television live! Not just live, either. It would do it with honest-to-goodness horses just like the ones John Wayne rode!

The problem of undertaking such an ambitious project had nothing to do with the script, the sets, or the actors. It was the horses. Not that they weren't well-trained and gentle; they just had never been on live television before.

Dealing with animals when situations are ideal is difficult enough. But when you add to it all the problems encountered doing a live television show, you're begging for trouble. The studios were hot, there was a constant glare from lights, the sudden movement of equipment could startle the animals, and once the show was on the air, it precluded the constant urgings and commands shouted by the animal trainers off camera.

Even dogs as well trained as Lassie could be a problem. For this reason there were several Lassies, each of whom performed different demanding stunts.

But in live television tricks and doubles weren't possible. Trainers couldn't shout commands, and cameras couldn't be stopped if something went wrong. And one night on *Medallion Theater*, something very terrible went wrong.

The script called for a fight between Charlton Heston and another important leading actor who played the villain. My job was to supply the sound effects when the actors smashed each other over the head with balsa wood chairs (I crushed small berry baskets), battered each other with bottles made of compressed sugar (I broke real glass), and looked like they were punching each other in the jaw (I hit my leather wallet).

After this, the fight spilled out into the dusty street where the horses were tethered to a hitching rail. For the fight out there, I supplied the recorded terrified snorts and whinnies of the horses.

It was a spectacular fight right up to the time when the fighters got too close to the frightened horse. One horse, his eyes rolling back in fear, began supplying his own snorts and whinnies. Suddenly, it reared back and pawed the air with its hoofs. When it came down, one of its hoofs struck the hand of the actor playing the second leading part!

With the air show literally minutes away, and this fight such an important part of the show, there was serious talk of canceling the show and replacing it with an old kinescope.

This was something neither the producer nor the sponsor (Chrysler Motors) wanted to do. A kinescope was a copy of a television show that had been filmed off a television monitor. As a result, the picture was of poor quality. And yet before television had live coast to coast transmission, this is what viewers were often forced to watch.

Someone suddenly recalled that Ken Utt, the show's stage manager, had been an actor. The problem was, how could someone without any rehearsal of either the lines or the actions do a half-hour network show live?

Utt, perhaps because of his stringent training as a stage manager and actor in the theater, had become somewhat familiar with many of the play's lines simply by working closely with the actors in rehearsals.

None of this explains how well Ken did that night on the show. The few times he couldn't ad-lib around the lines, or he forgot them, all the mikes were killed in the studio and Ken's assistant floor manager would call out the lines. It was one of the gutsiest performances I had ever seen in all the years I worked in live television.

After the show, Ken received the following telegram from the stricken actor: "This is the last time I'm ever going to let a horse step on me!"

CHAPTER 12

SFX Makes the News!

The phone in the CBS News Office rings, and the voice on the other end screams: "There's a fire burning out of control in a Brooklyn warehouse! There's chemicals in there! Get a camera here quick! But be careful! The whole damn thing may explode any second!"

And off the intrepid network news cameramen go! Ready to risk their lives to capture the fire on film so that you'll have something exciting, and hopefully dramatic, to watch on your six o'clock news.

When the fire story arrives back in the editing room, it's up to the newswriter, producer and editor to dig out the most informative pictures and story from the hundreds of feet of film shot of the fire.

In an often futile attempt to lend realism to many of these filmed news stories, the films were shot with the natural sound of the fire. However, supposing the director wanted to save the shot of a wall crashing down to end the story and wanted to begin the story with the fire engines arriving at the scene? To further complicate matters, if the director wants to cut away early (go to another scene) from fire engines, it will interrupt the natural sound of the engine's sirens.

That in a nutshell was the purpose that sound effects served on the news—to iron out the mistakes and glitches from your nightly news.

Just Use the Usual Fire Stuff

The majority of time spent in sweetening the news with sound effects was spent in the viewing room, not looking at finished news clips, but waiting for a CBS news courier on a motorcycle to come roaring in from La Guardia Airport with the unedited film.

Very often, because of the crucial time element, the editing would go on right up to air time and even *into* air time. This meant no opportunity to actually see what we would need in the way of sound effects. Our only clue would be

123

a vague hint from the director. "This is a story of a fire in Brooklyn. You know, the usual fire stuff. And, oh yeah! Be ready with a big chemical explosion!"

"Usual fire stuff," indeed! "Be ready with a possible chemical explosion?" This could mean everything from fire engines arriving or perhaps leaving; a building engulfed in flames, with timbers and walls falling, sirens screaming, high pressure water sounds for the hoses; and don't forget the possible chemical explosion! And all to be thrown together in ten minutes!

When we began sweetening the news, we learned there was never enough time to synchronize all the sounds. So instead of risking mistakes and drawing attention to the fact that the sound effect of our fire engine screeching to a halt didn't match the picture, we adopted a "less is more" policy.

Doing sounds for the television news was not like doing the sounds for radio's *Dragnet*.

Jack Webb was a stickler for authenticity. If the show required the clamor of a large city newsroom or the eerie stillness of a morgue, he would send a remote crew out and record them on a disc.

The sounds for television's news shows were different. They felt the picture was compelling enough to distract the viewers from what they were hearing, just as long as they were hearing "something." Something that was safe, unobtrusive and that replaced the deadness of silence that might mean their TV set had lost its sound.

It was therefore out of desperation that we searched for the one sound that would get us through everything from a fire in Brooklyn to the atom bomb. And we found it on a 78 RPM recording of a little known waterfall in darkest Africa, the Mogambi Waterfall.

When the record was played softly at a medium-slow speed it was the sound of the interior of a jet plane. At a slightly higher level, it was the sound of a city street late at night without horns. By playing at a slow speed and goosing (raising and lowering) the sound level in a rhythmic fashion, it could simulate just about any piece of machinery—or roaring chemical fire!

If the camera showed a closeup of a roaring fire or timbers and walls falling, we'd raise the sound level of the waterfall. This technique, helped by separate recordings of sirens, was about as ambitious as we ever got with a four-alarm fire. Although it might sound a little primitive compared to today's high-tech editings, we never were criticized, or even caught faking the news with sound effects.

This sneaky little practice, like most grievous sins, started out innocently enough. In the early days, all television news stories shot away from the studio were done on film. Often times, these films would come back unedited—either without sound, too long, mixed with other non-related stories, or containing material not acceptable for home viewing. It was then up to a film editor to cut into the film, discard all the film that *wasn't* going to be used, then put aside all the film pieces that *were* going to be used, and then put the pieces together so the story made sense! Did I forget to mention that the editor had to make these stories fit strict time restrictions so that the weather person could have his or her moment in the sun?

The perky weather girl and the humorous weather man are a creation of television. Long before there were comedy clubs, there were weather shows. And long before there were meteorologists, there were standup comedians. Tex Antoine, in New York, used to make weather fun by drawing cartoons. Before Pat Sajak decided to make his fortune spinning a roulette wheel, he predicted weather for KNBC.

The idea of giving time to someone so they can talk about the low and high pressures moving in was a fundamental one. If there was little news to talk about, you could always fill the time talking about what the weekend weather was going to be like. The fact that the predictions were so frequently wrong didn't matter; it gave the viewer a welcome break from the depressing news.

Those Awesome Editors

Today, all news stories done for television are shot on video tape. Not only is the quality of the tape as good as, if not better than, film, the important improvement lies in the editing process. Video tape today is edited with computers; early film was edited by hand, a tedious process involving a film splicer to cut the film and glue to put the film together.

Just to watch these skilled film editors at work under the tremendous stress of a news program's deadline was absolutely awesome! Did I forget to mention fast? Because if these film editors weren't fast under pressure, "awesome" wouldn't even get them a seat on the subway.

Perhaps if everything could be done the day before, or if the editors had the luxury of time, as their brothers and sisters had in theatrical films, everything would have been fine. But this was television—live television—and going on the air was never more than minutes or seconds away. Therefore, the real culprit when things went wrong on network news was not the camera person who shot the filmed story, or the editors, or the producers, or the directors. It was the old clock on the wall.

Sweetening the Bomb

Sweetening is a television term that means "to improve or add to something." Now you would hardly think that the sound of the atom bomb would need to be made louder, or more awesome, and yet that is exactly what was requested of me.

Bill Levitsky, one of the truly fine audio engineers with NBC in Hollywood, was often requested by such stars as Dean Martin, Frank Sinatra, and Elvis (for the *Elvis Presley Spectacular* from Hawaii) to mix their shows because of his music background and sensitive hearing.

It therefore came as no surprise to Levitsky when NBC selected him over a host of others to lend his ears in capturing the sound of an earth-rattling atomic blast.

It makes sense, doesn't it? Here was an audio mixer with an extensive musical background, a near perfect pitch, and the kind of talent that had some of the biggest singing stars requesting that he do their show. Certainly, then, he's the man NBC sends out into the Nevada desert to listen to the biggest boom the world has ever heard!

The actual televising of the detonation was being furnished by the Atomic Energy Commission. In addition, NBC sent their camera crews to cover their news commentators and to show local points of interest.

What the Atomic Commission wasn't furnishing was the sound. That was Levitsky's job. In that regard, he set out a number of strategically placed Schure Unidirectional Microphones in the hopes he would capture the tones of a bang that was capable of making molehills out of mountains.

Because of unfavorable wind conditions, the detonation was postponed on a daily basis for two weeks. This gave Bill ample time to adjust and angle his microphones so they were pointed in the optimum direction for an earth-shaking boom that was happening eight miles away at Ground Zero.

Bill was warned that if there were a last-minute shift in the wind, a horn would sound. If it did, and he was still alive to hear it, he wasn't to worry about the Schure microphones; he was to get into the vehicle he had been assigned to, head for the predetermined escape route and then haul ass!

Fortunately nothing so dramatic as this happened. But just prior to the detonation, the media personnel were warned to wear their sunglasses, to turn their backs to Ground Zero and to remain in that position for 30 seconds. At the expiration of the 30 seconds they were not to be alarmed if they felt a wave of hot air that was both suffocating and had the intensity of the fires of hell. Bill remembers distinctly that they didn't exaggerate on either account.

When the blast occurred, Bill was seated in the huge truck that was the electronic brain center for all of NBC's equipment. At the 30-second mark, it was as if the truck were hit by an earthquake. This huge truck, with tons of equipment, was simply lifted off the ground by this huge atomic fist, held there for interminable moments and then slammed back to earth in a display of power that had everyone in the truck vowing to go to church next Sunday.

Everything about the awesome atomic demonstration was a success—except the sound. It was awful. The sheer power of the explosion overloaded the mikes, distorting the sound so badly that it couldn't possibly be allowed to be associated with such a television spectacular! What would the television audience say of any such a disappointment?

Coming up with a more television friendly sound for the atomic blast was dropped into my lap officially at 5:30 P.M., which gave me approximately 30 minutes to come up with a sound the world has never heard and have it on the air for the six o'clock news.

When I previewed the picture of the blast, I was awestruck by the ponderous manner in which the clouds of smoke unfolded. Unlike dynamite, which has a quicker detonation, the atomic bomb seemed to be in no hurry. As the huge clouds of dirt and debris slowly billowed out at the base of the detonation, a funnel formed that served as a stem for the mushroom of pallid dust and smoke that had risen hundreds of feet in the air.

I had never experienced anything like it. Not during the invasion of Sicily, or Anzio, or Salerno, or the eruption of Mount Vesuvius, not even in a John Wayne movie. But in 25 minutes I had to come up with the sound no one in the world had ever heard!

This was one of the major problems in doing sound effects, to come up with "something." Something that would be convincing enough to match the magnitude of the picture the viewers would see, and the magnitude of the sound the viewers perceived.

The sound effects people doing Buck Rogers in radio had this problem long before the atom bomb. They too had to create sounds that had never been heard, sometimes for things that had yet to be invented! Can you imagine the disappointment if Cape Canaveral launched a space missile that didn't sound like those heard on Buck Rogers, first on radio and later in films? Perhaps that's what held back our space program—not the missiles themselves, but finding just the appropriate sound that came closest to that of radio's Buck Rogers.

In those early news days we were still using records. Although I had only three turntables, I had four pickup arms. This meant I could play four different effects at the same time. Three of the sounds I chose were a huge dynamite explosion, a wrecking ball smashing down a building, and the low, ominous rumblings of an earthquake. While the fourth sound was that of our old friend the Mogambi waterfall.

The one advantage the records and turntables had over tape was that each of those recorded sounds could be played at their most advantageous speeds and that was what I did. And, as luck would have it, no one ever complained about my faux atom bomb, sounding like a slowed down recording of the Mogambi waterfall.

An added thought just occurred to me. Wouldn't this be a great world if all wars weren't really destructive or devastating, but just sounded that way! Think of how cost-effective this would be in bombs alone! Now when countries went to war, all that would be needed were huge loudspeakers, ear plugs, and recordings of an African waterfall.

The Sports Shows

Although sound effects were never used to sweeten the weather, sports shows were different. Nothing too inventive or creative, just all kinds of crowd sounds, with plenty of cheers and occasional boos.

If ever there was an incident to explain the difference between live and taped television, it occurred when I was adding crowd sounds for a boxing show, hosted by Dennis James. The format of this program was to show famous fights and to have as a guest one of the fighters.

On this particular night the guest boxer was the Brown Bomber himself, Joe Louis. Louis was to have a highly publicized match in the near future with another fine fighter, Ezzard Charles.

Prior to the show, Louis entered the studio and the first thing he said to James was, "One thing I don't want you to ask me when we go on the air is how I'm gonna do against Ezzard Charles."

The show hit the air and, after introducing the often modest Louis, James smiled and asked, "Well Joe, how are you going to do against Ezzard Charles?"

The Frank Gifford Show

Sports in early broadcasting would be unrecognizable today. If the story involved an exciting sporting event, no cursing or obscene gestures on the part of the athlete was allowed.

If the camera picked up so much as a hint of a "damn" or "hell" being formed (let alone the big *F* word), the camera would get off the blasphemous athlete for fear of disillusioning the youth and sports fans of America.

This form of on-the-air censorship on the part of alert directors and camera operators was fine on the field of action, but this same type of care had to be exercised by broadcasters in the locker room as well.

Frank Gifford, who at the time was covering sports for CBS in New York, went to the Giants locker room to interview a player who had just intercepted a pass and run for the game-winning touchdown.

Gifford, having been a star halfback with these same Giants, was wise to the ways of the exuberant jock. So as a precaution, he explained to the player prior to going on the air with him live would he please not use any "damns" or "hells" while they were on the air.

The player flashed Gifford a smile of unbridled excitement and shouted: "Shit no! I'm not like all those other stupid motherfucker players!"

With the advent of audio tape, those of us in sound effects began moving away from being totally dependent on records. What was equally important was the introduction of the portable tape recorder. This allowed us to leave the studio and tape sounds in remote locations, like the time I was given the assignment of going to a New York Giants football game and recording the crowd sounds.

With my special media pass prominently hung around my neck, I boldly walked over to the New York Giants side of the field and stood in back of the bench. I was close enough to my gridiron heroes to touch them. And to think I was getting paid to do this job!

When I finally got down to work and started taping the various reactions from the crowd in response to a caught or a dropped pass, a long running gain or a quarterback sack, I noticed that each of the crowd sounds was punctuated enthusiastically by one of the Giants players.

It was either "Sheeet! That man can't play football!" or, "Sheeet! How could he drop that fucking ball!"

As I reluctantly moved out of earshot of my now slightly soiled All-American heroes, it seemed no matter where I stood on the field, there was some extraneous noise to spoil the crowd's reactions. If a jet wasn't flying overhead, a helicopter was. And if I wasn't bombarded by the noise from above, music from a makeshift band across the field more than made up for them. And if it wasn't the music, it was bullhorns, or the public address announcer intoning names or what yardline the Redskins or Giants were on. All of these sounds conspired to ruin the total crowd effect I wanted to record.

I finally realized I was wasting my time trying to get any realistic taped football crowd effects. Perhaps when baseball season started, I could tape that less rowdy crowd, mix it with the soccer crowd we had on records, and *voilà*! We'd have our genuine Giants football crowd!

Because the view from the Giants bench was still the best place to watch the remainder of the game, I put my tape recorder away and stood in back and off to the side of the bench.

I had no more than gotten there when a huge Giants lineman turned and asked, "Got a light?"

I stupidly asked, "What sort of light?"

"A light for my fucking cigarette!"

I couldn't believe my eyes. But there it was. A cigarette dangling from his lips. And there were several other players smoking as well! First I found out my heroes cursed; now I found out they smoked! What next? That they hated Wheaties?

So Much for Collectibles

A friend of mine was a big sports nut. He saved every *Sports Illustrated* cover he could get his hands on. And when he found out I was doing the Gifford show, he pulled out all the magazines that had a pro football player on it and handed them to me to have signed.

I told him it would take months. But nothing I said discouraged him from his scheme of making a killing with these future sport-collectible autographs.

I reluctantly took them, knowing how difficult it was going to be. I also knew the only cover I could reasonably expect to get signed was the one of Gifford being tackled by Chuck Bednarik.

When I went to work the next day, Gifford was preoccupied with a show idea that the film editor had come up with.

During a slow sports day, the editor had put together pieces of film with the most violent tackles and hits imaginable. He then orchestrated the film to the strains of the *Nutcracker Suite.*

Gifford thought it was great. He had even sent a copy of the film to the head of the Sports department and was now waiting for his reaction.

I felt this was as good a time as any to pull out the *Sports Illustrated* magazine with Gifford on the cover.

Gifford's cover graphically showed the violence that existed in pro football. His face was twisted over one shoulder, and his eyes were wide with fearful expectations of the hit he was about to get from Chuck Bednarik, which would temporarily interrupt his pro football career.

When I asked Gifford to sign the cover, I couldn't help asking him what was going through his mind at that moment just before he got hit. Gifford looked at it again, and I could have sworn I saw him flinch at the recollection.

"The only thing that flashed through my mind was, I'm gonna get killed! Fucking killed!"

And you know something? He almost was. Gifford received a serious concussion.

Just then the phone rang.

It was the head of Sports. He hated the film Gifford sent him. He thought the film frivolous, in bad taste, and more importantly, thought it trivialized the great game of professional football.

As Gifford hung up, he angrily picked up the magazine showing the picture of Chuck Bednarik's vicious tackle.

"If he thinks that film overdid the violence in football, I wish the hell that was him on the cover instead of me!"

With that, Gifford tossed the magazine on the desk. It was then that he saw the other magazines I had brought.

"What are those?"

I explained about my friend hoping to make a killing in the sport memorabilia market.

Gifford didn't say anything but I could tell that this type of sport fan wasn't his favorite.

He then picked up the magazines and fanned through them.

"Hell, half these guys are retired, and the other half I've already had on the show. But lucky for your greedy little friend I know how all of them sign their names. Got a pen?"

Those Trying Remotes

Although live political conventions never involved sound effects, I feel this story is worth telling.

One of the most highly prized jewels in the CBS News department's crown of newsworthy accomplishments was the presidential conventions held every four years. This was show-off time for the networks. No expenses were spared in an effort to get a hot story and beat out the other networks.

At a national political convention in San Francisco, CBS, NBC and ABC were there in force, each anxious to scoop the rival networks.

Networks pulled out all the stops for these political conventions. For instance, CBS even equipped golf carts with cameras so they could go careening off in hopes of getting the jump on the cursed competition.

Each cart contained a camera, its operator and an assistant tech driver. This of course was before the days of video tape and the handheld camera, so in addition to driving, it was the responsibility of the assistant tech to take care of the cumbersome but extremely important camera cables.

On one late-breaking story, the producer in the CBS control center sent our old friend Roy's golf cart off at breakneck speed to cover a late-breaking story of a fire.

As the golf cart went whizzing off to the conflagration, the all-important camera cable that was attached to the all-important control room began uncoiling as if the cart had hooked into Jaws!

But just as all good things must come to an end, so did the length of the camera cable. It ended not so much with a bang as it did in a shower of electronic sparks.

The director back at the CBS control center, thinking the sparks flashing on his monitor were the aforementioned conflagration, was ecstatic.

"We did it! We scooped NBC and ABC! Look at that beautiful goddamn fire!"

"Fire, my ass!" screamed the videoman. "That's a hundred-thousand dollar CBS camera going up in smoke!"

CHAPTER 13

Television's Two Biggest Embarrassments

In thinking back on all the thousands of shows I have done as either a writer or sound-effects artist in radio and television, I can recall many that were inspiring, informative, exciting, heart-warming, sad or funny. And I can recall two that might qualify as a couple of broadcasting's most embarrassing moments.

Since 1951, there have been many shows that I have worked on that have vied for the unenviable title of "all-time worst." These shows, however, at best—or, maybe, at worst—are little competition for the two I'm about to nominate.

What I'm talking about here are unadulterated stinkers. One of these embarrassments lasted only a brief day, while the other, CBS' *Strike It Rich*, had an agonizing run from July 4, 1951, until January 12, 1955.

What always comes to mind when a show such as this lasts so long is the issue of responsibility; that is, who the hell is to blame for these excruciating broadcasts? Was it CBS for putting it on? the sponsors for paying for it to be on? the public at large, who, in watching it, more or less mandate its airing?

The premise of this show was to help the downtrodden masses: people with money problems, health problems, and every conceivable other kind of problem. So far so good. Isn't that what many of the most respectable charitable organizations in this country do? And God bless them for doing it.

It wasn't, therefore, the apparently noble intentions of *Strike It Rich*, but the manner in which they chose to present it.

The show received thousands of letters each week from desperate people hoping that their tragic story was tragic enough to merit a chance to strike it rich. To some viewers it was television's noblest display of compassion; to others, it was further proof of television's lack of morals.

To get on, viewers were urged to write to the show, explaining exactly what their problem was. But instead of writing first, many, believing their lot was sufficiently bad to ensure a spot on the show, traveled to New York penniless in hopes of striking it rich and only to end up needing a bed to sleep on from the Salvation Army.

132

The theater *Strike It Rich* came out of was across the street from the *Garry Moore Show*. I can recall seeing crowds of contestants lining up early in the morning in hopes their story was compelling enough to get them on the show. I can also recall hoping the time would never come that I had to do that show.

Many of the production assistants who interviewed these unfortunate people could only listen to their heart-felt stories for little more than an hour. They would then be relieved, often leaving in tears from the legitimate stories they heard from the needy, or in anger from the few people who were faking it.

One of the features of the show was the "Heart Line." Viewers wishing to help the contestants would call in with some sort of help in the way of money, clothing, a baby crib—whatever.

In what may have been nothing more than an attempt to manufacture the show's aim for drama, phone calls from sympathetic viewers weren't connected to the phone on the stage. Instead, all calls would ring and be answered in the control room.

This is where Sound Effects came in. To indicate to Warren Hull, the show's host, that someone was calling on the "Heart Line," we would ring a sound-effect phone that could be heard on the stage. This in turn would cue the stagehand to start flashing a light behind the large red heart and give it a life-like appearance of "beating."

Warren Hull would then pick up the phone and relate to the contestant what he or she was going to receive.

During one memorable show, a handicapped contestant who had to wear heavy steel braces on his deformed legs was having difficulty walking across the stage. The producer, in an effort to make certain that no one missed the fact that this unfortunate person did indeed need heavy leather and steel braces to walk, began screaming at the director: "get a camera shot of the braces!"

The director, Matt Harlib, ignored the command and kept his camera on its widest shot covering the whole stage.

Again the producer screamed, "Goddamn it! The braces! The braces! Get a shot of the braces!"

The director became so disgusted by this demand, he tore off his headset, threw it on the console and replied, "If you want a shot of the braces, you get it!" He then walked out of the control room and never returned.

I got stuck with this show only once. But it was enough. Very often, the phone calls from sympathetic viewers didn't come as rapidly to the heartfelt pleas of Warren Hull as the producer wanted. When this happened, and because time in live television was always of the essence, the producer would yell, "Heart Line!"

That was my cue to ring the phone and start that big red light in back of that sympathetic red heart pulsating on stage. Then when Hull picked up the phone he would hear the producer shouting, "We're running late. Give the family fifty bucks and kiss them off!"

As callous as giving a desperate family $50 and then tossing them aside may sound, it was just the tip of the iceberg in coldness compared to this next television embarrassment.

The Specials?

The movies had their "Spectaculars," while television had what it liked to call its "Specials." Many times the shows were what they were billed to be. "A Sinatra Special," for instance, is a memorable example of the occasional truth in advertising. But one show I worked on was neither special nor even sincere; it was simply embarrassing.

In doing sound effects at NBC, I got stuck with my second exploitative production: a fund-raising telethon for a pastor wishing to spread the word of the Lord and, while he was at it, raise a little money.

Although I had worked on some of Oral Roberts' telecasts before he built his own studios in Oklahoma, they never involved deception or sound effects. This one did. And a whole lot more.

The only effect I had was that of telephones ringing, both singularly and in random groups, the idea being that this would give the viewers at home the impression that many people were calling in with their problems—and, of course, with their money pledges. The phones on the floor took the pledges while the control room took the calls from viewers with problems of a more personal nature.

These calls were of course all screened with the seven-second delay tape we talked about earlier. This kept the cranks off the air while providing the pastor's staff with an opportunity to select what problem they felt serious and titillating enough to pass on to the pastor.

Because of the strange technical setup, I was again positioned in the control room, this time a rather overcrowded and very busy control room. As I supplied the sounds of the mythical phones ringing off the hooks, production assistants were answering the real phones from the home viewers.

"Tell him someone needs prayers for their husband who is dying of some disease."

"What disease was it?" the producer demanded.

"I couldn't understand her too well. She was sobbing too much."

"Damn it, *disease* ain't interesting! What we want to know is what's causing the disease! And if they don't want to give it, say 'God is listening to you,' and hang up!"

All of a sudden one of the young production assistants yelled out excitedly, "I have a homosexual on the phone that needs some prayer to help him come out of the closet!"

"Bingo! That's great!" a voice answered.

But before he could relay this message to the preacher, another voice sang out: "I've got a man that's about to commit suicide!"

Upon hearing this, the normally stern voice became shrill with excitement. "Great! Put him through to the preacher and kiss off the homo!"

CHAPTER 14

Sounds Like Fun!

Although this story might be decried by many as apocryphal (even pooh-poohed by some), I ask only that you read it with an open mind. Recently, scientists collecting mineral deposits in a remote area of the Tibetan Mountains stumbled upon wall etchings that suggest sound effects have been around longer than anyone might have guessed.

After puzzling for a while over the etched images, experts at long last have pieced together the narrative the artists sought to relate. It seems a large animal was terrifying the inhabitants of a particular cave. Upon hearing the roar of this mysterious beast, the cave dwellers would scurry into their cave and cower in the dark, all the while wishing someone would come up with something to replace the boulder they'd been using to block the grotto's entrance; already these retreats had cost four men a hernia.

Finally someone did devise an alternative—and it was a beauty! It was made of solid oak, was as round as a circle and fit perfectly the opening of their cave. Now when danger threatened, all they had to do was slam the door and not open it until someone gave the secret knock.

Then one day a caveman—we'll call him Abe—was out chopping wood (just in case someone discovered fire) when a funny thing happened: his wife opened the door! Abe immediately demanded to know why she exposed herself to danger by opening the door. His wife, knowing what a kidder her husband was, replied, "Are you kidding? You gave the secret knock." He informed her he couldn't have, since he was in a nearby forest chopping wood! Abe was perplexed.

Suddenly the thought hit him like a thunderbolt! His wife had mistaken the chopping sound for a knocking sound! Wow! Abe was on to something, but he didn't have a clue what it was!

Wonderful and exciting things like this didn't go unnoticed by the other cave dwellers. They soon began imploring him to make other sounds, and he happily acceded. He started out small, doing baby cries, and worked his way up to frightening everyone out of their loincloths with his vocal impression of a saber-toothed tiger in heat.

Then one night Abe went too far. He left the safety of the cave and, as a practical joke, started doing his impression of the saber-toothed tiger out in the moonlight. He not only fooled the people in the cave into slamming their doors shut, he fooled a real tiger who was out looking for a good time.

As Abe continued roaring in the moonlight, the tiger came racing around the corner of the cave only to discover that Abe was no hot little number, but simply an early man making the *sound effect* of a tiger! The tiger got so angry at Abe for getting his hopes up that he ate him, loincloth and all!

This story may indeed sound untrue, or even spurious, but not to me. I once had a director on *Gangbusters* who wanted to do the same thing to me for missing a gunshot.

If you aren't familiar with the venerable old art of sound effects, the vague definition found in a dictionary might fool you: "SOUND EFFECTS: *Imitative, or artificially reproduced sounds such as thunder or an explosion...*"

"Imitative or artificially reproduced sounds such as thunder or an explosion"— *indeed*! Oh sure, that may be the case today. Maybe you can go to just about any toy store and buy something that has a micro computer chip that either grunts, whinnies, or moos. But is that sound effects?

There are companies that will sell you everything from an entire library of sounds down to a single reel, CD, or tape of sounds. But is *this* sound effects?

One such company that markets a sound-effect library is *Sound Ideas*. In addition to the usual "thunder and explosions," they even offer "peeing in a urinal."

Just think what radio's Lum and Abner would have done if they had at their disposal some of the sounds offered by *Sound Ideas*. Now instead of Lum always having to go in the back of the *Jot 'Em Down Store* to get some canned peaches for a customer, Lum could always say: "Abner? Watch the store for a minute, will you?"

"Where are you going, Lum, to get more canned peaches?"

"No Abner, to take a pee."

Becoming a Sound-Effects Artist

To become a sound-effects artist in radio took three years. This wasn't an arbitrary time frame; this was the considered opinion of no less an authority than a CBS vice president.

Now, if vice presidents are normally paid to cut costs, why did this particular vice president jeopardize his own job throwing CBS' money around for a bunch of nincompoops to learn how to knock on a door? The answer is that he didn't.

Even after you knew all the recorded and manual effects in the CBS Sound Effects department, you still weren't prepared to face up to the mental aspect of flying solo on a top-rated live radio show.

One of the gnawing fears that haunted every sound-effects artist was of being asked to do an effect that you hadn't a clue how to do. For instance, what would you do if the director requested the sound of a human body being turned inside out?

If this were your first time working alone, you might of course panic. Then you would begin frantically wondering if, in committing to memory all of the 7,000 recorded sounds and hundreds of manual effects sounds, somehow the sound of something so memorable and potentially revolting had fallen through a crack!

All this time, the director is staring at you, the assistant director is staring at you, the cast is staring at you, the musicians are staring at you, the audio mixer is staring at you, and even the guy who brought in the coffee is staring at you! But at least you can take comfort in the knowledge that if the rest of your life is filled with a moment as agonizingly long as this, you're going to outlive the giant redwoods.

If all this wasn't nerve-wracking enough, out of the corner of your eye you see the director edging toward the phone to put in a call to have you replaced.

As your mind races for a solution, you suddenly bump into a disturbing thought: "Is the director putting me on? Is this like the sound of snow falling on snow? A naked behind sitting on a marble bench?"

What do you think? Was the director having fun with his request for a human body being turned inside out? The answer is no. The recipe and directions: (1) Twist a pair of wet rubber gloves; (2) Slowly tear away the protective husk from ears of corn; (3) Scoop away, in a deliberate fashion, at an overripe muskmelon.

The ability to create sounds under the rigors of live radio was the first requirement of doing sound effects. The second was the ability to please and exude confidence with all the demanding people you were thrown in with.

Sometimes even the actors took potshots at Sound Effects. If you had the sound of an iceberg breaking up, there always seemed to be some actor born in the Klondike who would venture such timely information as "I come from Alaska and that sure as hell doesn't sound like no iceberg breaking up to me!"

One must always remember that the world is filled with people who have developed one-upmanship to a fine art. Broadcasting was no different. Knowing how to respond in an appropriate manner, if indeed it's in CBS' best interest (and yours) to respond at all, is what took the three years' experience the vice president had in mind.

Are You Kidding, Norman?

Over the years there have been many sounds requested that have pushed the sound-effects artist's imagination to the edge. The sounds of "hundreds of rats chewing through a lighthouse door," for instance.

This effect was called for on the radio thriller *Suspense*. The script was titled "Three Glass Keys" and was directed by Paul Robson.

Director Paul Robson listens attentively as CBS *sound artists Billy Gould, Cliff Thorsness and Russ Murray bite and chew on wooden berry baskets (photograph courtesy of Malachy Wienges).*

Fortunately, none of the artists got berry-basket wounds bad enough to require surgery. Can you imagine explaining to your dentist how you got them?

"Well, you see, Doc, here I was pretending to be a rat and chewing down this here lighthouse door…"

As unusual as creating the sounds of hundreds of rats is, I'm afraid it pales by comparison to the sound that was requested by Norman Lear, producer of CBS' controversial and innovative situation comedy *All in the Family*.

Although Lear frequently requested the sound of a toilet flush, he never had the temerity to ask for any sound that might normally accompany it. Whether this could be attributed to Lear's good taste or CBS' Broadcast Standards—that is, censorship—the fact is he never requested anything explicit or distasteful—at least not on television. Films, however, were a different story.

If you felt squeamish about the discussion of the peeing sounds and toilet flushes, Norman Lear's film *Cold Turkey*, starring Dick Van Dyke, will make you blush. In it, Lear hit a new high when he requested a fart.

After all, if Norman Lear could bring the toilet flush out of the closet, what was so disgusting about bringing to the silver screen the sound of a little pip-squeak of a fart?

Admittedly, if Edward Everett Horton, the extremely accomplished actor, could have listed the ability to produce a flatulent sound on cue in his resume, there would have been no need for Lear to listen elsewhere. But inasmuch as Edward Everett Horton couldn't, such sounds were required of Paramount Pictures' sound-effects editor, Paul Hockman.

If you find this subject revulsive, you'd find it very difficult to make your living pursuing the fine art of creating sound effects.

Now admittedly, a fart—pip-squeak or not—doesn't belong to the same class as the legitimate sound effect requested by radio's Arch Oboler, that of a "giant worm gobbling up the population of a small town." There's simply no comparison. All you needed for Oboler's request was a bowl of cooked spaghetti that you squished slowly between your fingers, keeping in mind you were a hungry worm gobbling up a town.

Pretending to be a hungry worm is what it took to create successful sounds. You had to *be* the sound you were creating. But for the sound Lear wanted, how can you be or imagine you're a fart? Not just any old fart, either. It had to be a *funny* fart!

Now, if you are Paul Hockman, who was nominated for an Academy Award for his sound-effects work on the futuristic film *Soylent Green*, the one thing you don't say to a producer with Norman Lear's clout is "A fart? Are you kiddin', Norman?" I did it once, not to Norman, but to Walter Gorman, the director of an early CBS soap.

My mistake with Walter arose from having worked with him several times in radio and always finding him to be polite and friendly with a good sense of humor. All that, I was soon to find out, was before television.

We were doing a scene in a barroom where all I had was the sound effects of a low hubbub (talking) of a small crowd. Then, as the bartender went off-camera to draw a beer, I heard Walter over my headset say, "I'd like to hear the sound of the beer being drawn please, thank you."

Now comes the second part of the art of sound effects: knowing when to keep your mouth shut. I certainly knew how to create the sound of beer coming out of a tap. But why even have it? It was such a meaningless off-camera sound that wouldn't be heard under my crowd sounds anyway. Therefore, instead of just doing it, I wondered, "Was he kidding me?" Unfortunately, I didn't keep that question to myself; instead, I heard myself responding in a rather jocular tone, "Are you kidding, Walter?"

Never have I heard a voice respond to a question so quickly or decisively. The words sounded as if they were bitten off and spit out.

"No, goddamn it, I'm not kidding! And don't ever ask me again if I'm kidding about *anything*. Is that clear!"

After a moment or two of loud silence on the headset, the assistant director reaffirmed in a whispered voice what by this time I already knew. "No, Bob, he sure as hell ain't kidding."

Walter had obviously misinterpreted my question as a challenge to his authority. And come to think of it, it probably was. But because this beer-pouring sound was not found on any record, I would have to do it manually. This meant making a phone call that every one of our equipment men dreaded, the call for a portable kitchen sink.

The CBS portable sinks were "portable" in the same sense as a bathtub is portable. And because no cab was big enough to accommodate it, the equipment man had to schlep the sink up Park Avenue by hand, though he would still put in a petty cash request for enough to cover the cab trip and a tip.

This business of the equipment men putting in a petty cash slip for cabs they never used was not so much a dishonest act as it was the outcome of a tacit understanding with CBS. The Sound Effects supervisor figured this petty cash tendered for a cab never taken was fair payment for the ridicule that the equipment man would have to suffer from curious New Yorkers as he wheeled a portable sink— complete with a shower head—up fashionable Park Avenue. Tourists often asked them to pose for pictures. (Horace Rea, one of the equipment men, received a letter addressed to him at CBS that read, "My picture of you won First Prize! Under the picture I wrote: 'New York has everything ... even the kitchen sink!'"

So it wasn't that I didn't know *how* to do the effect—I just felt it was a lot of trouble and work to go through for something that would never be heard under all the other sounds that were going on at the time.

This is one of the reasons it took a minimum of three years to become a bona fide sound effects artist. A beginner needed six months to learn the proper way to knock on a door (in at least 61 different ways), and two and a half years to study the psychology of production and agency people.

In a business that feeds on insecurities, everyone is looking for something or someone solid to hang on to. And if a director so much as gets a whiff of vulnerability in one area of your personality, the feeding signal goes out. You may be the best sound-effects artist in the world, but if you can't hold your own in a shoving match, you're in for a very stormy ride. And one of the true signs of inexperience is a response as dumb as "Are you kiddin', Walter?"

When Orson Welles requested the sound of grass being cut and then ordered a lawn of real grass to be delivered to the radio studio, did Bill Brown, the sound-effects artist, say, "Are you kiddin', Orson?" No, sir!

And when Madge Tucker, the writer-director of the delightful and imaginative radio show *Coast to Coast on a Bus*, asked Keene Crockett, her sound-effects artist, for the sound of "flowers in sunshine jumping up and bursting in full bloom," did Keene say, "Are you kidding, Madge?" No! He simply assembled his glass wind chimes, a slide whistle, and a toy xylophone and did it!

And when Red Skelton asked Ray Erlenborn, his sound artist, for the vocal effect of a flea, did Ray say, "Are you kiddin', Red?" No!

When Rudy Vallee, a non-smoker, appeared in *I've Got a Cigarette* and forgot

When you turned on the faucet to one of these portable sinks, it had the same musty smell that archaeologists must inhale when they unearth the tomb of a forgotten Pharaoh. But the sputtering sound the water made as the recirculating pump drove the combination of air and water out of the faucet matched perfectly the sound of a draft beer being drawn in a bar (photograph courtesy of Walter Pierson).

to take home his gift of a carton of Winston cigarettes from the show, then drove all the way in from Beverly Hills the next day to get them, did the prop man say, "Are you kiddin', Rudy?" No.

When John Frankenheimer was doing a story of a river and demanded that a large body of water be installed in a CBS Television City studio, did CBS ask, "Are you kiddin', John?" They may have spent many thousands of dollars later shoring up the studio floor so the weight of the water wouldn't flood Television City, but they never questioned his seriousness.

Nor when this same John Frankenheimer was doing *The Snows of Kiliman-jaro*, and he requested an expensive Land Rover, did CBS say, "Are you kiddin', John?" No! But when Frankenheimer saw the brand-new, right-off-the-showroom-floor Land Rover that CBS had gotten him, he was outraged. And when John requested a sledgehammer so he could trash the Land Rover to make it look like an authentic, African bush Land Rover, did CBS then ask, "Are you kiddin', John?" (In this case CBS should have because the old car that was being made to look like a beat-up Land Rover was still in the paint shop. Frankenheimer trashed a just-off-the-showroom-floor Land Rover loaned to CBS by the dealer.)

Paul Hockman must have learned his "Are you kiddin'?" lesson early in his career at Paramount Pictures, because when Norman Lear made his request for the sounds of flatulence, Paul never so much as flinched, or stifled a smirk. If he had, he would have been in bigger trouble with Norman than I had been with Walter.

After all, in the world of sound effects, where boinks, boings, bops, beeps, bashes and bedlam are all part of a day's work, what's so special about a little flatulent sound?

"Not just any little flatulent sound," Norman corrected with a sniff of indignation, "but an unpresumptuous, unobtrusive, elegant, genteel one that would befit the demeanor of a Zsa Zsa Gabor," or in this case, Edward Everett Horton.

Hockman went to every party and gag store, both legitimate and under-the-counter, on or off Hollywood Boulevard in search of Norman's quest. Although his findings were disappointing, he was hoping he could sneak one past Lear's critical ears. Instead, he got this response: "No, damn it! Those farts are neither elegant nor genteel, they're too loud and explosive!"

Then with his fingers crossed, Hockman played his hold card—a recording of our National Anthem, not accompanied by the Mormon Tabernacle Choir, but instead, a wide assortment of breaking wind noises.

As Lear listened intently to the National Anthem, he seemed duly impressed with the unusual manner in which the notes of the stirring music had been ingeniously orchestrated to accommodate a series of rhythmic and musically pitch-perfect farts. Although Hockman became encouraged when he heard Lear humming a few bars, Lear ultimately shook his head.

In desperation, Hockman called upon the ingenuity of all his fellow sound editors. But, alas, none of them had anything on tape or film that would even come close. However, the gauntlet that Hockman had thrown down to his fellow workers couldn't be ignored. If Lear's fart was out there, by God, they'd find it!

The group was encouraged by the work of Howard Beal, who had gone through similar trials with the legendary Cecil B. DeMille. Howard even related the story of working on the film *The Ten Commandments*.

DeMille wanted to add sound effects to a scene that showed the Israelites making bricks out of mud and water. Beal decided that the only way to achieve that effect was to get into a large tank of mud and water.

When DeMille listened to his soundman's creative efforts, he objected to a rustling sound. Beal explained the microphone must have picked up the sound of clothing. As a result, DeMille had him go back and do it again, this time without the noisome rustling clothing sound.

It therefore came as no surprise when the more experienced and film-savvy Beal told Hockman that Lear's request for the sound of a pip-squeak fart was nothing compared to having to make bricks for the Israelites bare-assed.

As Lear continued to veto the efforts of Hockman and his fellow sound-effects editors, an air of desperation permeated the hallowed grounds of Paramount.

Many of the editors even began taking their work home via handheld tape recorders. But none met the rigid requirements of Norman Lear's highly selective ear.

Finally, after presenting literally hundreds of rejected sounds, Hockman decided to discard the nitty-gritty method of acquiring the sound by resorting to the more artificial genre of wind.

Two weeks later, the Norman Lear production company received a petty cash bill from Hockman for $283.83. When the accountant asked Hockman for a more explicit explanation, Hockman wrote it down in two words: whoopee cushions.

But even these usually reliable party props met with failure, rejected because of what Lear claimed was their frivolous, light-farted sound. Again it was back to the drawing board.

When Hockman showed up in the Paramount commissary, he would scan the menu with an increasingly practiced eye in search of nature's windiest source: baked beans. If it was on the menu, Hockman, with his portable tape recorder hidden in his jacket's pocket, would sidle up to one of the tables where the legumes were being consumed, rest his excited finger on the record button and try to look nonchalant.

It wasn't long before the employees of Paramount got wise to Hockman's feigned acedia, and soon he and his crew were on the list of people to avoid.

To be seen with Hockman trailing behind you was a telltale sign that perhaps an embarrassing moment was about to happen. Those hardest hit were the young shapely starlets. Because of the unobstructed openness and acoustical excellence of what they normally wore, they made for obvious targets; as a result, the young stars stopped wearing their thonged bikinis.

Finally, out of desperation, Hockman assembled everything that could be rubbed, scratched, kicked, or twisted into making the elusive sound, but Lear again and again merely shook his head.

To add to his problems, Hockman's wife had read him a note from their son's teacher decrying their son's disgusting behavior in class. When Paul questioned his son about this alleged "disgusting behavior," it seems his son had the innate and uncanny ability to simply place his hand in such a manner under his armpit and produce the most "elegant little pip-squeak of a fart this side of Beverly Hills."

It should therefore come as no surprise that the next day, Hockman took his son and his pip-squeak of an arm to work with him, leaving his wife at home to explain to the school their son's absence.

CHAPTER 15

Getting Laughs
the Quiet Way

One of the fears that we share with our inscrutable cats is the fear of looking foolish. Have you ever seen how embarrassed a cat becomes when he trips, or finds himself stuck up a tree? If you haven't, it's only because their humiliated little faces are hidden under a protective layer of feline fur. But if we were quick enough, and the cat would hold still long enough, all we'd have to do is brush aside a small amount of fur from around the cheek area and we'd see it was beet-red with embarrassment.

This aversion to looking foolish and trying to hide it has been the basic ingredient in comedy since the days of Abe the caveman. Cave wives soon realized it was more ego-saving to laugh off their spouses' occasional love-bops with a club than it was to suffer the embarrassment of screaming "ouch!" Besides, what good would it do to complain about spousal battering? It wasn't until shortly after fire was discovered that someone came up with the idea of being a lawyer.

Although pain is indeed the by-product of a club to your head, it isn't the only pain we humans and our cats endure. In fact, physical pain by itself isn't funny at all.

An Early Lesson

When I was about eight years old, a group of neighborhood kids got together to make some candy money by putting on a backyard circus. We charged a nickel and wound up with an audience of ten sympathetic mothers and a total gate of 37¢. (One mother wanted to encourage us and paid seven cents, two said they thought it was free, and the other one left her pocketbook at home.)

Although a nickel doesn't sound like a lot today, back in those days it was about half of what the movies were charging for a double feature, the news and a cartoon. And if you were lucky, your neighborhood theater might even have air conditioning! Pretty stiff competition for a backyard circus.

We therefore counted heavily on the fact that we were live. We rouged our cheeks and noses and wore our parents' old clothes.

Although the audience comprised women who had given birth to the assembled youthful performers, they gave no hint they were getting their money's worth. We tried everything. We tumbled, did cartwheels, made funny faces—not so much as a motherly nod.

In desperation I even tried something I had no business trying: juggling croquet balls with a partner who wore thick glasses. By "juggling," I mean we simply tossed the rock-hard, wooden balls back and forth to one another.

As we tossed the balls back and forth, the audience was so quiet you could hear a cat purring two houses up the street. As I turned to see if the mothers had left en masse, my partner tossed a ball that knocked off my hat. It brought down the backyard!

What the backyard didn't know was that the ball, in addition to hitting my hat, had hit my head. Because we were finally on a roll, I didn't even feel the throbbing pain. But suddenly, a little girl in the show saw I was bleeding and screamed. The mothers all stopped laughing and rushed home for the iodine.

Although my cut of the gate came to only half a Baby Ruth candy bar, it taught me at an early age one of the first laws of physical comedy: "If you want to keep an audience amused, don't let them see you bleed."

W. C. Fields, the famous star of vaudeville and early films, put it a better way: "I try to hide pain and embarrassment, and the more I do, the better the audience likes it."

Comedians hide their pains in a number of ways. Some joke about it, others have things happen to them.

Failure on behalf of the comedian to react to pain in what might be considered an appropriate manner comes as a surprise to us. Comedy offers other surprises as well.

The Chaplin Way

Charlie Chaplin, the brilliant comedy star of both the silent and sound movies was once asked how he would go about filming the classic physical comedy bit, so often used in silent pictures, of the man in the high silk hat stepping on a banana skin and falling.

Did Chaplin think it would be funnier to show the banana peel lying on a sidewalk first and then show a man walking and stepping on it, or would he show the man walking towards the banana peel first and then stepping on it?

Chaplin, without a moment's hesitation, said, "Neither. I'd show the man walking towards the banana peel, have him see it. He then walks around the banana peel and falls into an open manhole."

This is an excellent example of "physical" comedy. But it isn't pantomime. The mime cannot use a piece of scenery or props, only body parts. I would therefore pose the question to Mister Chaplin of how he would go about miming his story.

It's one thing to see a man stepping into an open manhole when there's a banana peel to step around and a manhole to fall into, but how does a mime create this illusion with nothing but tights stretched over his birthday suit?

If you've ever wondered how anyone in their right mind writes a pantomime, you've come to the right place. Getting laughs from an audience without being able to say anything funny is not the easiest way to be funny—especially on live television. That's assuming of course someone who did pantomimes could even get on television—live or dead on tape.

The mere mention of the word *pantomime* struck fear in the hearts of television producers. To them, pantomime meant Marcel Marceau, and in their minds it was too artsy-fartsy for the average tastes of television.

Understanding the story a mime is trying to reveal takes a certain amount of concentration. In a darkened theater, without distractions, this strict attention usually goes with the price of admission. People there have paid to see the mime perform. This is not the case with a television audience.

The home viewer is often interrupted by the more pressing distractions of the baby crying, the telephone ringing or the dinner burning. With all these things going on in the home, how does someone doing a pantomime hold viewers' attention if he can't make any noise himself?

Dumb shows were popular as far back as Augustus' reign in ancient Rome. But even way back then, pantomimists knew that their art form was a tough ticket to sell. So instead of performing on a bare stage without the help of scenery or props, they added music and singing to help the audiences better understand the story unfolding in mime.

So if it was okay back then to punch up a pantomime with singing and music, why not also add some interesting or hopefully funny sound effects?

Why not, indeed. Didn't many of the silents add sound effects? And then when *The Jazz Singer* made the talkies a reality, didn't sound effects add to the zany antics of the Three Stooges?

Curly, Moe and Larry

The Stooges were products of the rough-and-tumble world of vaudeville. But even there, audiences didn't think there was anything funny about seeing someone bleeding. As a result, the Stooges made use of convincing props and sound effects.

Now Larry could hit Curly over the head with what looked like an iron bar, and have it make a hollow wood sound. This pleased the audience in two ways: the sound reassured the audience Curly wasn't hurt, and it surprised and amused them with what it implied about the content of Curly's head. And isn't the element of surprise a basic tenet of comedy?

The Stooges evidently thought so. The next time you see an old Stooges film, watch for the following mayhem and listen for the following sounds: knuckle crunches (cracked walnuts), eye stabs (violin plinks), broken body parts (twisted celery stalks). Now imagine how funny any of that physical violence would have been without the accompanying imaginative sounds.

The TV Pantomimists ... Kind Of

The first live television comedians weren't classic pantomime artists in the style of Marceau. Nor, to be honest, did they want to be. Where was it written that in order to do comedy requiring physical movements you had to be a Marceau clone?

Marceau was a product of the serious theater; the early TV comedians often came from a nightclub atmosphere where the only thing the audience took serious was drinking. Here, the comedians had to be fast and funny to hold the attention of the easily distracted viewers of early television.

The average audience watching live television was totally unaccustomed to seeing someone perform a pantomime. If they were old enough, they could remember Chaplin and Buster Keaton in silent movies.

But this was not the same. Chaplin and Keaton had the advantages of scenery, props, makeup, and costumes. Sid Caesar, Imogene Coca, Red Skelton and a young Dick Van Dyke didn't.

Although I never wrote pantomimes for Caesar and Coca, I did write for Red and Dick. Skelton at that time was doing his show on tape, while with Van Dyke, it was all live, very often painfully live.

Van Dyke started out like Jerry Lewis, doing a record act. Because the singers they were impersonating were on records, what made Lewis and Van Dyke funny was the way they mimed their actions to the singers' voices. This required both gesticulation and facial contortion, something they would use later when they moved up to doing physical comedy without the need to lip sync to recorded voices.

The Sound-Effects Artists?

There are sound-effects artists and there are those who did the *Andy Williams Show* on ABC television. Andy was the summer replacement show for another popular young singing star, Pat Boone.

During one memorable *Andy Williams Show* episode, I had written Van Dyke a narrative-pantomime about an irascible cat named Tabby.

In this sketch I decided that in addition to using sound effects, I would break all rules and have Dick talk. But, to my amazement, the dialogue wasn't what got me into trouble. Are you ready for this? It was the sound effects! Because of the network's and union's rules, I was not allowed to do them. It was on this show that my writing hat took on a healthy distrust for some sound-effects artists.

The *Andy Williams Show* was shot during the summer of 1958. As yet, tape was still not in general use, and so there was no such thing as post-production: this was still live television. But to be honest, I sure as hell wished it wasn't!

The sketch I had written was to be done on a bare stage, without props, and Van Dyke, in keeping with the true art of pantomime, wasn't allowed to add so much as a bushy tail to his outfit to suggest his felinity.

It was instead in his acting that Dick had to give the audience the vivid impression that he was just an overgrown cat. So maybe he talked, but everything else he did was mimed, and he had a little help from sound effects—goddamn little help!

My trouble with sound effects came when Van Dyke looked at his paws and decided that if he was ever to catch a mouse again, he had to sharpen his nails!

To indicate this, I had written, "Van Dyke takes his two hands and begins striking his fingernails together in the manner of a cymbal player in a marching band. Only in this case it's his fingernails instead of the cymbals that get struck." The directions to Sound Effects, then, read thus: "SOUND EFFECTS: THE CLASHING OF SWORDS IN SYNC WITH VAN DYKE'S MOVES."

Unlike the average comedy writer without my sound-effects background, the sound-effect cue that I wrote wasn't something I pulled out of the air. This is the sound that I would have selected if I were doing the show myself. But instead of hearing my requested sound of two clashing swords, I heard the faint clicking of two freaking *teaspoons*!

Because I was moonlighting as a writer from my sound-effects job at CBS, I had to keep my astonishment hidden under my writing hat. So instead of rushing up to the sound-effect area and venting my anger with something appropriate like: "What the fuck was that sound supposed to be!" I had to temper my displeasure with "Gee, that was an interesting interpretation of the sound I wrote, but don't you think it was just a tad too small for comedy?"

The sound-effects artist's explanation was brief and to the point: "Nope."

Perhaps it would have helped if he had looked up from the newspaper when he spoke, but he didn't.

"I know you're busy, but I wrote that sketch, and I thought it might get a chuckle from the audience if they heard something bigger when Dick hits his nails together—like something foolish and inappropriate from what the audience would normally expect—like surprise them with sabers clashing together?"

That got his attention.

He looked up from the crossword puzzle long enough to reply, "Hell's bells!

We own a cat and when Boots sharpens her claws, it sure as hell doesn't sound like no sabers banging together."

"But this is *comedy*!"

"So? What's that go to do with the way a cat sharpens its nails?"

Obviously this man did the sound effects for the Pat Boone musical show, because he didn't have a clue about comedy.

This, unfortunately, often happened when a comedian was a guest performer on other, noncomedy shows: you were forced to work with sound artists who lacked that special talent it took to get laughs with sounds.

To avoid such trouble when we performed similar sketches on other shows, we decided to solve this problem with some desperate measures.

The solution we came up with was almost as dangerous as the problem. We decided that instead of just taking a chance that we might get lucky and get a good sound-effect artist (there were plenty out there), we'd record the sounds ourselves on a long-playing 33⅓ RPM record, and Van Dyke would mime to the sounds.

The acid test for our mime to sounds on a record would soon come when Van Dyke was asked to appear on the *Tonight Show*, starring Jack Paar.

Van Dyke, having started out in show business as one of the *Merry Mutes*, was accustomed to miming to records. However, he soon found out that miming to a singer was far easier than miming to noises, especially on the *Tonight Show*.

One of the problems all comedians face is whether or not they are going to get laughs. It would be nice if the laughs were loud and long, but if not, laughs of any length would do.

Our problem was more complicated. In miming to the sounds on records, it was imperative that Van Dyke hear the recorded sound effects. If he was to mime getting his foot in a bucket, he had to know when to make a movement with his foot to indicate it was indeed in a bucket. If his timing was right, it would appear as if when Van Dyke shook his foot, his foot was somehow magically making the bucket sounds.

If, for instance, this business with the bucket got a laugh, how long would it be? If it was very short, it would slow down his movements waiting for the next sound to occur; if the laugh was too long, Van Dyke wouldn't be able to hear the next sound and it would throw his timing off so that he'd be out of sync with the other sounds. In other words, we had to decide just how funny this sketch really was and space the sound effects far enough apart to accommodate the audience's reactions.

Prior to going into a recording studio, Van Dyke would mime the moves, and I would time what I thought would be a reasonable time to allow for laughs. The problem was that the more he did the sketch, the less funny it seemed.

We finally decided enough was enough, and I arranged for a studio at CBS where I could lay the sounds down on a record. Van Dyke could then rehearse at home with the record, and hopefully he'd have the precise timing down perfectly in time for his first appearance on the *Tonight Show*.

That night, when Paar introduced Van Dyke's sketch as a special kind of "pantomime," even on the control room speakers, I could hear a moan from the audience at the mention of the word *pantomime*.

This audience disapproval lasted only until Van Dyke mimed to the first sound effect. And the more the audience became accustomed to this relatively new form of comedy, the better they liked it. They began laughing longer and louder!

Our nightmare was happening! The audience was enjoying the sketch so much that they were drowning out the recorded sound effects that Van Dyke had to react to!

It was bad enough they were giving five-second laughs where I had allotted three-second pauses, but now they were laughing where I hadn't even left a pause!

Suddenly, in a fit of panic and anger, I screamed out something that I doubt had ever been heard in the *Tonight Show* control room from a comedy writer.

"What the hell are you laughing at? It ain't that goddamn funny!"

How Could You Do That Awful Thing!

In writing comedy for live television you could always expect a certain amount of things to go wrong. For people like Gleason, Moore and Berle you had to be careful what you wrote for them to say. With the pantomimist, it was what they didn't say.

The premise of this next sketch involved Van Dyke coming home after having a little too much to drink and trying not to wake his wife, or their big, sleeping dog.

If you recall, this is the sketch for which Ed Sullivan gave away the ending the night we did it on his show.

When my agent read it he thought it was very funny. But his main concern was, "Where the hell are you going to get a dog like that that won't kill Van Dyke?"

"We don't need a dog, just the sound of the dog. It's a pantomime, Bill."

"I know it's a pantomime! But you're still going to need that big damn dog!"

That should have been a clue to me that I was in trouble.

When Van Dyke read it, he too thought it was funny and wanted to do it on the *Ed Sullivan Show*. And since you already know how Ed introduced it, and the ending, I thought you might like to see a pantomime in print.

Although we weren't concerned about where we were going to get that "big damn dog," I just wanted to make certain the home audience didn't think we had harmed the invisible one!

The following is the actual script that I wrote for that memorable night on the Sullivan show.

Sneaking Home Late at Night
A Pantomime

Except for the one chair center stage, the stage is without scenery or props. We open on a stage in semi-darkness. When Dick Van Dyke makes his entrance, we follow him with a spotlight wide enough to pick up his movements.

*Music: Three o'clock in the morning. Estab, bg and out.**
SFX: Off car drives up and skids to stop. Car doors open and slam.
DICK [SLURRING]
   Good night, Charlie!
Dick staggers slightly as he emerges from the upstage shadows.
SFX: Footsteps in sync with Dick's. Key sounds.

Dick stops, takes keys out of pocket and has difficulty finding right one in darkness. Puts key in mouth and strikes match.
SFX: Match strike.

Holds lit match in right hand and puts the book of matches in pocket. A look of dismay comes over him … can't find the keys! Hurriedly pats pockets with left hand. Suddenly gets foolish look. Crosses eyes and sees keys in his mouth. Holds the keys up to match and burns fingers! Angrily stabs key at door lock and misses!
SFX: Loud door chime.

Dick quickly puts finger to lips to quiet the sound. Carefully puts key in lock.
SFX: Key in lock.

Turns doorknob and slowly opens door.
SFX: Loud wood squeak. Follow action.

Inches door open slowly in, stops and starts. Finally can't risk any more noise. Turns sideways and squeezes through door. Cautiously closes door.
SFX: Door close.

Looks upstairs to see if he woke wife. A smug smile of triumph comes over face. Takes one step and falls over a table.
SFX: Short Fibber crash.

Looks upstairs fearfully. Not a peep! Again success. Rights overturned coffee table with effort.
SFX: Table sounds.

Starts returning glasses to table.
SFX: Glasses hitting table. Follow biz.

Returns three glasses in this fashion. As he returns the fourth, he glances upstairs and misses the table!
SFX: Glass crash.

Can't see where broken glass is. Needs some light. Takes a step and reacts to the loud sound of his shoe stepping on the broken glass.

*Estab—Establish (sound or music) in the clear.
bg—Background (sound or music) to a lower volume level.
Biz—Business (physical action).
Sync—Synchronize.

SFX: *Loud crunch of broken glass.*

Takes another, more cautious step. Again he hears the loud sound of crunching glass!

SFX: *Follow action with glass.*

This time he carefully lifts leg high and moves it in a circle, trying to decide where it's safe to step without making noise. Slowly lowers it and a look of triumph comes over face ... no glass crunch! Takes a step down, and as he does...

SFX: *Loud metallic clump of wastebasket. Follow biz.*

Dick hobbles in circle trying to shake it off.

SFX: *Wastebasket bangs and clangs.*

Finally succeeds in removing wastebasket.

SFX: *Loud cork pop followed by clatter of wastebasket banging to the floor.*

Dick screws up his face and clenches his eyes shut in fear of discovery. When nothing happens, he tiptoes for several steps, arms in front of him sleep-walking fashion in hopes he doesn't run into something ... he does.

SFX: *Loud clank of metal.*

Dick reacts and rubs his head. But at least he found the lamp. Goes hand over hand à la kids choosing up sides in baseball. Finds the metal chain lamp pull. Pulls it down.

SFX: *Lamp chain pull ... follow action.*

As he pulls the chain, he gets a quizzical look. Does long unscrewing of light bulb.

SFX: *Light bulb biz.*

Finally gets bulb out. Peers inquisitively into light socket. Sees something. Tries to remove it by blowing it out.

SFX: *Blowing air in sync with biz.*

Is unsuccessful. Takes index finger and pokes it into socket in an effort to remove the object.

SFX: *Loud electric spark gap!!!*

Camera reverses polarity as Dick's face contorts in pain! Finally yanks finger out!

SFX: *Cork pop and spark gap out.*

Dick sucks finger and angrily kicks lamp.

SFX: *Lamp crashes over ... right on the sleeping dog! Recorded sounds of angry snarling and vicious barking!*

Dog grabs Dick's ankle with a snarl and jerks him around in a circle. Dick gets a look of desperation! Reaches in coat pocket, gets booze bottle and pulls out cork.

SFX: *Cork pop.*

As dog continues dragging Dick around, Dick takes drink.

SFX: *Gulping sound.*

Dick starts to put bottle away, then suddenly he gets a maniacal look à la the transition from Jekyll to Hyde. Although the dog is still snarling and pulling Dick around, he takes out glass from pocket, and then, holding the glass under his arm, gets some ice cubes from other pocket and drops them into glass.

SFX: Ice cubes in glass.

Dick sticks finger in glass and stirs it.

SFX: Ice cubes and liquid being stirred.

Holds drink out to dog in a friendly, smiling fashion.

SFX: Barking and snarling out abruptly.

Puts left hand under the dog's chin—he's as big as a Great Dane—and gives him drink.

SFX: Lapping liquid followed by long "slurp."

Dick gives dog big, toothy smile and after a beat, watches dog pass out.

SFX: Thump of dog falling to floor.

Dick opens door.

SFX: Door opens.

Picks up dog and staggers under the weight. Gently puts him outside. Tips hat and bows politely, then turns and reenters house … and slams the door shut!

SFX: Door slam.

Dick "leans" against door and fans himself with his hat in relief.

SFX: Door chime.

Frowning quizzically, Dick turns and opens door.

SFX: Door open … followed by snarling and barks.

Dick slams the door and this time locks it, closes four bolts, and just for good measure, quickly nails the door shut!

SFX: Follow above action—and good luck!

Dick tiptoes over to stairs. Removes shoes and does Marceau bit of "climbing stairs" in pantomime.

SFX: Slight stair squeak in sync with steps.

Suddenly gets look of pain as he steps on something! With effort he pulls it out and tosses it away.

SFX: Loud clang of a large railroad spike.

Dick reacts to noise. Takes three more steps and hears…

SFX: Two loud cuckoos from clock.

Dick quickly removes hat and jams it over clock!

SFX: Two more cuckoos in a muffled, choking fashion. These are done vocally.

Dick continues to climb for two more steps and stops. Cups hand to ear.

SFX: Snoring off—another vocal.

Puts hand on doorknob and eases it open.

SFX: Door open … snoring gets louder.

Closes door carefully. Tiptoes into room, mimes taking off jacket and tie. Pulls down pants and leaps in the air in pain!

SFX: *Loud boing.*

Dick gets sheepish look. Forgot to take off suspenders! Does biz. Yawns, stretches, scratches and pulls back "covers" to his "bed" chair. Gets on chair and leans over and gives his wife a goodnight kiss.

SFX: *Juicy vocal kiss.*

Dick's smile turns sour. Does Stan Laurel frown of concern. Takes his hand and rubs it up and down his face, feeling the stubble of his beard.

SFX: *Scratch of sandpaper in sync.*

Reaches over and repeats biz with wife. Now Dick is really worried. Reaches over and quickly gets wallet out of pants. Flips it open and reaches over and turns wife's head with hand. Makes hurried comparison to picture of her in wallet … it's definitely not his wife! … his room! … or even his house!! Jumps out of bed, grabbing for clothes and hurriedly miming putting them on!

SFX: *Vocal of gruff, sleepy man's voice.*

VOICE
Hey! Who are you?!!!

In a panic, Dick runs to door, miming the fact his pants are only around his knees, yanks open door…

SFX: *Door open and dog barks.*

Turning from this new threat, Dick does what any sensible drunk would do if they got into the wrong house—dives out through the window!

SFX: *Huge glass crash!*

Cut to black.

Music: Playoff.

After my taking all these pains to make the pantomime as clear as possible, the producer got a letter the following week from an irate woman who mistook Dick's giving the dog a drink for out-and-out poisoning! "What the hell," she wanted to know, "is funny about poisoning a poor dog!"

These were some of the problems of writing comedy—and especially pantomimes—for live television. If the all-important audience that you depended on for your timing and, hopefully, for your laughs, wasn't blocked by a phalanx of equipment and engineers, it was confused by Special Effects. And if it wasn't that, it was the clock, or people thinking you poisoned a dog.

After having written comedy for live television for so many years, is it any wonder I welcomed the opportunity to write for a show that had the safety and convenience of tape? But as I was soon to learn, even safety and convenience come with a price. And it came in the shape of the world's funniest clown, Red Skelton.

CHAPTER 16

Red Skelton:
The Name Says It All

In 1969 the fat hit the fire. I was doing the *Captain Kangaroo Show* when there was a booming, metallic announcement on the studio talk-back (studio public address system).

"Bob Mott, you have a call in the control room from [*long pause*] HOLLY-WOOD!"

Suddenly the studio erupted in a series of *whoooooos* and *ooooohs* at the mere mention of that most magical of all towns located somewhere across and beyond the Hudson River.

As I made my way to the control room I couldn't for the life of me figure out who it was. The only person I knew out there was Dick Van Dyke. But I hadn't heard from Dick since he began starring in his own series.

It was Bill Holbin, the director-producer of the *Red Skelton Show*. I knew Holbin from New York where he had directed, and I had written for, the *Andy Williams Show*. He wanted to know if I'd be interested in writing the pantomimes for Skelton.

Would I be interested? It was what I'd been praying would happen.

I first saw Red Skelton in 1938 at New York's Paramount Theater. At that time he was the warm-up act for the real attraction, a skinny singer named Sinatra.

After the movie and stage show, both Skelton and Sinatra begged the first ten rows of screaming bobby-soxers to have a heart and leave so that the thousands of kids that had been in the rain for hours could see the show. But, just as their kids would one day storm the *Ed Sullivan Show* when the Beatles, Rolling Stones, Three Dog Night, or Elvis Presley were appearing, so too those future mothers refused to budge out of their seats and just kept screaming adoringly at Old Blue Eyes.

Doing comedy on the same stage with Sinatra was not the most enviable place to be. Shelton, however, felt right at home.

One of the reasons for Skelton's success, in addition to enormous talent, was his great respect for his audience, regardless of their ages. He knew from experience emceeing the grueling walkathons and doing comedy for unruly burlesque and nightclub crowds, that no matter who was seated in the audience, they had the power to decide whether he worked or went hungry. But entertain them he did! He got laughs from everything from outrageous jokes to bone-shaking pratfalls and from being "a mean widdle kid" to gaining 35 pounds doing his famous "Dunkin' Donut Routine." And as often as I had been to the Paramount Theater, no comedian ever impressed me or made me laugh so much as Skelton did that day.

Would I be interested in writing for Red Skelton? I started at CBS in 1951; it was now 1969. It took 18 years for that phone to ring. I was now 45 and pretty much at the top of my game in sound effects. I had all the security in the world, and all I had to do was wait another 20 or so years and I could retire with a good pension. But, then again, I was also going out of my mind with boredom!

It was the old story: you go to work, have a few beers, watch a little television, go to bed and when you wake up, you're 65.

Television was rapidly leaving New York and moving to Hollywood, the land of wine, honey, and big-name stars. All that was left in New York were the soaps, game shows, Ed Sullivan, and my show for the past ten years, *Captain Kangaroo*.

From a Sound Effect department that had once boasted 26 people, only six remained. The rest had either been transferred to other departments or had retired and not been replaced.

To appreciate how few six is, consider that radio's version of *Moby Dick* had eight sound people doing that one show. Now there were less than that number to take care of all the shows that came out of New York! And of the shows that were left, only Kangaroo offered a creative challenge. If you call doing carrot crunches for a hand puppet named Bunny creatively challenging.

It was time to move on.

Red Skelton

Even among such great live radio and television laugh-makers as Jack Benny, George Burns, Gracie Allen, Ed Wynn, Fanny Brice, Jimmy Durante, Milton Berle, Redd Foxx, Carol Burnett, Lucille Ball and Jackie Gleason, Red Skelton was unique. And to be unique in a business that fairly wallows in uniqueness took some doing.

Red's humor was neither witty, smart, satirical, deprecating, nasty, sarcastic, sophisticated, or smart-ass. It was all about having fun. Red was a clown. Whether he was radio's Mean Widdle Kid or television's Clem Kadiddlehopper, the country bumpkin Sheriff Deadeye or sheriff San Fernando Red, he was still Red Skelton.

Even when he was Gertrude and Heathcliff, the dim-witted seagulls, he was Red Skelton.

When Skelton moved to television on September 30, 1951, he added Freddie the Freeloader, a good-hearted, well-meaning character that was not unlike Charlie Chaplin's "Little Tramp." There were other similarities as well. Although Freddie never spoke, he wore a tattered costume, clown-like makeup and worked in a set with props. This television version of a silent movie was referred to as the "Silent Spot."

The Silent Spot was not to be confused with Skelton's pure pantomimes (or, as Skelton used to refer to them, "panto*mines*"). This is what I was hired to do—or attempt to do: write Red Skelton's television pantomines.

Getting Located

During the weeks before pre-production, I began searching for an apartment that would accommodate a family of six. After weeks of frantic searching, one almost fell in my lap. I was getting my hair cut and got in a conversation with my barber. I happened to mention how difficult it was to find a four-bedroom apartment when the gentleman in the chair next to me said his son-in-law had just such a place in—are you ready for this?—Beverly Hills! Oh sure, Beverly Hills? I had seen *The Beverly Hillbillies* on television, and if they think I could afford one of those mansions...

As it turned out it wasn't a mansion, or even as large as my house back in New Jersey, but it was furnished and in Beverly Hills! What's more, it was something I could afford! Although the house was small, it was in a very nice neighborhood of other small, well-kept homes. But the important thing was that my daughters lived in the area that allowed them to go to Beverly Hills High School!

It seems Beverly Hills was very picky about who went to their school. Some parents who lived out of the Beverly Hills district rented empty apartments they never set foot in, just so they could show the school officials proof that they "lived" in Beverly Hills.

Here I was, writing for Red Skelton and living in Beverly Hills! No more Kangaroo, no more wearing two hats, and no more live television! No more dealing with the ineptness of Special Effects, no more Ed Sullivan's introductions, and no more audiences trying to look around the rear ends of cameramen to see what Van Dyke was doing. This was the big time! Or was it?

Hollywood Spoken Here

While I was waiting for my family to come out from Hackensack, New Jersey, I attended my first big-time party peopled by agents, producers and network executives. As I entered the house, I hadn't had time to order a drink from the bar at poolside when an attractive woman sidled up to me and asked my reason for being invited to this power party. I was hoping someone would do that, because I was tickled pink to be selected to write pantomimes for the consummate clown of all time, and all too happy to tell folks about it. But I didn't want to appear too pleased with myself, so I decided to play it Hollywood cool.

"Hollywood cool" is a look of haughty unpretentiousness. To pull the look off, it should be accompanied by a slight furrowing of the brow to indicate interest and an unwavering look in the eyes to show sincerity. If accompanied by a slight condescending smile, the overall effect should superficially convince your audience that you're really "one of them." But be careful. If you're too attentive or too accommodating or otherwise let on that under all this show business facade you really are a nice guy and you really are interested in who they are and what they have to say, they'll lose all respect for you and consider you nobody important.

Therefore, instead of telling this lady I was writing the *Red Skelton Show*, I condensed it: "I'm writing for Red."

There was a fleeting look that seemed to ask "Who the hell is Red?" behind her sunglasses, but she didn't dare speak it. But since it hadn't sent any signals to her database of possible ways of getting ahead in this cold, cold town, she flashed a smile and sauntered off.

Her place was taken by a gentleman determined to show the world the very latest in cosmetic teeth capping. After a perfunctory greeting, he asked what got me an invitation to the party. This time I dropped the subtle act and hit him with my big guns.

"CBS. I write for Red Skelton."

The man lifted his eyebrows and said, "Oh, after all these years he's still on the air? Amazing."

I could see I was in trouble with this guy. But before I could play his game, he asked me the second most often asked question in Hollywood.

"Where do you live?"

Now I had him! I smiled and loftily replied, "Beverly Hills."

Back in New Jersey this would have at least raised an eyebrow or two. But here, under the California evening sky, with candles floating in an azure-colored swimming pool, all it did was beget a second question.

"North or south of Sunset Boulevard?"

This was something that was never explained on *The Beverly Hillbillies*. After thinking a moment of where the hell Sunset Boulevard even was, I finally replied "South." He gave me a condescending smirk, grabbed a backup glass of white wine from the bar and left.

Even though "South" was where I actually lived, it obviously wasn't the correct answer. So just for the hell of it, my next answer would be different.

I didn't have to wait long. As soon as this woman wearing heavy makeup, slacks and a man's necktie found out I was new in town, she popped the big "where do you live" question. This time I smiled with confidence. "*North* of Sunset Boulevard." In response, she lifted one tattooed eyebrow and asked, "In the Hills?"

I had enough. Retaining my now practiced smile, I answered, "Doesn't everyone?" I quickly followed this with "But not at the bottom of the hill, or even the middle of the hills, but right at the tippy top where on a clear day I can reach up and shake hands with God!"

She uttered an unladylike obscenity and gave me an even more unladylike gesture with her middle finger and moved off to find people who really knew how to play this strange game of Hollywood's.

Welcome to the Big Time

When I entered CBS on that very first day, I was met by Arnie Rosen, a very talented writer I worked with on the *Garry Moore Show*. To give you an idea of the mind of a comedy writer, instead of shaking my hand, he held out his arms as if to give me a Hollywood hug, but instead began giving me a police frisking and demanded roughly, "Got anything funny on you?"

After Arnie offered his congratulations on my finally making the break from sound effects and wishing me luck with Skelton, he headed for his headwriter's job with Carol Burnett, and I headed for the elevator and the Skelton office.

The first thing I noticed about the elevator was the red telephone. It seems that Skelton was once stuck in the elevator without any means of outside communication. The next day there was a telephone in the elevator. A red one.

The first Skelton writer I encountered was Mort Green. Mort had a smile and personality to charm the birds out of a tree, but God help them if he got his hands on them!

After he introduced himself, he wanted to know what I did as a writer that was so special since there were so many writers out of work in Hollywood? And didn't I also do sound effects at CBS?

Perhaps Mort was good to his parents, his wife and children, and gave to the church, but he suddenly was a pain in the ass to me. But having been around many writers before Mort, I chose to see how much of a pain in the ass he wanted to be. I could only hope the rest of the writers weren't like him.

In answering Mort's question regarding my two-hatted career, I told him about working with Holbin on the *Andy Williams Show* and that he brought me out to write Skelton's pantomimes.

Mort jumped at that. "No, kid, me and Dave O'Brien write the Silent Spots *and* pantomimes!" He then snapped his fingers and continued. "I know! My agent was asking Skelton for a big raise. So when they were reluctant to go that high, my agent told them that unless they met my price, I wouldn't do the show."

He then gave me a long quizzical look. "Don't you get it? They brought you out here as a backup in case I didn't sign. But I did. So where does that leave you?"

It left me thinking Mort Green was a bigger pain in the ass than I originally thought.

The Second Day

Perhaps I had still suffered from jet lag on the first day, because on the second, the other seven writers seemed quite friendly. Especially Dave O'Brien, Mort Green's writing partner. Dave had come to Hollywood in the early thirties and got a job as a stuntman in the old Pete Smith specials (still shown on cable).

Dave started doing stunts when he considered falling off a roof an easy way to pick up $25. Because of this stunt background, he began writing physical comedy for many of the early film comedians.

The other writers had equally interesting backgrounds and were every bit as quirky and friendly as Dave. Bob O'Brien (Skelton's head writer) had worked with Bob Hope, and written for the *Eddie Cantor Show* and *I Love Lucy*.

Artie Phillips was the writer for the Ann Sothern radio series, *Maisie*, and the *Phil Baker Show*.

Seaman Jacobs wrote for the Jack Paar radio show. Jacobs told me he was turned down for the Henry Morgan radio show with the excuse that Morgan's wife didn't think Jacobs' writing was funny. Later, when Morgan divorced his wife, he gave as his reason: "She didn't have a sense of humor." Jacobs and his partner, Freddie Fox, wrote for *I Love Lucy*, *Love Boat*, and God knows how many more. Jacobs also created the wacky *F Troop*.

Freddie Fox wrote for the *Judy Canova Show* and for Bob Hope. Fred was probably one of the few writers who told Hope he no longer wanted to write for him. That in itself may not be unique, but how he did it was.

Fred tended to stammer and stutter when he got excited. And when Hope started calling him on the phone at all hours of the day and night for last-minute jokes, Fox finally had enough. "Bbbbbob, you can ttttttake your jjjjjjob and shh-hhhh..." Hope suddenly interrupted with, "It's okay, Fred, I get the idea," and hung up.

George Balzer, unlike the rest of the writers, had only one real credit. But fortunately it was with Jack Benny and lasted over 25 years!

Bob Orben started writing comedy at the age of 18. Since that time he has written 49 books on the subject, published a monthly newsletter containing topical humor, written for Dick Gregory (a political activist-comedian) for six

From the left: Artie Phillips, Fred Fox, George Balzer, Mort Green, Dave O'Brien, Sy Jacobs, the author, Polly Mitchell (the writers' secretary), and Bob Orben. Bob O'Brien is missing (author's collection).

years and edited Gregory's two books, *From the Back of the Bus* and *What's Happening?* In addition, he was appointed a special assistant to President Gerald Ford.

After the monologue, Skelton would do his "Gertrude and Heathcliff" spot. Heathcliff and Gertrude were two goofy seagulls who told jokes. And in order for Skelton to sound like seagulls, he had to look like a seagull.

He would muss up his hair, shape his hat lengthwise to represent a seagull's bill, fold his arms and tuck them under his armpits to represent wings, cross his eyes and finally affect a couple of goofy voices to begin the bit.

HEATHCLIFF	Gertrude, did you hear what Willie the Nearsighted Worm said when he fell into a bowl of spaghetti?
GERTRUDE	No, Heathcliff. What did Willie the Nearsighted Worm say when he fell into a bowl of spaghetti?
HEATHCLIFF	I love you! I love you! I love you!

(*Red delivers each line in a different direction.*)

Now it was one thing for Skelton to look as silly as he did on stage doing the jokes, but what about the poor soul who had to write them? When I asked Orben, this was his reply.

"You can't write the jokes without feeling like a seagull. But because I couldn't look like a seagull like Red could, I used to fold my arms into wings and go around my apartment walking like one. That is, I did until I saw my lady neighbor across the way watching me through her window."

When the Skelton show went off the air and I was doing sound effects at NBC, I found Orben was telling the truth from that great authority on seagulls, Johnny Carson.

What made this conversation so unusual was that no one at NBC was allowed to strike up a conversation with Johnny Carson. And yet despite all the horror stories I heard about him, he was very pleasant.

Our conversation took place outside his office next to the *Tonight Show* studio. He had a few minutes before he was due in the studio and was killing time with a cigarette. Since I was working in the studio next to his and had also come out into the hall to have a cigarette, I decided to say hello.

Perhaps if I had asked him for an autograph it would have been different, but he smiled and nodded. So rather than just stand there like a couple of dummies, I asked him point blank whether it was true that at one time he wrote the seagull jokes for Red Skelton?

At first he looked at me funny and then replied, "Not only did I write them—they almost cost me my first marriage. You can't write the damn things unless you get in front of a mirror, cross your eyes and look like a nut. My wife finally said she took me for better or worse, but not for a couple of seagulls."

Getting to Meet the Legend

Writing a funny pantomime is difficult enough, but writing one for Skelton was really a challenge. Skelton had been doing pantomimes on television for the past 19 or so years. In live television years, if your show was on weekly, a television "year" lasted for 39 weeks. If Skelton did one pantomime each week for all the years he was on, that came out to 741 pantomimes. Add to that number all the pantomimes he did before television in theaters, burlesque, nightclubs and state fairs!

With this in mind, I was anxious to get with Skelton to discuss what mimes he had already done, what mimes he'd like to do and, for God's sakes, to meet the man!

Although Skelton had a home in Bel Air, he spent most of his time in Palm Springs. With the show just two weeks away from going into production, I decided to give Bill Holbin a call about setting up my meeting with Skelton.

After Holbin finished laughing, he told me Red would not only not want to meet me, but if he ever even saw me and found out I was one of his writers, I would be fired!

Having always worked closely with the people I had written for, this news about one of Skelton's idiosyncrasies struck me as both unusual and bewildering.

Comedians are notoriously insecure. They need every sign of approval they can get, no matter how seemingly insignificant. Why else would Skelton finish a show at the Sands Hotel to a standing ovation and then come backstage asking, "How did I do?"

As disappointing as it was for me not to personally meet a man I had admired for so many years, I consoled myself with the fact that at least I would learn a great deal watching him during one of his rehearsals.

And what rehearsals! If radio's *Gunsmoke* had their "dirty" Saturdays, Skelton's day was Monday. Many CBS employees juggled their work schedules to allow them to attend a Skelton rehearsal. And he never disappointed them. I couldn't wait for Monday to come around so that I too could sit in the audience and once again see Red. Only this time, not as a 14-year-old kid back at the Paramount Theater in New York. Now I was one of his writers!

As my big day arrived, I told the other writers I was skipping lunch so I could go and watch Red rehearse. When they finished laughing, they told me if Red ever found out I was one of his writers, I would be fired *tout de suite*.

At first I thought they were joking. I knew he didn't want to meet me in person, but how would he know I was in the audience? That, I was told, is the chance I would be taking.

These were just a few of the obstacles I was facing as the new 45-year-old kid in town. There were more.

As I turned in my first script to the secretaries to be typed up, I noticed they put my effort at the bottom of the pile. When I asked why they had put what I sweated over at the bottom, they gave me a smile that was more like a suppressed, conspiratorial giggle.

"To tell you the truth, because Red rarely does the pantomimes that are written for him, we've been told if we're faced with a deadline, to save the pantomimes until last."

First I couldn't talk to Red, second I couldn't watch Red, and now I was told that what I was writing didn't have a snowball's chance in hell of being done!

Skelton got along fine with everyone on his show, just as long as they didn't write for him. Here he is with his sound-effects artist, Ray Erlenborn (photograph courtesy of Ray Erlenborn).

We Finally Meet Face to Face

Despite all the warnings, I did get to meet Red Skelton face to face—sorta.

One evening, as I was walking to my car, I decided to take a shortcut past a section of parked cars that was set aside for CBS' biggest stars, one of course being Red Skelton.

His car was the fairest of them all. It was a shiny, deep-maroon 1930s Rolls-Royce. As I walked around this magnificent automobile, I saw this tall man wearing a full-length black mink coat. It was the car's owner, Red Skelton! Standing beside him was Guy Della Cioppa, his executive producer.

At first, neither of them saw me. But I saw them. And what I saw was unbelievable. Here was the world-renowned clown trying to open the door of his hundred-thousand-dollar antique Rolls-Royce with a motel wire coat hanger!

I didn't know what to do—offer to help, turn and run, hide my face? And then I heard Della Cioppa saying the forbidden words: "Red, this is Bob Mott." Thank God he left off the magic word, "writer." Red smiled, shook my hand warmly and said, "Bob, you wouldn't happen to have an extra key for a 1937 Rolls-Royce?" Before I could think of a bright, witty, funny, or even appropriate answer, the locksmith's truck pulled up and I was saved the trouble.

It was funny: after all the years of being such a big fan of Red's and wanting to meet him, or even, God help me, write for him, it took a locked vintage Rolls-Royce for us to meet face to face!

I Finally Write for Skelton!

When my first script finally did get typed, and it finally did get read by the head writer, he telephoned me and said he wanted to see me in his office at once!

Had I blown my writing career already? As I entered O'Brien's office he handed me my script. It was riddled with red marks. "Never submit another script like this again if you want to keep writing for Red." As I looked closely at what was circled in red, it seemed to be the same word: *son.*

I looked at O'Brien. "What's wrong? Are you looking for a funnier word than *son?*"

O'Brien neither smiled nor laughed.

"Never use the word *son* on the Skelton show. Red's only son died of leukemia."

Now it was my turn to get upset. "Then why wasn't I told about something as tragic as that?"

"You should have been, and I thought you were. But since you weren't, you have been now. Another thing: Red has difficulty understanding a written script. So Holbin puts it on audio tape and lets Red listen to what you wrote. Which makes you the first writer to do pantomimes for radio."

Red's talents were unique. He did pantomimes, but he wasn't a Marcel Marceau, or even a Dick Van Dyke. He told jokes, but he certainly wasn't in a class with Bob Hope. But one thing he could do better than any of them (along with making you wet your pants laughing) was make you cry. This put him in a class with Charlie Chaplin. And wouldn't those two have made a pair: Skelton's Freddie the Freeloader and Chaplin's Little Tramp.

Red was basically a clown. Not only would he drop his pants for a laugh, he would eat his necktie. Once while having lunch at Hollywood's Brown Derby, Red cut up his necktie, put it in a Caesar's salad and ate it!

Another example of his desire to make everyone laugh was the time when Universal Studios called together all their stars for the annual year-end studio picture. Skelton, arriving late and breathless, neither apologized to the assembled stars nor sneaked sheepishly to his seat. Instead, he jumped up on a chair and in a voice still out of breath from running, called out to the biggest stars in Hollywood: "You can all go home now; the part's been casted!"

In writing Red's pantomimes, I learned Red, unlike Marcel Marceau, had no formal training in the classic style of pantomime. He even lacked the skinny litheness of a Dick Van Dyke.

What Skelton did have that more than made up for any mime shortcomings was his face. He could shape it into all the dozens of characters he played, from a "mean widdle kid" to a punch-drunk fighter. And yet basically it never changed. It was always ready to make you laugh, cry or forgive him for his outlandish behavior.

The Importance of a Hat

When Red did his pantomimes, he never used costumes, makeup or props. The only exceptions were a chair and his hat. To Red, a hat was an extension of his personality. The way he wore it told you who he was. Marty Ragaway, one of

This photograph shows Red doing a pantomime I wrote about the owner of a new sports car. Now, to you and me Red is wearing a fedora, but to Red, it's a peaked racing cap that identifies him as a member of the elite sports car family. The reason Red has that expression on his face is, after shifting his car a dozen times to get just the right speed, an elderly pedestrian makes him come to a stop so he can very slowly walk across the street (author's collection).

A picture of Red dating back to his radio show. Even then, Red would turn his hat upside down for his Widdle Kid character. Notice the childlike look on his face as he plays with some of the sound-effect "toys" (photograph courtesy of Pacific Pioneer Broadcasters).

Skelton's writers, explained Red's need for his hat this way: "Red couldn't get into the character unless he was wearing the hat of that particular person."

I couldn't agree with Ragaway more. I feel that when Jacqueline Kennedy decided to go to church with a lace handkerchief on her head instead of a hat, she did more than give the millinery industry a collective heart attack, she took away one of society's great communicating tools: a hat.

Unlike today, where style dictates we emblazon some designer's name across our chest or butt, at one time everyone wore hats. The former tells everyone that you're au courant, while the latter reveals who you are.

Red's hat was an expensive Italian import that could be molded, punched, kicked, pummeled or jumped on. Despite being able to take this punishment, the hat in itself was just a hat. Its value was how it was worn and how it made Red feel.

"He's Got a Million of Them!"

Skelton had a joke file that rivaled Milton Berle's. This made Bob Orben's job of coming up with new jokes for Red as difficult as my coming up with new pantomimes. And yet, when Orben started writing for Red in 1964, he at least got to meet and talk with him!

After knocking and being given permission to enter Red's dressing room, Orben found Red stretched out on a chaise lounge, resting his back. After years of doing pratfalls into vaudeville orchestra pits and on television, it had finally caught up to Red.

After introducing himself, Orben told Red he'd be writing his monologues and asked whether there was any special way he'd like them.

"Funny" was Red's only suggestion.

Actually, that wasn't Red's only suggestion. Red would decide what the weekly monologue was to be about, and it was up to Orben to write it and make it funny.

It was then my job to call Orben, find out what the subject of the monologue was going to be, and write a pantomime and hopefully make it funny.

In other words, I couldn't just come up with any funny idea for a pantomime; it had to be one that was on the subject of Red's monologue.

If one of Red's monologues ran long, I would have to write a very short pantomime, like the one you're about to read.

In writing pantomimes for Skelton, I tried to use as few words as possible. One reason was to save space, and the other was because Skelton hated to read.

So instead of indicating that Skelton was to "yell angrily," I would simply write "jaws." This meant that Skelton was to mime moving his mouth angrily. You'll see "jaws" in all my Skelton pantomimes.

Skelton

Tonight I'd like to do a little pantomime about the latest sport-craze among some of the more athletic husbands and wives in this country—mountain climbing.

SFX: *Wind*

Red inches toward the edge of mountain top and looks down. He has to hold his hat firmly on his head to keep it from blowing away. Gets frightened looking at the height. Then jaws down at his wife that he'll get her up! Spits on hands, rubs them together, grabs rope and unwinds it from peg on the ground. His wife's weight causes him to cross his eyes in pain. Struggles to turn his back, puts rope over shoulder, and fights a tugging seesaw battle to keep from falling over the edge. Finally starts pulling her up hand-over-hand by rope. It's tough work! Stops. Takes one hand off rope, removes his hat, wipes his forehead on sleeve, spits on it and takes other hand off rope so he can rub them together to dry.

SFX: *Slide Whistle Down.*

Red suddenly looks at empty hands and panics. Runs to edge of cliff, looks down, does sickly take, and puts his hat reverently over his heart.

Music: Playoff.

As short as this last pantomime is, if space permitted, I could show you four more drafts I submitted until it finally pleased the head writer enough to submit it to Skelton. But then, on several occasions, what I wrote so pleased the head writer that he'd turn it into the longer Silent Spot, leaving me a few hours to come up with something else.

This was all part of being one of the Skelton writers, and I enjoyed it thoroughly. Especially the night that John Wayne was the guest and I was asked to come up with this coin joke for Wayne. Now it's one thing to write pantomimes for Skelton, but to be asked to write a *joke* for John Wayne? Does it get any better?!

The writers had written a western sketch for Wayne and Skelton. Wayne is in a bar having a drink and suddenly we hear Red's standard opening for Red's western character, "Deadeye."

SFX: *Galloping hoofbeats*

DEADEYE: Whoa … whoa… [*pleading*] Aw, come on, horsie, please, whoa!

SFX: *Loud screech of brakes followed by whinny!*

As Red rushes into the bar where John Wayne is seated, he slams a silver dollar on the bar and tells the bartender he needs some change for the parking meter.

With that Wayne picks up the silver dollar, tosses it in the air, pulls out his pistol and shoots it. Suddenly a shower of nickels comes down.

WAYNE [*casually*]

Is that enough, Pilgrim?

The one subject that all writers could count on was holidays, especially Christmas and Thanksgiving. Now it's one thing to talk about Christmas, but how do you write a pantomime about Christmas?

The one Christmas pantomime I knew I couldn't write about was trying to get a Christmas tree to stand up straight; that one had been done to death by everyone.

Therefore, the one I wrote involved Red taking out last year's Christmas lights and trying to untangle them. This gave Red a lot of moves and an opportunity for a number of different facial expressions.

Here's part of that pantomime. I called it "Christmas Lights."

Music: Light and festive mood. Hold in background.

Red has a childlike smile of happiness as he looks at his tree. Goes and bends, or fluffs up a branch.

SFX: *Follow action with rustle of branches.*

Red turns and opens large cardboard box.

SFX: *Follow action with cardboard box flaps.*

Red's smile fades to sick look as he slowly pulls out the tangled mess of Christmas lights.

SFX: *Tinkling of glass bulbs. Keep in and follow action.*

Red puts part of one string over shoulder, another string over other shoulder, and one string under chin. Keeps hauling up other strings. Ducks head through opening of one loop, high-steps leg through other loop.

Red, in trying to find the ends of the lights, puts parts of one string in mouth, over head, under arms, between legs, moves one leg through the loop, the other leg through the other loop.

This action starts slow and deliberate, but gradually increases in speed and intensity.

Red gets a cat-like look on his face as if the lights are now a ball of yarn. His hands are now paws as he strikes out at what he thinks is the end of a string of lights. These moves become faster and more fiendish until Red now finds himself hog-tied.

With head bent low, and because one string of lights is caught under his crotch, Red is forced to take short mincing steps as if a bouncer in a bar were about to give him the old heave-ho out the door!

Red jaws angrily at the invisible bouncer's hand that has him grabbed tightly by the seat of his pants!

He now is bent over in hunchback fashion. His hands become twisted, and his eyes flash about with a crazy gleam! Red is now the hunchback of Notre Dame!

Because of the snarled and twisted lights, Red can only drag his now lifeless leg to one side as he fights to free himself from the many clinging arms of an octopus! But the more he fights, the more entangled he gets! He is now dragged to his knees. He twists and rolls à la Houdini trying to get out of a straitjacket! He begins jawing angrily at his predicament, when we hear…

Music: Celesta plays "Tis the Season to Be Jolly" (as if this is Red's conscience reminding him of the season).

Red ignores his celestial conscience and continues jawing!

Music: Celesta plays same song a little more persistently.

Red now even angrily jaws at the celesta!

Music: This time "Tis the Season to Be Jolly" has the scolding authority of an organ!

Red, frightened by this ominous music, becomes very humble and apologetic. Gets sweet, angelic choirboy look. Red, trying to be calm, climbs clumsily back to his feet. Red, out of the corner of his eye, sees a way out! He grabs some of the light strings and begins wiggling out of them à la a woman taking off a girdle.

Other lights he gathers in two hands and rolls them down his legs as if they were silk stockings.

For the last string, Red reaches both hands in back and unfastens them à la brassiere. He's free!

Red quickly plugs the lights together and skips merrily around the tree à la maypole fashion. Gets to end. Takes it over to wall socket. Looks happily at tree and plugs in his beautiful Christmas lights!

Red's look of happy expectancy fades into a quizzical frown. No lights. Red jiggles wall plug. Nothing. Goes to tree and taps some lights. Nothing.

Finally unscrews one light. Looks into socket … can't see anything. Gets socket closer … closer. Looks up at ceiling for better light, and when he returns head down, his nose gets stuck in light socket!

SFX: Loud crackling of electricity!

Red's eyes cross in excruciating agony! Finally, with one mighty pull…

SFX: Cork pop.

He's free! Red jaws angrily at the lights, and the tree in general! Suddenly hears…

Music: Celesta— "Tis the Season to Be Jolly."

At first, Red resists the music. Continues jawing angrily.

Music: Celesta plays a short piece as if to say, "Come on, Red, calm down. It's Christmas."

We play the music until Red finally succumbs. His face takes on a peaceful look. Picks up box and opens it. Takes out small object and smiles. Turns it and makes winding motion with hand.

SFX: Small winding sound.
Music: Music box— "Come, All Ye Faithful."

Red places angel at top of tree. And as he stands back, smiling, and at peace with the world, the camera slowly goes in on Red's joyful face.

Music: Segue from music box to big orchestration of "Come, All Ye Faithful." Swell music to finish.

And that's what it was like writing for Red Skelton. One minute his nose is stuck in a light socket, and the next, his face reflects the childlike joy of Christmas.

In spite of all my doubts and fears, Red never did fire me; CBS fired Red. And although writing for Skelton could be very difficult and demanding, if I have any disappointments at all, it was the day I got the news of Red's cancellation.

I've often thought that whatever communication he withheld from his writers, he gave his audiences in full. It was an ongoing love affair whether he was playing the Iowa State Fair, Las Vegas, or to a bunch of prewar screaming kids at the Paramount Theater.

Red, unlike most comedians, wanted more from his audience than just laughter. He wanted something better. He wanted to make his audiences happy. And personally, I can't think of anyone who did it better, or received more satisfaction in doing it.

CHAPTER 17

Television's Most Despised People

Laughter is not to be confused with "laffter." *Laughter* comes from the hearts of people enjoying themselves; "laffter" comes from a lifeless machine capable of spewing out "laffs" with just the flick of a finger. I should know; I was once a finger-flicking-laff man.

If in your naïveté you think one of the most difficult and challenging tasks you face in life is finding just the perfect man or woman of your dreams, or the perfect mutual fund, or the perfect auto mechanic, or even the perfect martini, try finding the perfect laugh—that one laugh for any and all occasions.

Well I've got good news for you: Your search is over! There ain't one. If you think that a laugh is a laugh is a laugh, both you and Gertrude Stein are all wet, because I spent a career searching for one.

Welcome to the wild and crazy world of canned laughter! Yes, folks, meet the high priests of ha-ha! The often criticized and much maligned magicians of mirth! The artists who have a funny bone for a finger! The chosen few who sit behind closed doors and dictate to the world of television viewers not only *what* is funny but for how *long* it's funny. You don't believe me? Then just listen to the peals of laughter coming from the ancient reruns of *Gilligan's Island*!

Look on the bright side: isn't deciding what is and what isn't funny on television these days adding just one more stress to your already stressful life? When you come home at night and flop on the couch, wouldn't it be a whole lot easier if that difficult decision-making process were done for you? Well, then, just sit back and relax, and join the carefree merriment of laughing along with the rest of the often dear-departed laughers entombed on the tapes or CDs of today's high-tech laff machines. Aw, c'mon! People that have gone to their just rewards can't laugh! Oh no? Not only can they laugh, but they can also chuckle, giggle, titter, guffaw, scream, howl, ooooh and aaaah! Even now, as I watch my fat cat, Max, pawing sand over his poop, I'm reminded of what I had to paw laffs over in my days of "sweetening" comedy shows.

A "sweetening session" is a time to forgive and forget all the mistakes that were made in taping a television comedy show. I say "taping" because that's what made all these sweetening sessions possible. In the good old rough-and-tumble days of live television, you didn't have anyone telling you what was funny. You either laughed or you didn't. And that was the problem. (What people want to watch a comedy show at which even the studio audience isn't laughing?)

To solve this perplexing problem, producers had a difficult choice. Either make their shows funnier by getting better scripts and more talented people or make viewers *think* what they're watching is funny.

The answer came when one producer read that laughter is supposed to be contagious. He also read that if you laugh, the whole world laughs with you. Unfortunately, the producer understood this to mean that people will laugh at *anything*. All they need is to hear someone else laugh first, like a claque.

Claque is from the French word *claquer*, meaning "to applaud." It is normally used to describe someone who applauds—and laughs—for a price.

Live broadcasting wasn't the first to use claquers as a way to inspire audiences to think they were enjoying themselves—vaudeville was. Even there, the very idea of leaving it up to audiences to decide what is and what isn't funny was barbaric! What did they know about comedy?

Radio also used this same rationale as an excuse to hire laffers and applauders. And then, as a safeguard to make certain the claquers knew what to laugh at, the show's comedy writers sat in the audience and added to the hilarity.

According to Max Eastman, author of *The Enjoyment of Laughter*, there are three laws of humor that must be obeyed if you expect to extract laughs from an audience.

The first law of humor is that things can be funny only when we are "in fun."

The second law is that when we are in fun, a particular shift in values takes place.

The third law is that being in fun is a condition most natural to childhood, and children at play reveal the humorous laugh in its simplest and most omnivorous form. To them, every untoward, unprepared for, unmanageable thing, unless it is calamitous enough to force them out of the mood of play, is to be enjoyed and laughed at.

If what Max Eastman says is true, how do you know the people who have been standing in line for hours to see your radio or television show are "in the spirit of fun?"

Simple. You do what all red-blooded producers do: you make damn sure the audience *gets* in the spirit of fun!

Ever since Marconi invented radio, comedy shows recognized the value of getting an audience in the proper mood to laugh with something called a *warmup*. One sure-fire way involved offering a five-dollar bill to the first couple in the audience who could break a balloon. Think it's easy? Just wait and see.

After selecting several men and women (it helped the laughs if they were both fat—very fat) the person doing the warmup, usually the announcer, explained *how* the couples were to break the balloons in order to win the five bucks.

He would then have the couples stand, not nose to nose, but belly to belly, and place the balloon between them! (Now do you see why fat people are funnier?) It was their job to break the balloon without using their hands, or any other part of their body except their ample tummies.

In the beginning they would simply press their bodies against the balloons, hoping their combined weights would do the trick. When this failed, they would begin moving their bodies back and forth in an undulating motion that bordered on wickedness. Then, as the allotted time to break the balloons began running out, and with it the loss of five bucks, they would throw propriety to the wind and become more frenzied and lascivious in their bodily activities. So much so that if it weren't for the balloons keeping the seeming coupling couples apart, they could have been arrested for fornicating in public.

All this activity was timed to reach a climax—so to speak—ten seconds before the show went on the air. If at that time there wasn't a winner, whoever was doing the warmup would puncture all the balloons, and the show would go on the air amid screams of laughter, proving to the listeners, or viewers at home, that their search for the Holy Grail of a good time was over. And the sweaty contestants? They would have been hustled offstage, given an armful of sponsor products and kissed off.

In addition to all these pre-broadcast shenanigans, most shows had a canned warmup speech given by the announcer or, sometimes, even the producer. So return with me to early live broadcasting and listen to one of those patented warmups:

> Now when I want you to applaud, I'll wave my hand. Now what I don't want you to do is wave back. No, nobody at home can hear you waving. Waving is like smiling, they can't hear that either. What they can hear is real loud laughs and real loud applause. So you men out there, in order to be able to laugh real loud, I want you to loosen your belts. You ladies loosen whatever it is that won't make you come apart. Now when I signal you to applaud, or you see the sign APPLAUSE flashing, clap as fast as you can. Clapping fast makes it sound like there's twice as many people here in the studio. Oh, I forgot to tell you: I know it's cold outside, but here in the studio we pay a lot of money to make sure the studio is nice and warm and cozy, so get those gloves or mittens off! Make those listeners at home hear you! Then when you get back home you can say, "Did you hear me? I was on the *Take It or Leave It* show!" And just so you do applaud and laugh real loud, one of our production staff will be watching you! And the one that laughs and applauds the loudest will get a fabulous prize! [The fabulous prize also always turned out to be a sponsor's product.]

After having rehearsed the audience numerous times in the proper way to laugh and applaud, they would ask the audience, in the spirit of friendliness, to turn around and shake the hand of the person in back of them. And when the audience members did, they of course found themselves facing the back of the person behind them! Loud laughter ensued.

If all this wasn't enough to get an audience warmed up, the announcer would end his spiel with this crowd pleaser. "Okay, audience, we have ten seconds to go— if anyone has to!"

Claques Go on Record

In addition to claques, some live radio shows even attempted to add crowd reactions recorded on 78 RPM sound-effect records. To give you some idea of the types of crowd sounds there were to choose from, here is a list of some of those audience records in the CBS Sound-Effect Library. (See Appendix I for a more complete list of records.)

100	A General Confusion
	B Applause
101	A General Confusion
	B Laughing
102	A-B General Confusion ("Concert Hall")
103	A Cheers
	B Clashing of swords
111	A-B Cheers, laughter, applause
113	A Applause; cheering
	B Excited crowd (baseball or football)
114	A Applause
	B Model T Ford—continuous
	Model T Ford—start; run; stop
	Dog (collie) barking
116	A-B Cheers
120	A Laughter (men and women, mixed small group)
	B Laughter (men and women, mixed large group)
122	A Angry mob
	B Applause (small and large group)

As you can see, sweetening a show with the above crowd sounds might be a little tricky if you have to worry about hearing a collie barking or a Model T Ford starting up, instead of the intended applause. It might also become irritating listening to only two laugh records for any and all jokes.

These sound-effect crowds were never intended to be used in place of a live audience's reactions. They were made to be used on dramatic shows and mixed with the reactions from the live actors. If the show's budget could afford a large cast, the records sounded great; if the cast was small, the records sounded, well, recorded.

One comedian who decided that only two laugh records weren't acceptable was Milton Berle. Yes, the future Uncle Miltie was way ahead of his time. Berle went to the expense and trouble of recording a series of different types of laughs on records. He then gave each one a number. These numbers not only indicated what type of laugh each one was, but how long the laughs lasted.

Prior to the show, Berle would give the sound-effects man (Parker Cornell, NBC–Hollywood) a script outlining to him where and what laugh numbers he wanted used. Then during the show, Cornell would go in the control room and play the laugh record where it was indicated in the script. Because the laughs were done in the control room and not heard out in the studio, guests appearing on the show accustomed to taking their timing from the studio audience now had to wait, whether the studio audience was laughing or not, for the laughs added by Cornell in the control room.

One interesting insight on how the powers of denial protect the ego: after the show, Berle would listen to a recording of the air show he had just done (with the added laughs) and never failed to respond, "What a great show! Listen to those laughs!"

While Here in New York

Despite New York's sophisticated reputation, those of us in sound effects at CBS lagged woefully behind Hollywood when it came to sweetening shows. New York was the city most influenced by the live theater, while Hollywood was most influenced by, well, Hollywood and the film industry. Films could be edited and things added to make them better; the theater was live. Therefore, while Hollywood was looking for ways to add stuff to live radio and live television, New York continued trying to get laughs the old fashioned way, by earning them.

My first experience of adding audience reactions came on a game show, *To Tell the Truth*. On this particular day, a howling blizzard was roaring up and down the overcast Great White Way. Instead of the normal flow of cars and taxis on Broadway, New Yorkers were braving the snow on foot, or schussing to work on skis. It was not a good day for tourists to be out and about.

This shortage of possible audience members posed a problem for the producers. The opening of the show and the lead-ins to commercials called for the sound of an audience applauding wildly. And even adding a number of claquers (the show's small production staff) did not make the sparse audience sound like an audience of 500 people applauding wildly.

In desperation, Mark Goodson, the producer and co-creator of the show, along with Bill Todman, asked if I had any recorded applause I could use to fill the void. I knew that the applause records we had in our library wouldn't be appropriate, so I gave him a choice of two special applause recordings done by the British Broadcasting Company: the applause that Prime Minister Winston Churchill received when he addressed the English Parliament, or the applause Adolf Hitler received when he announced he was going to conquer the world. When Goodson asked me what the difference in the two applauses was, I told him that the Hitler applause came with a sprinkling of lusty "*Zeig Heils.*" Without hesitation, Goodson opted for Churchill.

I often wondered how the legendary Winston Churchill would feel if he found out the raucous applause he received from the British Parliament was now being used to replace a snowbound game show audience!

Although Goodson's reason for adding applause was somewhat justified by the weather, the convenience of having a ready-made applause at your disposal was too much of a temptation for any red-blooded producer. Other excuses to use the recorded applause soon followed: "The audiences are too small, because the cameras and boom mikes blocked their view." "It was raining out." "It was Tuesday."

As much as producers wanted to augment live audiences with recorded sounds, two things held them back. One was the odious disclaimer they were forced to flash on the television screen: "Reactions from the audience were augmented." The other deterrent was sound quality: the applause records soon became scratchy from overuse.

Of the two, it was the scratchy records that kept the producers honest. Indeed, when you considered the number of viewers who knew, or even cared, what "augmented" meant in this context, and added to that the number of viewers who didn't pay any attention to disclaimers, there seemed to be little downside to flashing the message on the screen.

Television Turns to Tape

When television went to tape, all the advantages that post-production offered film were now in television's grasp—and more! In film, audiences never got to see all of a director's mistakes; in live television, nothing could be held back. Every flubbed word and wrong camera shot was heard and seen by viewers the moment it happened. Now, through the magic of post-production, all those mistakes could be corrected with one quick slice of a razor blade.

As we all know, nothing comes without a price. So when the videotape operators took those razor blades and began editing, they ran into a few problems. And the only way they could solve them on comedy shows was by adding canned laffs.

In 1956, Ross Murray was one of the pioneer tape editors at CBS. Here's his explanation of the problems those early editors faced:

> One troublesome videotape gremlin was caused by the fact that the picture and sound were not positioned at the same point on the videotape. The four recording/playback heads on the small rotating disc were separated physically from the audio record/playback head by nine inches, which accounted for a six-tenth of a time lag in audio.
>
> This wasn't noticed unless the sound was continuous—like laughter and applause. In that case, the edit was very noticeable.

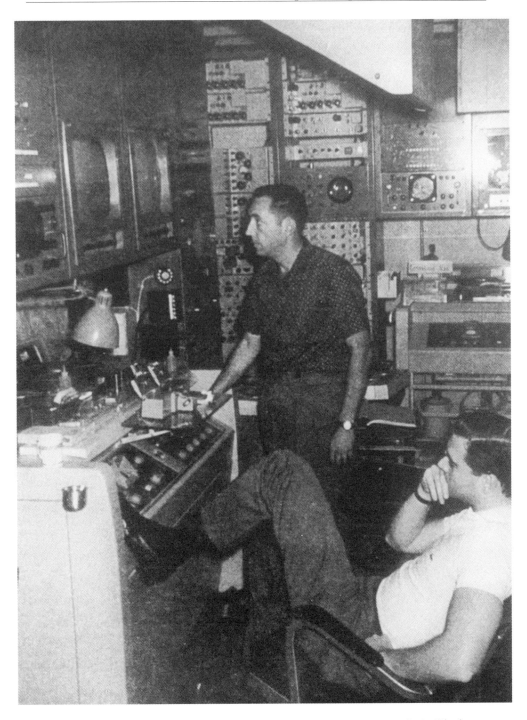

A young John Frankenheimer watches CBS' *Ross Murray perform his magic for* **Playhouse 90** *(photograph courtesy of Ross Murray).*

So add "technical difficulties" to all the other reasons why producers were so anxious to add canned laffs to their shows.

It was for these technical reasons that Monty Fraser, an NBC West Coast sound-effects artist, discovered that when he was sweetening a show and a tape pop occurred, if it was too short to be covered with laffs or applause, he could cover it with the sound of a nervous cough he had isolated from the audience tape and put on a separate cassette.

He used one cough for a short pop and a smoker's double-cough for a more sustained glitch.

Fraser recalled that in one difficult sweetening session, the tape required so many coughs due to tape-edited pickup shots and obscenities that when the show went on the air it sounded like the audience suffered from advanced cases of tuberculosis.

The Infamous Black Box

Charlie Douglas was an engineer at KNX in Hollywood. While there, he built and perfected what is generally acknowledged as the first laff machine.

An early CBS version of a multiple head tape laff machine (photograph courtesy of Walt Pierson).

Little is known of this mysterious machine because of Douglas' fear of it being copied. He kept a wary eye and a large padlock on it at all times.

Douglas' secret was so well guarded that each time there was a technical problem with it, he would take his black box out of the control room to repair it.

One producer, exasperated with the amount of time this took, shouted to Douglas, "You and the black box stay—we'll leave!"

The ability to play a number of different audience reaction tapes in one unit, *at the same time*, was the technical breakthrough needed in order to make realistic audience reactions a reality.

Douglas actually recorded on tape the reactions of the audiences he was going to be augmenting. These were broken down into a continuous applause, a three-second starting applause, and a three-second ending applause.

So much for the applause tracks. The laff tracks were more involved. These he broke down into the following categories: Large laughs, medium laughs, small laughs, giggles, chuckles and titters.

Each of these tapes was placed on its own rotating disk that passed in front of a playback head that was controlled by individual volume controls. By cross-fading from one track to another, the operator could fulfill the not-so-funny comedian's impossible dream.

Although Douglas' black box got the jump on the industry by augmenting laughs on such shows as *I Love Lucy*, help was soon to come from an improbable source—the Disneyland Magic Kingdom.

As it happened, one of the problems Disneyland faced was how to disseminate the hundreds of instructions, announcements and other vital bits of information the "guests" (Walt Disney insisted the paying public be referred to as "guests") needed as they stepped into never-never land. Using the little people who were parading around in their sweaty little costumes disguised as rodents wasn't the answer. Nor was it cost-effective.

The solution to the theme park's informational problem came with the invention of a continuous loop cartridge machine by a young engineer named Lou MacKenzie.

Now if you took the boat ride through the African jungle, for instance, when the boat passed a certain point on the river, an electronic solenoid would be activated and the head of a ferocious looking rhinoceros would suddenly lift out of the water. This in turn would activate a MacKenzie tape of a terrifying rhinoceros roar, which in turn would trigger your three-year-old daughter to scream, wet her pants and drop her $20 Mickey Mouse hat in the Congo River.

The working system of the tapes in the MacKenzie were too similar to Charlie Douglas' black box to be ignored. And so CBS finally decided to give the MacKenzie a try at doing both sound effects and audience reactions.

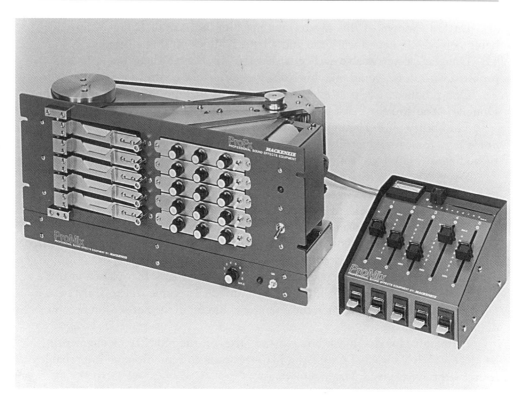

The MacKenzie Continuous Loop Machine (photograph courtesy of MacKenzie Labs).

Laffs Come to New York

Ed Sullivan, of course, always did his show live. But because of the vagaries of live television, and especially the vagaries of the live *Ed Sullivan Show*, every once in a while an act would be canceled in rehearsal and a replacement needed immediately. Rather than go through the panic of rehearing these new acts at the last minute, it was decided to tape a number of different acts and have these tapes available for any and all emergencies.

Why Tom Buchanon and I were selected to "sweeten" the show, God only knows. To begin with, we had never heard of the word *sweeten*, which was a Hollywood term. And secondly, the only thing we knew about this prototype MacKenzie Repeater was how to turn it on and what buttons to hit. We knew little or nothing about how the machine worked or what was inside it that made it work.

The first taped stand-by act that we were asked to sweeten was a circus act involving trained bears. All that was needed was applause as the bears made their entrance. The rest was already on tape.

During rehearsals our MacKenzie tapes worked fine. But when we went to do a "take" (a recording), the cartridges began spitting out our applause tapes in messy, twisted piles! Neither one of us had any idea of what was wrong or, more importantly, how to fix it. We slid open the glass door that separated the audio part of the booth from the video portion and apologized to the director for the "minor" delay. (*Minor*, hell! It was a catastrophe!)

While the director explained to Sullivan that there would be a few minutes' delay, we opened the MacKenzie with the desperate hope that merely by doing this it would somehow demonstrate that we knew what the hell we were doing. Fortunately, both Tom and I saw the problem immediately! Our applause tapes were twisted and intertwined around a confusion of imposing-looking electronic parts.

As we continued to stare at our electronic disaster, the director kept calling over in an increasingly agitated voice, "How much longer, guys?"

Tom had more nerve than I did, so he answered, and we hoped his voice wouldn't reflect the panic we felt. "We see the problem," he called out bravely. What Tom's seemingly assured voice didn't disclose was that "seeing" a problem is not quite the same as "fixing." Neither of us had a clue what to do.

The next voice we heard was that of Sullivan calling from the stage. "What's the holdup? I haven't got all night…"

Out of the corner of my eye I saw a lone turntable. I had brought an old applause record just in case of some unforeseen disaster. And if this wasn't an unforeseen disaster it was close enough. As I called over to the director to give us another minute, Tom shot me a look of utter disbelief. I then opened my briefcase, showed him the record and told the audioman, Bobby Miller, to open up the pot to the turntable.

Slamming the cover of the MacKenzie shut, Tom went through the motions of pushing buttons while I, with my back to the director, played the Prime Minister Churchill applause record.

With the completion of the sweetening, a grateful director came in and praised us, and the MacKenzie, for fine work!

When the director left, the audioman simply shook his head in disgust. "You sound-effect guys would take the pennies off a dead man's eyes." If he only knew.

Sanford and Son

Aaron Rubin was one of the class producers in television. He started his career as a comedy writer for the legendary Fred Allen in radio and later wrote for *Your Show of Shows*, starring Imogene Coca and Sid Caesar. Among his producing credits was *Gomer Pyle, U.S.M.C.* and, of course, *Sanford and Son*.

What made Rubin stand out as a producer was his insistence on making certain all the laff tracks and reactions we used were actually taken from the *Sanford and Son* audience. What's more, he never imposed his will over that of the studio audience.

If a joke or a situation didn't get a laugh when it was done in the studio, it didn't get a laff in sweetening. The only exceptions were when there had been technical delays during the taping and several audience members were forced to leave because of the late hour.

Because *Sanford and Son* was one of the first shows to have an all-black cast, it attracted a largely black audience anxious for both the show and Foxx to succeed in a largely white-dominated television. If this was a breakthrough for Foxx, it was a breakthrough for his race as well. As a result, the show had a very responsive and supportive audience.

Was the show funny? Very funny. All the time? Well, most of the time. Was the audience enthusiastic? Very. And although most of the humor was devoid of racial overtones, every once in a while there would be a line or a look on the part of Foxx that hit home with a segment of the audience that understood its true meaning.

The ensuing laughs weren't in a strict sense laughs; they were the audience's way of communicating to Foxx that they understood and enjoyed his inside joke's implied meaning. We marked those simply "Foxx laffs."

At one time the laff tracks that Douglas used sweetening the *I Love Lucy* show could have been interchanged with the laughs used on Jackie Gleason's *The Honeymooners*. Just as the laughs used on *The Brady Bunch* could have been interchanged with *Father Knows Best*. Those days are no longer around.

All in the Family probably started it. Can you imagine finding a laugh track from *The Beverly Hillbillies* that would be suitable for the audience's surprised (shocked?) reaction when Sammy Davis, Jr., kissed the bigoted Archie Bunker? Or the laughter that greeted the sound effect of an Archie Bunker toilet flush?

One of the problems with this type of humor is that the person sweetening the show has to use laughs that match those on the tape from the live audience. As a result, there is no such thing anymore as a "typical audience."

Chico and the Man had much in common with the Redd Foxx show. Both were breakthroughs in ethnic comedy series. And whereas Foxx attracted a largely black audience, Freddie Prinze's popularity among the Hispanic section of Los Angeles bordered on hero worship. This meant, in addition to having every conceivable kind of laffs, we had to have other libraries containing every conceivable kind of laffs for a particular ethnic audience.

As a result, it was time to give all those good folks that had been residing on tapes in our laff machine all those years a decent burial. Their days of laughing at *My Three Sons*, the *Brady Bunch*, and *Gilligan's Island* were over. May they rest in peace.

Who Are Those Funny Fellows?

With the introduction of computers, razor blade editing became obsolete. No longer was it necessary to depend on the skills of the tape editors—or the laff men and ladies. Now with the push of a button, complicated editing that formerly took hours could be done in seconds. And without the risk of a bad edit, a pop or having to use a nervous cough!

Audio equipment also improved. No longer were laffs done with the limitations of the MacKenzie. Nor did producers have to depend on the timing and dexterity of laff men to manipulate a number of tapes to produce a desired result. Computer driven CDs solved all those old-fashioned methods.

With each succeeding sweetening session, not only did our equipment and laff tracks improve, but producers began becoming increasingly involved with judgment calls, deciding what was, and what wasn't, funny. Suddenly, being a laff person with a keen sense of humor was more of a detriment than a plus.

Ray Erlenborn, CBS–Hollywood and Charlie Douglas were two of the first laff men to sweeten shows in early television. Douglas worked on *I Love Lucy* and Erlenborn on Red Skelton's show.

Because of Erlenborn's comedy background on stage and in films, he was one of the most sought-after laff men during the earlier days of sweetenings. One reason for his popularity may have been his understanding of comedian-audience interaction, which he developed as an adolescent. "From the time I was nine years old up until I was fourteen," he recalls, "I performed along with other juvenile entertainers from Seattle to San Diego. During the five years when I did as many as five shows a day, I would spend all my free time watching the other comedians on the bill. I got to the point where I would stand offstage and mimic their timing until I knew where every laugh came in every routine used by over a hundred comedians."

When I asked Erlenborn how much of an advantage his background as a comedian gave him, he simply shrugged and replied, "Only in the early days. Later on, if I wanted to keep doing audience reactions on many of the shows, I had to keep my sense of humor under my hat."

Tom Buchanon, also of CBS, was another excellent sound-effect and laff man. Like Erlenborn, Buchanon had a show business background that allowed him to cultivate the sense of timing he'd later need sweetening shows. In addition to being a juvenile actor in radio, he was the son of a prominent director and producer with the prestigious advertising agency Young and Rubicam. Buchanon recalls that his laff man skills were developed indirectly from his acting experiences: "I learned my timing from being a young actor on radio in both dramatic roles and commercials. If you can't do your lines in thirty seconds on a thirty second commercial, having a father as the director isn't going to get you a job on a commercial."

Tom recalls how his first experience on the *Sonny and Cher Show* would draw upon his entire store of skills—and patience:

> For whatever reasons, only the musical portions of the show were done before an audience. This meant that all the audience reactions for the comedy sketches came from the machine. In a way this was good. There wasn't the problem of

matching your laughs with what little laughs the audience may have given a joke. On the other hand, it could be a nightmare.

My first problem occurred when Cher twitched her right eye. The producer, standing behind me, yelled, "You missed it!"

Without turning, I answered, "Missed what?"

"Cher's eye twitch!"

"I just thought she had something in her eye or it was a nervous tic."

"Hell no! The audience loves it! It isn't a scream but it's a big laugh!"

For the life of me I didn't know how the producer knew the audience "loved" it, because there was no one in the audience. Very often producers get confused as to what the "audience" loves and what the writers and production people love. Anyway, I gave Cher's old eye-twitch shtick a laugh—not too big, not too small. Just something appropriate for an eye-twitch.

The laughs were no more out of the machine when I heard her voice again. "No, no, no! Wrong type of laugh! This is a woman's thing. Give me a woman's laugh."

Believe it or not, I did have a cart of laughs where women were predominantly heard. And, believe it or not, she bought them on the first pass of laying them in. But I wasn't out of the woods yet. She then ordered me to save that laugh because there were so many more eye-twitches coming up!

To understand how lucky I was to hit the right laugh on the first try, a laff cartridge often contains a dozen different laughs. Although they are all similar, they are not all alike. The only person on God's earth that can tell the difference of course is a nit-picking producer in a post-production room.

When the next eye-twitch came up, I again gave Cher a hearty women's laugh, but it wasn't the same women's laugh I had given her earlier—similar, but not the same. And the producer told me so. I therefore had to play all of the twelve laughs until we came to the one laugh out of twelve that the producer liked. Which meant if I was a beat slow or fast laying that one laugh on tape, we had to play all of the laughs again until that one laugh recycled.

I'll spare you the rest, but that one sweetening session lasted for 24 hours! And when it was over, the producer stretched, yawned and smiled [saying], "Great sweetening. This is the shortest time it's ever taken!"

On another occasion, Buchanon was sent to post-production to sweeten a show that had been shot without an audience. As the tape began rolling, the producer in back of him called out cheerfully, "Make it funny."

As the tape continued to roll, Tom hadn't put in so much as a snicker. "What the hell are you doing!" cried the astonished producer. "Where are the laughs?" Tom, without turning replied, "I'm saving them for something funny to happen." "Something funny!" she barked back. "That's what you're here for—to *make* the damn thing funny!"

Perhaps the most blatant rejection of reality happened between a producer of a comedy show pilot and an NBC vice president in charge of comedy development.

During the studio taping of the show, no one in the audience laughed or so much as smiled. Most just got up and left before it was over, including the lady from NBC Comedy Development.

A few days later she received a phone call from the producer of the ill-fated pilot begging her to come to the post-production room. Hoping for a miracle she hadn't witnessed in the studio, she reluctantly agreed.

When she arrived, the producer greeted her with unbridled enthusiasm. "Wait 'til you see it. You're gonna love it!"

What she saw and was supposed to "love," was nothing more than the edited version of the dreadful show she had walked out on in the studio! Turning angrily to the producer, she complained, "It's the same show! All you did is add machine laffs!" The producer, undaunted by her tone of voice, nodded his agreement and bubbled enthusiastically: "I know! But did you hear *those* laughs! I *told* you the damn show was funny!"

CHAPTER 18

Is It Sound Effects or Foleying?

Foley is the movie version of radio's sound effects. It refers to the art of creating effects on film with your hands, feet, or other expendable body parts. I say "expendable" because when your art form demands that you splinter doors, shatter bottles, break windows, shoot off rifles, and wield razor sharp knives, swords, or machetes, the creativity that goes into making the noises demands risk-taking.

The reason for the inclusion of a film term in a book about live broadcasting came about when I was doing sound effects on *Chico and the Man* at NBC. During an early rehearsal, a young producer came into my sound-effects room to give me some script changes.

As he turned to leave, his eyes suddenly swept over the various manual effects in the room: a 1932 Ford car door, a glass crash box, a screen door, a genuine Las Vegas one-armed-bandit slot machine and a dozen other smaller manual effects neatly positioned on shelves and in drawers around the room.

The young producer's eyes widened with the excitement of a child on Christmas morning. When he wasn't opening and slamming the vintage car door, he was seeing what he won on the slot machine.

"What the hell are all these things?"

The question came as a shock. First I turned to see if he was kidding. But he wasn't. And yet I still couldn't understand how anyone, especially someone in television, wasn't aware of the role that these manual effects had played in making the Golden Age of live radio so truly golden. Then I saw how young he was. My 1932 Ford car door was probably older than his grandfather.

"We used all these effects in radio."

Before I could continue, his eyes opened wide and he almost shouted, "Jeezchrist! You did radio!"

He made it sound like I invented it.

"Did you ever do that guy that yelled, 'Hi yo, Silver'? What was his name?

"The Lone Ranger."

He snapped his fingers. "That's the guy!"

Guy? He called the Lone Ranger a *guy*!

"Name some other radio shows you did!"

"To begin with, I didn't do the Lone Ranger. That came out of—"

"Whatever!" He then eyed me suspiciously. "Name some of the shows you did Foley on."

"Sound effects," I corrected. "In radio it was called—"

"Whatever! Name some."

"I did quite a few."

"Name some."

I couldn't figure out if he was just in a hurry, impatient, or simply a pain in the ass. But very often, producers were all three. And despite his age, he was a producer. I started with "*Perry Mason.*"

"Hold it! That was a television show!"

"But it was a radio show first."

"Well I'll be damned! Name some more shows you did."

Rather than just naming some more shows, I decided to jump to the one show that even the producer, as young as he was, had to be familiar with.

"I also did *Gangbusters.*"

"You did *Gangbusters*?"

I knew that one would get him. In response, I simply gave him a modest nod.

"*Gangbusters* was a *radio* show? Hell, I just thought it was an expression! Like 'coming on like gangbusters!' You know what I mean?"

An expression! *Gangbusters* an "*expression*!" I felt the hairs on the back of my neck stiffen. It was unthinkable that this action-packed drama was now being remembered as nothing more than an *expression*!

Didn't he know that Saturday night wouldn't have been Saturday night without the exciting sound effects of marching feet, machine guns and sirens? Or without Phillips H. Lord's G-men screeching off in cars in search of the nation's worst criminals? I could have saved my breath. He was playing the slot machine again.

"No bullshit, now—you know how all this Foley stuff works?"

"In addition to knowing how this *stuff* works," I answered with righteous indignation, "I know how to get sounds out of them! Only back in radio we didn't call it Foley. We called it—"

"Could you make the sound of a milkman leading his horse walking slowly on cobblestones?"

Was he serious? I told him I could even make the milkman's horse walk, trot, gallop or, if in a pinch, fart!

If I hoped to startle him, I failed miserably. He took my announcement as a fact of life. But what I had told him was true. How a sound so obviously flatulent ever got on a commercial sound-effects record back in those primrose days of live radio I have no idea, but it had. And according to Ray Kemper, CBS–Hollywood, he and Pat Hanley, also of CBS, had often used it during the *Gunsmoke* "dirty Saturday" rehearsals.

Veteran Foley artist Ken Dufva poised to either shoot, stab, or give himself a nasty cut. Ken started at Paramount Pictures as a film editor. Then, as the art of Foley became increasingly popular, he switched to Foleying and created sounds for over 400 films, including **Star Trek: Generations, Clear** *and* **Present Danger** *and* **Robocop** *(photograph courtesy of Ken Dufva).*

But back to our excited, wide-eyed young producer.

"No bullshit, now! You really can Foley?"

"No bullshit. I really can."

Instead of responding, he turned his back and began rummaging in a drawer where some of the smaller sound effects were kept. Turning, he held up a small lyre-shaped metal instrument about three inches long containing a metal tongue that was plucked while being held in the teeth and used to produce small, tremolo sounds.

"What the hell was this used for?"

"To make small boings."

"What was it called?"

"A Jew's harp."

His eyebrows shot up. "A *Jew's* harp? And nobody complained?"

"About what?"

"About it being called a Jew?"

"That was the name of it. It was a traditional instrument in Israel."

"I know, but why wasn't it called something less ethnic, like a Hebrew harp?"

"Because its real name is Jew's harp, and back then it never seemed to bother anyone. Like Polish sausages, Irish stew, Hungarian goulash, French kisses…"

The young producer wasn't even listening. He quickly dropped the harp back in the drawer and pulled out two less politically controversial sound effects: my battered, old sound-effects shoes that I used for doing footsteps. As he turned them over, I beat him to the punch.

"The heels are made of wood to give a good solid sound when we did footsteps in radio for men and women."

The young producer just shook his head in amazement. "Amazing! To think you did Foley way back in radio! Freaking amazing!"

I just nodded and replied, "Ain't it the freaking truth."

Before It Was Called Foley

In 1951, Jack Foley, a sound-effects editor for many years with Universal Studios, was working on a film titled *Smuggler's Island*, starring Jeff Chandler. Upon the film's completion, the director wasn't satisfied with the sound of the Pacific Ocean. He therefore called on the talents of Foley to make the ocean water sound "wetter."

When Foley viewed the scene requiring the effects, he found it involved a pilot (Jeff Chandler) who had crash-landed in the Pacific. Foley decided that rather than do the waves and boat-paddling sounds in the more conventional and time-consuming method of using the sounds from Universal's library of film sounds, he would do the water effects live in the studio manually with a large tank of water.

When the director screened the work Foley had done, he was so impressed with the efficiency and speed of this technique that he sang the praises of Foley to anyone who would listen.

And listen they did. It wasn't long before all the young Hollywood directorial lions began requesting that the sounds for their films be done the way "Foley" did it. And thus was born unto Hollywood a new and wonderful buzzword to set the cleansed apart from the unwashed multitude.

In fairness to all the sound-effects people that labored in films, it should be observed that Jack Foley neither invented nor improved this technique. And Jack would be the first to admit this fact. His name simply became identified with doing synchronized sound effects manually.

Ed Bernds, who directed some of the *Three Stooges* shorts, was at one time a sound mixer. In 1929, Columbia Pictures decided to make the silent film *Submarine* into a sound movie of a sort by adding sound effects. Bernds recalled working all night on the sound-dubbing stage trying to sync noises *live* while watching the action on the screen.

One other name that precedes the term *Foley* is MacDonald—Jimmy MacDonald. If anyone should be given the credit of enhancing the art of synchronizing effects live to films, it should be this artist.

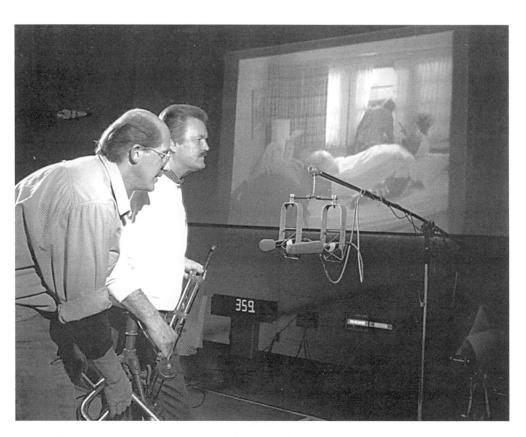

Above: *Bob Kline, WOR, goes all the way in making the sound of water not only wetter, but noisier. To the radio sound-effects artists over at WOR, this splash tank was referred to as the "Queen Mary" (photograph courtesy of Barney Beck).*

Opposite, top: *Ken Dufva (right) and his partner David Lee Fein caught in the act of Foleying. Dufva and Fein have to keep their eyes on the large screen for any signs of movement that might require sounds from the props they're holding. As a safety factor, and for convenience, the sounds that Ken and David are making are recorded on audio tape. If for any reason they don't match exactly with those on the screen, or the sounds are too soft or too loud, the sequence is done over until it meets with everyone's satisfaction.*

The reason for the double mikes is that the scene they're doing is in stereo. What David creaks and squeaks on the left, Ken creaks and squeaks it on the right (photograph courtesy of Ken Dufva).

Opposite, bottom: *Dufva and Fein demonstrate how to do what perhaps God found unnecessary—make the Pacific Ocean sound wetter (photograph courtesy of Ken Dufva).*

MacDonald, like many of the early sound-effects artists, started out as a drummer. In 1934, MacDonald's band was hired to do the music for a Mickey Mouse cartoon. After providing the normal assortment of drummer's *traps* (*traps* is short for "contraptions")—the slide whistles, wood blocks, wind whistles and bird twitters—MacDonald became interested in his drummer's ability to provide sound effects, rather than music.

Although being a drummer was a tremendous help to MacDonald in capturing the correct speed and rhythm of various sounds, he still had to be aware of the seven other components that go into the making of a sound: pitch, timbre, harmonics, loudness, attack, sustain and decay (the time it takes a sound to completely fade).

When any sound, no matter the source, has a similar amount of these nine components, it will sound the same. Is the sound of a gunshot not the same as that of a car backfiring? And hoofbeats—don't two coconut shells pretty much sound the same? Or can't the sound of gentle waves be made with rolling BBs carefully around the head of a bass drum?

Helping MacDonald with the sounds in those early Mickey Mouse cartoons was the orchestra. At that time it was customary to synchronize the actions in a Disney cartoon with either sound effects or music.

The Mickey Mouse cartoons, perhaps more than other cartoons of the day, were characterized by their use of this technique. Because of that, music written to synchronize with the action in a film was called "Mickey Mousing."

Today, there are all types of electronic equipment that can bend and twist sound waves at the touch of a key, whereas MacDonald had to painstakingly hunt and peck his sounds from household objects and junkyard discards. However he did it, he did it well, and often: the Disney Sound Effects Library contains 28,000 sounds—give or take a dozen—attributed to the creative mind of Jimmy Mac-Donald.

In addition to all this, when Disney got tired of doing the voice of Mickey Mouse in the mid-forties, MacDonald took over doing the falsetto voice of the moneymaking little rodent.

So Is It Sound Effects or Foleying?

There is absolutely no difference between the way the art of sound effects and the Foley art is done. They both had their humble beginnings from vaudeville and people like Tommy MacDonald and Ora and Arthur Nichols.

If you compare the efficiency and results of the two ways of doing sound effects, Foley wins, hands down. But think of the downside of Foleying. What it gains with high-tech equipment and working in nearly ideal acoustical isolation, it loses in the human factor.

This photo was taken about the time that MacDonald was working at Disney. Pictured from left to right are Ora Nichols, Van Brackel, Walt Pierson, Max Uhlig, Henry Gauthier and Vic Rhubei. Ora Nichols and her husband Arthur were responsible for starting the first Sound Effects department at CBS (photograph courtesy of Walt Pierson).

The Foley Stage

Foleying today is done in the relative seclusion of a post-production sound stage. There are no directors, actors, musicians, curious clients, client's guests or fascinated audiences watching your every move. Normally the only other person in the studio is the Foley mixer.

The Foley mixer, like the audio engineer in radio, is responsible for adjusting the sound volume and balance of the various sounds the Foley artists create. The advantage that the Foley mixers have over the radio engineers is that, while radio was live, Foley is taped (and taped and taped and taped—ad infinitum).

Once the sounds are on tape—and there can be many tapes—he then sends them to the sound editor, who transfers the Foley sounds onto a master sound track that will also contain the actors' dialogue and music tracks. Three sound tracks are used so they can be edited individually without disturbing the overall sound of the master tape.

The Radio Studio

The heart of any radio show, large or small, was the control room. It was here that the director had the final say about both *what* was said and *how* it was said over the air.

Seated next to the director was the second most important person in the room, the audio engineer. It was his job to pull switches and turn knobs in a certain way so that all the words and sounds the director approved of got to the transmitter and out over the air.

These two were the sound-effect artists' mortal enemies. The director criticized how, when, and what we did, while the audio mixer made damn certain our sounds conformed to the FCC's (Federal Communications Commission) rigid laws of how loud or how soft our sounds could be.

In live radio, because the actors, musicians and sound-effects artists were all in the same studio at the same time, it was up to the audio person to balance the three together into one homogeneous sound.

Not having the actors or musicians in the same studio with us in live radio was unthinkable. Each of us was dependent upon the creative energy of the others.

A show like *Sorry Wrong Number* was a joy to work since there was no creating special sound effects and hoping the director would buy the sounds you created. And yet, even with a sound as simple as a phone ring, there were some directors who would find something wrong with it.

The Visual Directors

The visual directors of radio were by far the most difficult to work with. These were the ones whose eyes took dominance over their ears; in other words, what they saw influenced what they heard.

Even though we used actual telephone bells for the ringing sound, because the bells weren't attached to a telephone, a visual director would complain the ringing didn't sound like it was coming from a telephone.

And if you were unlucky enough to have the sound of a bubbling volcano in the same script with eating a breakfast of oatmeal, you knew you were in big trouble.

The director might accept the sound of boiling a pot of oatmeal for the sound of boiling a pot of oatmeal, but he sure as hell wouldn't accept boiling the same pot of oatmeal (closer to the microphone) for the sound of a bubbling volcano!

Barney Beck, whose regular show at WOR was *The Shadow*, was asked to do a Christmas radio show with a director noted for her reputation as one of those "visual directors." Upon nervously reading the script, Barney was relieved to find the only sound called for was that of a crackling fire in the fireplace. Knowing

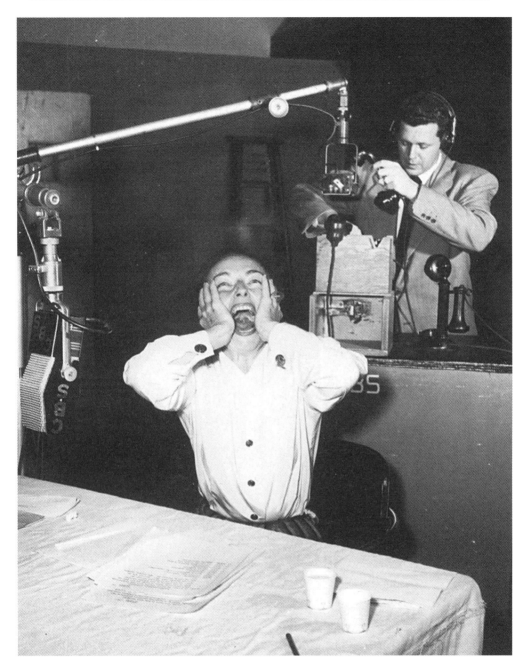

The relation between the actors and Sound Effects often became extremely intense. Shown are Agnes Moorehead and David Light, doing the radio thriller **Sorry Wrong Number.** *David is dependent on Agnes for his cue lines to ring the phone, and Agnes is dependent upon David to ring the phone at just the precise moment. Too soon or too late would affect her performance (photograph courtesy of David Light).*

Obviously they were both happy with what the other did. Although it could be terribly stressful doing sound effects live in this manner, the rewards, as you can see in this picture, were worth it (photograph courtesy of David Light).

that even a diehard visual director couldn't complain about the time-honored use of cellophane for the fire effect, Barney was lulled into a false sense of security.

Therefore, when the cue came, Barney gently crackled his cellophane with little fear of abusive criticism. Then, as Barney began putting the cellophane away for the air show, the director requested an additional sound that wasn't in the script. Such last-second demands were the reason sound-effects people drank.

"Barney, on page 22, I want to hear the sound of Beth unwrapping her present. Let me hear what you're going to use for the sound of cellophane."

Working in the same radio studio, at the same time with the actors and musicians, created its own headaches. In addition to the visual directors, there was always someone who felt obligated to give his opinion of what an effect should sound like, especially if the effect was a difficult one. (Remember that actor from Alaska criticizing my iceberg sound?)

Although I'm sure these comments weren't always made to embarrass the hell out of us, they were made often enough for us to want to see what radio would be like without actors.

What really annoyed us was that the actors were often right. Many of the effects did sound terrible. But there was a reason.

When you worked at a network you didn't do just the *Jack Benny Show* or the *Lone Ranger*. Often times, if you were doing prime-time programs, you might do five shows in a week, while those who did the soaps normally squeezed in two soaps in one day.

This meant that in spite of the hundreds of manual and recorded effects, there were always some sounds that were better and therefore more in demand. These of course were grabbed first by the artists who did the shows that had the highest ratings. This left the artists with the lower-rated shows the unenviable job of trying to "sell" (get approval for) effects that were not their first or even their third choice.

The art of selling effects in live radio was sometimes harder to do than the actual effects. Especially if you were dealing with a tough director who was influenced by what they saw you using.

Barney Beck of WOR recalls trying to get approval from a visual director for the sound of a punch.

"I punched my leather wallet with leather gloves and without leather gloves; I punched my wallet with bills in it and without them. I punched sandbags, hit a baseball catcher's mitt, even smacked a bowling pin with a rubber mallet—nothing satisfied her. And she let me know it."

"I don't get the feeling that those punches really hurt!" she complained.

Barney, still nursing his sore knuckles, replied, "But I've hit everything I can think of—except maybe you."

Barney remembers "Even though I said it with a big smile, she still kicked me off the show."

Ray Erlenborn demonstrates the fine art of "selling" his sound effects for the **Texaco Star Theater** *back in 1939. The two people seated on the left in the control room are unidentified, while the unimpressed director on the right is Ed "Archie" Gardner of* **Duffy's Tavern** *radio fame (photograph courtesy of Ray Erlenborn).*

Layering Sounds

Doing sounds manually in radio usually meant doing them one at a time. If, for instance, Barney had four or five hands, he could have satisfied the picky director. He could have punched his wallet, whacked the catcher's mitt, slapped the boxing glove and smacked the bowling pin with the rubber mallet all at the same time!

That's what *layering* sounds means—adding one or more sounds on top of one another to achieve a totally new sound.

For the punching sounds heard in the *Raging Bull* and *Rocky* movies (all four of them), Ken Dufva didn't have to resort to selling, because the film's director wasn't interested in how Ken went about making the sounds, or even what Ken used; he was interested only in how they enhanced the excitement of his film's fight scenes.

If you recall, the accepted way of doing a punch in radio was to hit your wallet with your fist. Contrast this with the way Dufva assembled and layered the sounds of his punches:

> For many of the punching sounds, we used boxing gloves and hit ourselves on the legs, arms and chests. We then used the gloves to hit tires, a rubber mallet to smack a piece of 6" × 6" block of wood, and a baseball bat to pound an old leather saddle.
>
> We would then start all over again and hit them a number of different ways for variety. After we taped a number of those sounds, my partner, David Lee Fein, and I would strike two different objects at the same time—David hitting the tire while I smacked the saddle.
>
> When we were finally satisfied with the sounds we had made, we'd send them to Frank Warner, the sound-effect editor. He would then play our sounds on one tape and add other sounds to our hits to give them a bigger sound. Some of the sounds he added to our punches were a piece of a clap of thunder, a lion roar, or a gunshot to make it sound like the requested "shattering" punch on the jaw!

Layering becomes even more elaborate for sounds such as explosions, those modern movie staples:

> In creating the sound of an explosion we may use as many as eight tracks or more. Each sound that we do gets its own track. For instance, for the sound of a building exploding we would *lay down* [record] the following sounds:
> Track #1. We may splinter some wood.
> Track #2. Pieces of wood falling.
> Track #3. Large glass bulbs and panes of glass shattering.
> Track #4. Pieces of glass raining down.
> Track #5. Rocks and bricks falling.
> Track #6. Dust (sand falling).
> If the sound is in stereo, we do it all again for the left side. That brings the sound of the explosion up to 12 tracks, and usually, many, many more according to the needs of the picture.

Layering Sounds the Old-Fashioned Way

In live radio, we layered sounds in one of two ways, either with the help of other artists or with records. (See the appendix for the recorded sounds common to all the networks.)

If, for instance, we wanted to create the sound of a dinosaur, we first had to decide what a dinosaur sounded like. After that, we'd mix recordings of a lion roaring, an elephant trumpeting and a tiger snarling. We would then play the records at a slower speed and this became the standard sound for all radio dinosaurs.

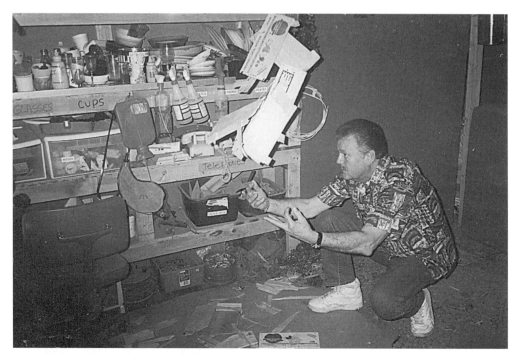

Ken tosses the pieces of wood that will become Track #2 in the overall sound of the explosion (photograph courtesy of Ken Dufva).

Interestingly enough, the public must have bought this sound, because even Spielberg, with all the advantages of computers, didn't dare change such a widely accepted sound when he made his blockbuster *Jurassic Park*.

Doing sound effects on a busy radio show often required providing multiple sounds at the same time, which is just another way of layering. Only, when many of the sounds have to be done manually, it requires additional hands. Sometimes 16 of them!

The record number of sound artists used on one show at CBS in New York was eight. The show was *Moby Dick*. Although using so many artists might seem excessive, it wasn't. Not if the director wanted to hear every squeak of a windlass, every luft of a sail, every creak of an oarlock. Indeed, it often took several people to create the lush sounds that evoked for the radio listener the images that were the true purpose of any radio sound effect.

What was it like working with several other sound-effects people? Crowded as hell! It almost required the talents of a Busby Berkeley to choreograph where everyone stood without getting goosed by Ahab's harpoon, or an errant épée!

What act do you think of when I mention the word *condom*? Well, I suppose you could use it for that, but Ken Dufva stretched one over a microphone and placed it in a tank of water to create underwater sounds for the movie *The Hunt for Red October*.

Sound-effects artist Tommy Evans operates NBC's *answer to cutting down on the number of artists needed for the sound of a wagon train. The eccentric offsets on the revolving drum activate the hooves in proper rhythm. Surfaces under the hooves were interchangeable to simulate different terrains (photograph courtesy of National Broadcasting Company).*

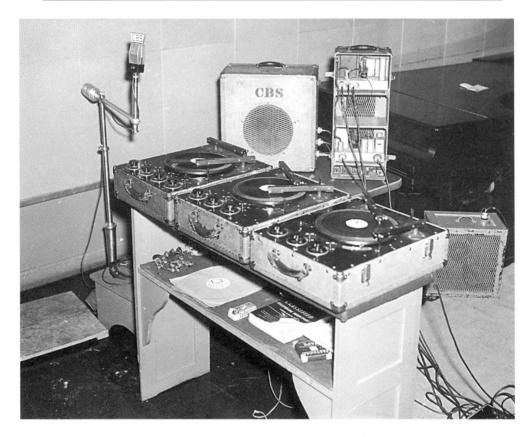

This photograph shows the turntables we used for layering an explosion in radio. If we couldn't do it with three records, we'd request a sound artist to play additional records on another turntable console (photograph courtesy of Malachy Wienges).

And when the movie *Ghostbusters* needed the sound of "ghosts seeping through a keyhole," Ken got a glob of Jell-O, wrapped it in a towel, and by squeezing it in a certain way, convinced moviegoers that ghosts were indeed squeezing through the keyhole.

The demand for unusual Foley sounds are more numerous and demanding than they ever were in radio. Despite the fact that the Foley artists do the sound effects for a visual medium, the improved speakers in the theaters, the larger screens and the increased use of camera closeups demand a greater number of effects.

Is It Junk or Sound Effects?

If you've ever moved, had a garage sale, or simply decided to clean out your attic, you know what a difficult job it is to get rid of things. And if you want

This photograph reveals how many swords it took to make **The Prisoner of Zenda** *sound authentic on the radio. Helping out with the swordplay is movie star Ronald Colman (fourth from left). In the background is the control room where the director watches every parry and thrust the sound artists make. Shown from left to right: Parker Cornell, Virgil Reimer, Bob Conlon, Colman, Fred Cole, Tiny Lamb and Floyd Caton (photograph courtesy of NBC).*

to make the job impossible, have a sound-effects artist—Foley or radio—help you.

What you may have thought was junk, the artist might look upon as a priceless treasure. Like that useless, hideous clock you received from your mother-in-law. You know the clock I mean—that pink and gold, fat-cheeked cherub with the timepiece stuck like a jewel in the belly? The one that chimes out the hours by flapping its wings? Useless? Hideous? Perhaps. But only a Foley artist knows the true value of a wing-flapping old cherub's clock chime!

No doubt about it: Foley artists are a resourceful bunch. It simply boggles the mind what sounds a couple of these folks can produce with a few basic materials and a little space to lay them out. Consider, for instance, the myriad possible sounds of footsteps. Well, Foley artists can cover nearly the entire range with a few square feet of concrete, slate, gravel, sand, carpet, linoleum and dirt. Further, with a few rocks, they have nearly all they need for rugged, outdoor sounds in an action-packed adventure flick. And what about snow, you ask? That's done by rhythmically squeezing a chamois bag of cornstarch with your hands. For the sounds of dogs running or walking over a hardwood floor, simply slip on a pair

Top: *Jack Amrhein, CBS–New York, shows sentimentality doesn't enter into a radio sound-effects artist quest for the perfect clock chime (photograph courtesy of Malachy Wienges).*

Bottom: *And what kind of monstrous father would steal his only son's bazooka water gun? Why, a Foley father, of course! In this case, David Lee Fein (photograph courtesy of Ken Dufva).*

If you look closely at these cluttered shelves, you'll find items you've heard in dozens of movies. See that punching bag? That did some serious punching sounds for the movie **Rocky.** *And the shoes in those baskets? They walked in the footsteps of some of Hollywood's biggest stars! (Photograph courtesy of Ken Dufva.)*

of large cotton work gloves that have rivets fastened to the fingertips for the sound of the dog's nails hitting surfaces.

And because the Foley artists have the time, budget and equipment that allows them to layer effects, one artist can do the footsteps for a man *and*, on another track, do the steps for a woman. Then in post-production both tracks would be mixed together for the sound of the man and woman walking together.

In live radio, this was impossible. As a result, if a show was too cheap to have more than one artist doing the separate steps, you might be forced, as Michael Eisenmenger of NBC-Chicago was, to do the work (see photograph on page 210) of two people.

Another thing that the sound-effect artists of live radio and television shared with their brethren Foley artists was the need of vocal artists. Some sounds simply defied mechanical, electronic or manual re-creation.

One of the most memorable examples of vocal artistry involved Brad Barker, the man who, in addition to all of his work in radio, television and cartoons, created MGM's signature lion roar—with his own voice!

On one radio show the script called for a ferocious grizzly bear breaking out of an airplane's cargo cage at 25,000 feet. Now, in all the records we had in sound

Revealing that Foley artists aren't the only ones with tricks up their sleeves, Michael Eisen-menger accompanies himself with a pair of women's high-heeled shoes (photograph courtesy of Robert J. Graham).

effects, there was nothing that even came close to the sound of a snarling, growling, roaring bear gone wild. But Barker was able to get out of something as unbearlike as an empty, conical shaped, cardboard orange-juice container everything he needed to create the effect of the scariest bear you've ever heard! He threw back his head, his body stiff and erect, his face blood red, as one terrifying roar after another erupted from that simple orange juice carton! So compelling was his performance, I found myself caught up in the grizzly's anger and frustration, and I began shaking his iron cage (an iron jail gate) with an intensity I only hoped matched that of Barker's electrifying and terrifying performance.

Which, Finally, Was Better?

For sheer technical excellence, the Foley done in film beats the sound effects of live broadcasting all hollow. But still, given the choice between films and live radio, I think I'll take the camaraderie of radio. Even if it means gnawing on wood for "The Three Glass Keys," being stabbed by an epée on *The Prisoner of Zenda*, or even goosed by a harpoon on *Moby Dick*! Compared to live radio's energy and excitement, Foleying for films doesn't even come close!

A Few Final Words

That's what it was like working on both sides of the microphone and camera during the Golden Age of live broadcasting.

Were those days really all that golden? That's for you to decide. As for me, if the phone rang tomorrow and it was live broadcasting calling, I wouldn't hesitate to ask just three questions: Do I bring my typewriter? my wooden-heeled shoes? or both?

Robert L. Mott
Arroyo Grande, California

Appendix:
Recorded Sound Effects

The following records were common to all the networks during the days of live radio and television. Although many of them have been destroyed, some of these old recorded sounds are now in computers or on compact discs. And isn't it nice to know that some sounds will never fade away, that they just become new again? Spelling and enumeration have been left as in the original document.

Voices and Applause

100-A	General confusion
B	Applause
101-A	General confusion
B	Laughing
102-A-B	General confusion ("Concert Hall")
103-A	Cheers
B	Clashing of swords
104-A-B	Restaurant noises [This record bore the following admonition: "Don't use second cut. Contains copyrighted material."]
105-A	Baby crying
B	Screams; snores; typewriters
106-A-B	Mumbling (female) (mixed)
107-A	Children laughing, playing
B	"Don't use this side" [another warning]
108-A-B	Crowd (football game)
109-A-B	Excited crowd (ball game)
110-A	Players warming up (baseball)
B	Crowd (ball game)
111-A-B	Cheers; laughter; applause
112-A-B	Fight (male) (mixed)
113-A	Applause; cheering

114-A	Applause
B	Model T Ford: continuous
	Model T Ford: start; run; stop
	Dog (collie) barking
115-A-B	Boos; hisses; wails (mixed)
116-A-B	Cheers
117-A	Confusion (large crowd at sports event)
B	Same
118-A	Confusion of voices (women)
B	Confusion of voices (small and large group of men)
119-A	Conversation and laughter (women)
B	Conversation and laughter (men)
120-A	Laughter (men and women, mixed small group)
B	Laughter (men and women, mixed large group)
121-A	Confusion of voices (mixed)
B	Same
122-A	Angry mob
B	Applause (small and large group)

Automobiles and Motorcycles

200-A	Auto: 4-cylinder, door shut; start; run
B	Auto: crashes
201-A	Auto: 6-cylinder, door shut; start; run
B	Auto: 6-cylinder, continuous running
202-A	Auto: continuous running
B	Auto: start
203-A	Auto: starter; shifts; run; stop
B	Auto: approach high speed, stop; pass at high speed
204-A	Auto: Model T Ford, continuous running
B	Auto: Model T Ford, crank, start
205-A	Auto: 8-cylinder, continuous running
B	Horns (various types)
206-A	Auto-races: passing at high speeds
B	Auto-races: continuous (dirt track)
207-A	Auto-races: passing at high speeds
B	Auto-races: start; idle; pull away
208-A	Auto (7 cuts): door; start; idle
B	Approach, squeak of brakes
209-A	Plane crash; auto-skid; auto crash
B	"Don't use this side"
210-A	Auto: start; shift gears; horn
211-A	Auto: (5 cuts) Model T Ford; crank; start; idle
B	Auto: approach; pass; recede; continuous running

212-A Motorcycle: start; run; stop; start; idle
   B   Motorcycle: approach and stop; start and pull away; passing at high speed

213-A Explosions
   B   Air hammers; tire skids (30-seconds long)

214-A Tractor: Fordson, ploughing
   B   Tractor: idle; shift and plough

215-A Auto—Packard: start and backing; tire skid and stop
   B   Diesel—electric train: arrive; stop; start run

216-A Moving car (in traffic)
   B   Moving car (no traffic)

217-A Packard: start and run
   B   Baby cries

218-A-B Auto: start; run; stop

219-A Auto races
   B   Airplane crashes; auto-skid crash

220-A Auto: starter; start and idle
   B   Old model auto: continuous

221-A Auto: continuous (old-model car)
   B   Auto horns

222-A Model T: starter; start and idle
   B   Auto horns

223-A Model T: start; idle
   B   Auto horns

224-A Model T: starter; start and idle
   B   Model T: continuous

225-A 7 ton-truck: start; run; climb steep grade; gear shift
   B   7 ton-truck: fast; idle continuous; slow; idle; clashing of gears

226-A Tractor: continuous
   B   7-ton truck: start; shifting gears; stop

See also: 611   Tractor: start; run; stop
            114-A   Applause
                B   Model T: continuous
                    Model T: start; run; stop
                    Dog (collie) barking
             504   V-8 Ford continuous running
             800   Same record as 213
             750   Tractor
             914   Auto horns
             604   Auto horns

250-A Motorcycle: start; run; stop; start and idle
   B   Motorcycle: approach and stop; start and pull away; passing at high speed

251-A Police squad car: start; run; stop
   B   Police squad car: start; pull away; approach and stop; pass at high speed

252-A Police motorcycle: start; run; stop
   B   Police motorcycle: pass at high speed; start; pull away; approach and stop

See also: 604   Fire siren; ambulance or police bell; auto horn

Airplanes

300-A	Planes: take-off; fly; land
B	Flying in circles
301-A	Plane: flying overhead (single motor and tri-motor)
B	Plane: take-off; single motor; twenty planes passing overhead
302-A	Plane: single motor; zooming and swooping
B	Landing and idling
303-A-B	Plane: takeoff; circling
304-A-B	Plane: Challenger
305-A	Plane: battery starter; takeoff and fly (Douglas)
B	Battery starter; start and idle; taxiing and revolutions up (Douglas)
306-A	Plane: flying; landing; idling (Douglas)
B	Plane: single-motor army landing and idling; single-motor Stinson landing
307-A	Plane: single-motor army; motor missing; wind in strut; landing
B	Plane: single-motor army overhead
308-A	Planes: diving and zooming (Army)
B	Planes: 13 in formation landing (Army)
309-A	Planes: 13 overhead in formation (Army)
B	Plane: (4) cuts take-offs
310-A	Planes: aerial dogfight
B	Planes: aerial dogfight with ground fire
311-A	Plane: starter; idling; take-offs; flying (Army)
B	Plane: idling and take-offs
312-A	Plane: idling; full power continuous
B	Plane: flying in circle (single motor)
313-A	Plane: power dive and crash (3 cuts); take-off
B	crowd effect (small group)
314-A-B	Airplane idling (motor boat?)
315-A	Planes: single-motor take-off
B	Planes: tri-motors take-off
316-A	Planes: airplanes racing
B	Burros braying

See also: 209   plane crash

Trains

400-A	Passenger: approach; pass; recede
B	Freight: approach; pass; recede
401-A	Passenger: start and leave station
B	Freight: continuous; passing
402-A	Passenger: distant whistle
B	Passenger: enter station; stop; standing

403-A Passenger: standing in station; start; whistle; leave
    B Railroad station: miscellaneous trains

404-A Passenger: pass at high speed with whistle
    B Freight: pass at high speed with whistle

405-A 20th-century train

406-A-B Passenger: continuous inside coach

407-A Railroad terminal
    B Idle engine with bell and without bell

408-A Passenger: approaching and passing with crossing bell; approaching and pass-
        ing without bell

409-A Local passenger locomotive
    B Train: to stop and pull out; idle engine with bell and steam; crossing bell

410-A Fast passenger locomotive: start and continuous run
    B Passenger: start; run; stop; inside train

411-A Passenger: start; run; stop; inside train
    B Passenger: continuous inside train

412-A Passenger: start; run; stop; inside train
    B Passenger: continuous inside train

413-A Freight terminal
    B Train whistles

414-A Train: start; run; stop

415-A Train: pass in tunnel; pass; stop

416-A Roundhouse: running with whistle

417-A Zepher: enter station and idle; leave
    B Zepher: crossing whistle; enter station and leave

418-A Streamliner: enter station and leave
    B Gasoline electric: idle; bell; whistle; leave
        Passenger: approach, whistle; leave

419-A Motor train: approach; pass; recede
    B Stop and start

420-A-B Motor train: European train-start; run; stop

421-A-B Passenger elevator; underground train

422-A Train: Diesel engine
    B Sante Fe steam engine

423-A Santa Fe Chief steam engine
    B Santa Fe local freight

424-A Train: gas-electric local
    B Santa Fe local freight

425-A Southern Pacific Owl: enter station; stop; stand; start; leave
    B Southern Pacific Sunset Ltd.: whistle and pass; approach and stop; whistle;
        start; leave

See also: 215 Diesel electric: arrive; stop; leave
            1120 Passenger: start and run
             750 Elevated trains

909   Freight: start and run
913   Railroad bell

Weather, Rivers and Trees (Crashing and Being Chopped)

500-A   Surf: waves and backwash
    B   Surf on rocky shore
501-A-B   River rapids
502-A-B   Waterfalls
503-A   Rainfall
    B   Rainfall and thunder
504-A   Thunder crashes
    B   V-8 car: continuous running
505-A   Thunderstorm
    B   Wind and hurricane
506-A   Howling winter winds
    B   Blizzard: howl of wind
507-A   Wind howling
    B   Rainstorm
508-A   Storm at sea
    B   Seawash and breakers
509-A   Steady rain
    B   Lap and wash of water
510-A-B   Wind effect
511-A   Heavy surf
    B   Heavy surf and foghorn in background
512-A   Howling wind; rain and wind
    B   Same
513-A-B   Thunderstorm; brook; lapping water
514-A   Walking in snow and underbrush
    B   Chopping through ice on river
515-A-B   Thunder; carnival
516-A   Rapids
    B   Waterfall; wading in stream
517-A   Windstorm
    B   Thunderstorm
518-A   Gale of wind
    B   Underground explosions
519-A   Thunder: one heavy bolt; four heavy bolts; six heavy bolts
    B   Flood disasters: bridge crashes and washes away; dam breaks; roar of the
         flood
550-A   Chopping and tree crashes
    B   Sawing and tree crashing
551-A   "Don't use this side"
    B   Chopping and tree crash; outboard boat

See also: 1019   Sawing wood with a handsaw; driving nails

Fires and Fire Trucks

600-A	Fire truck: approach; stop; passing
B	Same
601-A	Fire truck: passing with siren and bell
B	Fire apparatus: continuous
602-A	Story of a fire (contains music; [warning:] "obtain copyright clearance")
B	A.D.T. fire alarm; electric siren
603-A	Trucks and crowd (large fire)
B	Fire and crowd; pressure hose
604-A	Siren; bell; auto horns
605-A	Campfire
B	Fire: burning; extinguishing it with water
606-A	Idling engine pump
B	Fire truck: with siren and bells; bell only
607-A	Fire truck: continuous run and stop
B	Metropolitan fire truck: continuous run and stop
608-A-B	Alarm; engine; phone bell; siren
609-A-B	Fire apparatus
610-A	Fire burning: continuous
B	Fire apparatus; fire and walls crashing
611-A	Fire apparatus and tractor
B	Do not use this side

See also: 751   Fire
               251   Fire

Traffic

650-A	42nd Street and Broadway
651-A	Indianapolis 500 (with newsboys)
	Indianapolis 500 (without newsboys)
652-A	Times Square
653-A	Small city
654-A	34th Street and Broadway
656-A	Crowd (wrestling match)
B	Street cars

See also: 908   Traffic

Boats

700-A	Outboard motorboat: start; run; stop; waves slapping against boat
B	Large motorboat: start; run; stop

701-A   Speed boat: start; idle; run; stop
    B   Diesel tug: continuous run; boat whistles

702-A   Engine room (with signal bells)
    B   Boat whistles

703-A   Engine room: pull out and signal bell
    B   Boat whistles

704-A   Landing and signal bells
    B   Firing boilers

705-A   Paddle wheel: running continuously
    B   Boat through lock with whistle

706-A   Ferry: loading and docking
    B   Ferry: docking

707-A   Harbor noises

708-A   Foghorns
    B   Harbor foghorns; radio beacon in background

709-A   Fishing boat: continuous
    B   Motor boat: continuous

710-A   Harbor noises
    B   Boat whistles

711-A   Steamer sailing: crowd and whistles
    B   Same

712-A   Harbor sounds: foghorns
    B   Harbor sounds: bell buoy

713-A   Wild birds
    B   Ship's engine room

714-A   Airplane maneuvers
    B   Diesel boat effect (bow wave)

See also: 314   Airplane idle (motorboat)
           551   Outboard motor
                   Steamboat siren

Machinery and Construction

750-A   Woodworking machines
    B   Woodworking machines (4 cuts)

751-A-B   Machinery: constant (fire crackling)

752-A   Woodworking machine (3 cuts)
    B   Sawmill

753-A   Newspaper press
    B   Saw matrix roller linotype

754-A   Drilling oil well
    B   Same

755-A   Corliss steam engine
    B   Small steam engine

756-A	Tractor running
B	Same
757-A	4-cylinder gas engine; pump
B	Hoist engine; air drill; pile driver
758-A-B	Excavator
759-A	Construction
B	Elevated trains
760-A	Manufacturing noises
761-A	Well and pitcher pump; lawn mower
B	Chicks and hen
762-A	Riveting (3 cuts)
B	Construction
763-A	Anvil; hand lawn mower
B	Steam shovel; power lawn mower
784-A	Electric drill: in wood; in metal
B	Hacksaw; file

See also: 213   Air hammers
                611   Tractor: start; run; stop

War

800-A	Explosions
B	Air hammers; tire skids (30 seconds)
801-A	Manual of arms and firing (infantry)
B	Marching and firing
802-A	Cavalry (4 cuts)
B	Artillery fire (3 cuts)
803-A	Battle
804-A	Machine guns
805-A	"Don't use this side"
B	Machine guns (6 cuts)
806-A	Tank
807-A	Whistling shells; distant cannon
808-A	Distant and close cannon
809-A	Distant cannon; close machine gun
810-A	32-calibre automatic pistol
B	16- and 12-gauge shotguns
811-A	Cannon; machine gun; tank
812-A	Automatic pistol shots
813-A	Warfare: historic battle
B	Warfare: modern battle
814-A	Warfare: machine guns
B	Warfare: shells; ricocheting bullets

815-A   Rifle and pistol shots
   B   Infantry marching

See also: 1128   marching feet

Whistles, Bells and Clocks

900-A   Big Ben
   B   Telephone bell; clock ticking
901-A-B Church bells
902-A   Small steam whistle
   B   Medium steam whistle
903-A   Large steam whistle
904-A   Large and small wildcat whistles
905-A   Large steam chime
906-A   Train; boat; steam whistle
907-A   Household clocks; Big Ben
908-A   Clock chimes
   B   Traffic
909-A   Freight train: start and run
   B   Church bell; train bell; cuckoo
910-A   Clapper; buoy; tympani; roll of drums ("could be used as drums of African savages")
911-A   Church bells
912-A   Boat whistles
   B   Applause; cheers; laughs
913-A   Gong (6 cuts)
   B   Railroad bell; church or school bell
914-A   Work siren; auto horn
   B   Steamboat siren

See also: 409   Crossing bell
                413   Train whistles
                604   Siren; bell
                606   Fire-truck bell
                608   Alarm; phone bell; siren
                702   Boat whistles
                710   Boat whistles
                1004   Alarm clock strikes

Carnival

950-A   "Beautiful Danube"; "Sidewalks of New York"
   B   Carnival
951-A   Carnival
952-A   Carnival
   B   County fair

953-A	Amusement park; roller coaster
B	Shooting gallery
954-A-B	Carnival; thunder

See also: 515 Thunder; and carnival

Miscellaneous

1000-A	Popcorn popping
B	Bacon frying; coffee percolating
1001-A	Bowling alley
1002-A	Coal going down chute
B	Pick and shovel in gravel
1003-A	Blacksmith's shop
1004-A	Sewing machine; vacuum cleaner
B	Alarm clock strikes
1005-A	Fireworks
B	Night noises
1006-A	Breaking dishes
B	Crashing glass; piano
1007-A	Walking on duckboard and mud
1008-A	Walking on gravel road
B	Team and wagon on gravel road
1009-A	Walking and running through underbrush
B	Pick and shovel in gravel
1010-A	Footsteps in gravel
B	Running in gravel
1011-A	Footsteps in water
B	Running in water
1012-A	Footsteps on pavement
B	Window shade; window opening
1014	Restaurant: general confusion; dishes in kitchen
	Newspaper editorial room: telephones; typewriters; copy boys

See also: 514 Walking in snow and underbrush
906 Steam
Fireworks
Night noises

Animals and Birds

1100-A	Redbird (2 cuts)
B	Miscellaneous songbirds
1101-A	English songbirds
B	Nightingales
1102-A	Birds and rattlesnake
B	Silver gulls

1103-A	Cows and calves
B	Calves
1104-A	Pigs and hogs
B	Mules
1105-A	Chickens
B	Baby chicks
1106-A	Chickens
B	Same
1107-A	Blackbirds; nightingales; canaries
B	Ducks; hens and cocks; cat
1108-A	Monkeys and birds; hyena scream; panther and monkeys
B	Screams and boos mixed
1109-A	Horses on dirt road
1110-A	Horses on turf and cobbles
1111-A	Hyenas and lions
B	Miscellaneous wild animals
1112-A	African lions
B	American pumas (or mountain lions)
1113-A	Chimpanzees
B	Lions and chimpanzees
1114-B	Hacksaw; file

See also: 213   Air hammers
               611   Tractor: start; run; stop

1115-A	Bears
1116-A	Gibbon monkeys
1117-A	Pygmy elephant
B	Elephant and hippopotamus
1118-A	Frogs
1119-A	Hog calling; harness race
B	Horse neighing; fireworks
1120-A	Passenger train: continuous
B	Bulldog; puppy begging; puppy lapping milk
1121-A	Sheep and lambs
B	Same
1122-A	Dog bark; baby crying; angry mob
B	Same
1123-A	Wolves and coyotes
B	Animals in zoo
1124-A	Sheep; rattle of buckets
B	Poultry house (roosters and geese)
1125-A	Horse and sleigh
B	Horse and sleigh: continuous
1126-A	Canaries
B	Crowd at bird show

1128-A	Pack of hounds
B	Tramp of marching feet
1129-A	Dog barks; 2 dogs (hunting scene)
B	Puppies whining
1130-A	Dogs barking: 4 dogs; 2 dogs and a puppy
B	Puppies barking
1131-A	Barnyard
B	Milking cows
1132-A	Dogs barking (25 or 30 excited dogs)
B	English bulldog: puppies; barking; whining
1133-A	Geese; angry horned owl
B	Coyotes and timber wolf; fox-terrier puppies
1134-A	Angry bulldog barking
B	Beagle hound
1135-A	Cats: fighting; meowing
1136-A	Chickens: rooster crowing; hens
B	Turkeys
1137-A	Cattle: cows and calves mooing
B	Range cattle: bawling, mooing
1138-A	Barnyard
B	Horses; 1 horse walking
1139-A	Walking in snow
B	Horse and wagon in snow
1140-A	Horse and buggy: continuous
B	Night noises
1141-A	1 horse: continuous (dirt)
B	2 horses: continuous (dirt)
1142-A	Wolf howling; lobo wolf
B	Wolf howling; answering mate; wolves barking
1143-A	Lobo wolf: continuous
1144-A	African lions: roaring and grunting
B	African lions: roaring
1145-A	Mountain lion; Gibbon ape; mountain lion screaming; Gibbon ape
B	Asiatic leopard; Sumatran tiger; 2 leopards snarling; leopard roaring; tiger snarling
1146-A	African lions: 2 lions snarling and fighting
B	2 lions snarling and growling; 1 lion roaring and grunting
1147-A	African lions roaring and grunting; 1 lion
B	Several lions roaring
1148-A	Horse galloping on turf and on gravel; troop of horses passing at gallop; cantering on turf
B	Horses trotting on hard ground and on turf; cantering on gravel

Radio

1200-A	Teletype: one machine; several machines
B	Tuning radio receivers; short-wave code; static
1201-A	Radio code transmissions: 3 frequencies
B	Old Navy-type transmitter; telegraph sender
1202-A	Sound introduction for news broadcast with news boys calling "Extra!" with and without code and teletype
B	Sound introduction: for war news; for sports news; for weather report; for comic news

Bibliography

Bacon, John. *How Sweet It Is.* New York: St. Martin's, 1985.

Barnouw, Erik. *A Tower in Babel.* Vol. 1 of *A History of Broadcasting in the U.S.* New York: Oxford University Press, 1966.

Brooks, Tim, and Earle Marsh. *The Complete Directory to Prime Time Network and Cable TV Shows.* New York: Ballantine, 1979.

Creamer, Joseph, and William Hoffman. *Radio Sound Effects.* New York: Ziff-Davis, 1945.

Dunning, John. *The Encyclopedia of Old-Time Radio.* New York: Oxford University Press, 1998.

Eastman, Max. *Enjoyment of Laughter.* New York: Simon and Schuster, 1936.

Foxx, Redd, and Norma Miller. *The Redd Foxx Encyclopedia of Black Humor.* Pasadena, Calif.: Ward Richie, 1977.

Harvey, Rita Morley. *Those Wonderful, Terrible Years: George Heller and the American Federation of Television and Radio Artists.* Carbondale, Ill.: Southern Illinois University Press, 1996.

Lewis, Marlo, and Mona Bess Lewis. *Prime Time.* Los Angeles: J.P. Tarcher, 1979; distributed by St. Martin's.

Ludes, Ed, and Hallock Hoffman. *How to Create Sound Effects for Home Recordings.* Pasadena, Calif.: Castle, 1946.

McGill, Earle. *Radio Directing.* New York: McGraw-Hill, 1940.

McLeish, Robert. *Radio Production: A Manual for Broadcasting.* Oxford, England: Focal Press, 1994.

Marx, Arthur. *Red Skelton.* New York: Dutton, 1979.

Mott, Robert L. *Radio Sound Effects: Who Did It, and How, in the Era of Live Broadcasting.* Jefferson, N.C.: McFarland, 1993.

____. *Sound Effects: Radio, TV and Film.* Oxford, England: Focal Press, 1990.

Perret, Gene. *Comedy Writing Step by Step.* Hollywood: Samuel French Trade, 1982.

Sanford, Herb. *Ladies and Gentlemen— The Garry Moore Show.* New York: Price Stern Sloan, 1976.

Taylor, Glenhall. *Before Television: The Radio Years.* South Brunswick, N.J.: A.S. Barnes, 1977.

Turnbull, Robert. *Radio and Television Sound Effects.* New York: Rinehart, 1951.

Weiss, Elizabeth, and John Belton, eds. *Theory and Practice: Film Sound.* New York: Columbia University Press, 1985.

Wertheim, Frank Arthur. *Radio Comedy.* New York: Oxford University Press, 1979.

Whelan, Kenneth. *How the Golden Age of Television Turned My Hair Grey.* Walker, 1973.

Index